CLIMATE-INDUCED DISASTERS IN THE ASIA-PACIFIC REGION

COMMUNITY, ENVIRONMENT AND DISASTER RISK MANAGEMENT

Series Editor: William Lee Waugh, Jr.

COMMUNITY, ENVIRONMENT AND DISASTER
RISK MANAGEMENT   VOLUME 22

CLIMATE-INDUCED DISASTERS IN THE ASIA-PACIFIC REGION: RESPONSE, RECOVERY, ADAPTATION

EDITED BY

ANDREAS NEEF

*Development Studies, School of Social Sciences,
University of Auckland, New Zealand*

and

NATASHA PAULI

*UWA School of Agriculture and Environment, and
Department of Geography and Planning, University of
Western Australia, Australia*

United Kingdom – North America – Japan
India – Malaysia – China

Emerald Publishing Limited
Howard House, Wagon Lane, Bingley BD16 1WA, UK

First edition 2021

Reprints and permissions service
Contact: permissions@emeraldinsight.com

British Library Cataloguing in Publication Data
A catalogue record for this book is available from the British Library

ISBN: 978-1-83909-987-8 (Print)
ISBN: 978-1-83909-986-1 (Online)
ISBN: 978-1-83909-988-5 (Epub)

ISSN: 2040-7262 (Series)

ISOQAR certified
Management System,
awarded to Emerald
for adherence to
Environmental
standard
ISO 14001:2004.

Certificate Number 1985
ISO 14001

INVESTOR IN PEOPLE

CONTENTS

LIST OF TABLES, FIGURES AND PLATES

TABLES

FIGURES

PLATES

LIST OF CONTRIBUTORS

Carl Adams	Tearfund, New Zealand
Ashley Bartlett	University of Auckland, New Zealand
Lucy Benge	University of Auckland, New Zealand
Kahukura Bennett	Fairtrade Australia New Zealand, New Zealand
Bryan Boruff	University of Western Australia, Australia
Chanchhaya Chhom	Royal University of Phnom Penh, Cambodia
Savuti Henningsen	University of Western Australia, Australia
Gracie Irvine	University College London, United Kingdom
Andreas Neef	University of Auckland, New Zealand
Meg Parsons	University of Auckland, New Zealand
Natasha Pauli	University of Western Australia, Australia
Renata Varea	University of the South Pacific, Fiji
Mark Williams	University of Western Australia, Australia

ABOUT THE CONTRIBUTORS

Carl Adams holds a Master of Arts in Development Studies from the University of Auckland. His interests include humanitarian coordination and bureaucratic impediments in disaster responses. He has recently worked in Bangladesh as Country Director with Swiss-based humanitarian agency Medair and now works as International Director with Tearfund New Zealand.

Ashley Bartlett holds a Master of Science in Environmental Management from the University of Auckland. Her interests lie in the intersection of climate change adaptation and sustainable development in the Oceania-Pacific region, and the ways in which marginalised people's knowledge can be incorporated into climate change resilience and adaptation planning.

Lucy Benge holds a Master of Arts in Development Studies from the University of Auckland. Her research interests include disaster-induced migration and displacement, climate change adaptation, disaster recovery and community-centred approaches to risk reduction and education.

Kahukura Bennett holds a Master of Arts in Development Studies from the University of Auckland. Her interests lie in the intersection of gender and sustainable development in the Pacific Islands. She currently works for Fairtrade Australia New Zealand.

Bryan Boruff is a Senior Lecturer in Geography at the University of Western Australia. His expertise lies in the application of geographic information system (GIS) and remote sensing technologies to the study of environmental hazards. His research interests encompass risk and vulnerability assessment, population health, sustainable livelihoods, urban and regional development and development of spatially enabled eResearch tools.

Chanchhaya Chhom is a Founder of Plankton Media, a social media platform for ecotourism and green messages in Cambodia. He has worked on projects and research in public policy, political analysis and within the energy and environmental sector, through the Royal University of Phnom Penh and Green Move Consulting. He is an accomplished author of Khmer poetry and songs.

Savuti Henningsen holds a Master of Environmental Science with a specialisation in Land and Water Management from the University of Western Australia. Her research interests lie in environmental management and statistical analysis of environmental data. She is a Tutor at the University of Western Australia and Murdoch University.

Gracie Irvine holds a Bachelor of Science with Honours in Physical Geography from University College London. She currently works in environmental consulting in London and specialises in the assessment of daylight, sunlight and overshadowing.

Andreas Neef is a Professor in Development Studies at the University of Auckland. His current research focusses on adaptation and resilience to climate change, climate-induced migration and displacement, post-disaster response and recovery and land grabbing. Most of his recent research has been conducted in Southeast Asia and the South Pacific.

Meg Parsons is a Senior Lecturer (Environmental Management) within the School of Environment at the University of Auckland. Her research examines the intersections between colonialism and climate change adaptation, and the ways in which Indigenous peoples' knowledge and experiences can be incorporated into climate adaptation plans and actions.

Natasha Pauli is a Lecturer in Geography at the University of Western Australia. Her research examines human–environment interactions in a range of settings from urban streetscapes to smallholder agriculture, with an emphasis on understanding how people perceive and manage ecological relationships under changing environmental conditions.

Renata Varea is a Research Associate with the School of Geography at the University of the South Pacific, Fiji. Her research interests include sustainable climate change mitigation strategies in Fiji. Her current research examines the effects of climate change and development on ecosystem services and the livelihoods of women, youth and minority groups in Ba.

Mark Williams holds a Master of Environmental Science with a specialisation in GIS from the University of Western Australia. He works as a Spatial Analyst for a Western Australian state government agency, where he uses spatial methods and technologies to help make communities in Western Australia more resilient to hazards.

PREFACE

Asia-Pacific is the world's most disaster-prone region, accounting for about half of the climate-related displacements of 19 million people that occurred globally in 2017. Climate-related, fast-onset hazards, such as floods, cyclones and typhoons, have claimed more lives, displaced a higher number of people and caused more damage than in any other world region over the past 20 years. In addition, Asia-Pacific countries are extremely prone to slow-onset climate-induced processes, such as sea level rise and extended droughts, as global atmospheric greenhouse gas concentrations continue to rise. Among these countries are several low-income nations, with persistent poverty in rural and coastal areas. The cost of short-term response to and medium- to long-term recovery from climate-induced disasters falls disproportionately on the poorest and most marginalised communities within the Asia-Pacific region. At the same time, long-term adaptation processes to climate-related hazards at the household and community level remain poorly understood. Increasingly, adaptation strategies need to address the challenges of multi-risk environments, whereby climate-related disaster risk is just one of many risk factors, alongside other potential environmental hazards as well as socio-economic and political–institutional risks.

This volume presents richly detailed qualitative research from diverse contexts across the Asia-Pacific region and adds to scholarship on the trajectory of community resilience and adaption to climate-related hazards. Drawing on case studies from Cambodia, Fiji, Solomon Islands and Samoa, the chapters examine various response, recovery and adaptation strategies at the local level, incorporating the perspectives and knowledge of affected individuals, households and communities.

The main questions addressed by the contributions in this volume are as follows:

- What are the perceptions among individuals, households and communities regarding the impacts of climate-induced disasters on their livelihoods?
- Is the post-disaster context the right time for implementing new development agendas and effecting social change?
- Which groups within coastal and rural communities are most vulnerable to climate-induced disasters? Are vulnerability and resilience gendered?
- Are disaster-affected communities involved in decision-making by humanitarian NGOs around post-disaster response and recovery processes?
- What are the factors that enhance or constrain disaster response and recovery by communities and organisations?
- Can scientific/expert knowledge and Indigenous/local knowledge be integrated to enhance community-based disaster risk management and climate adaptation?

- What types of adaptation practices and strategies have individuals, households and communities developed over time and how effective are these in a multi-risk environment?
- Are there trade-offs between individual adaptation mechanisms and community-based approaches to climate adaptation?
- How has planned relocation been constructed as a climate adaptation strategy among government actors and within intergovernmental agencies?

The editors acknowledge the financial support of the Asia-Pacific Network for Global Change Research for a three-year collaborative research project on 'Climate change adaptation in post-disaster recovery processes: Flood-affected communities in Cambodia and Fiji' (CAF2015-RR10-NMY-Neef; CAF2016-RR05-CMY-Neef; and CAF2017-RR01-CMY-Neef) and the University of Western Australia's Research Collaboration Award RA/1/1200/755 'Risk, resilience and recovery: A participatory approach to integrating local and scientific knowledge for disaster preparedness of communities in flood-prone catchments in Fiji' which laid the foundation for this publication project.

We are particularly indebted to the scholars who made invaluable contributions to this volume by reviewing the various chapters, namely, Alexandra Peralta, Chanrith Ngin, Clare Mouat, Jamie Gillen, Karen Paiva Henrique, Lucy Benge and Sarah Prout Quicke.

A common message from the chapters of this book is for greater recognition and acknowledgement of local preferences and practices in disaster risk management and climate change adaptation. We hope that this volume gives voice to the wealth of local knowledge and views expressed by participants in the research, and demonstrates the importance of the social and cultural context in which post-disaster response and recovery efforts and community-based climate adaptation approaches take place.

Andreas Neef
Natasha Pauli
Editors

CHAPTER 1

CLIMATE-INDUCED DISASTERS IN THE ASIA-PACIFIC REGION – FROM RESPONSE AND RECOVERY TO ADAPTATION

Andreas Neef and Natasha Pauli

ABSTRACT

Multi-risk environments pose challenges for rural and coastal communities in the Asia-Pacific region, particularly with regard to disaster risk management and climate change adaptation strategies. While much research has been published on disaster response and recovery for specific climate-related hazards in the region, such as cyclones, floods and droughts, there is a growing need for insight into how communities respond, recover and adapt to the multiple, intersecting risks posed by environmental, societal and economic change. This chapter frames the body of new research presented in this book from the perspective of multi-risk environments, paying particular attention to concepts central to the disaster response and recovery cycle, and rejecting the notion of a distinct boundary between climate and society. Further, this introductory chapter foregrounds the importance of cultural values, power relations, Indigenous knowledge systems, local networks and community-based adaptive capacities when considering resilience, recovery and adaptation to climate-induced disasters at the community and household level. Overviews of the research presented in this book demonstrate a diverse range of responses and adaptive strategies at the local level in case studies from Solomon Islands, Fiji, Cambodia and Samoa, as well as implications for policy, planning and management.

Keywords: Disaster; hazard; climate change adaptation; resilience; Southeast Asia; Pacific Islands

Climate-Induced Disasters in the Asia-Pacific Region: Response, Recovery, Adaptation
Community, Environment and Disaster Risk Management, Volume 22, 1–9
Copyright © 2021 by Emerald Publishing Limited
All rights of reproduction in any form reserved
ISSN: 2040-7262/doi:10.1108/S2040-726220200000022001

INTRODUCTION: THE MAKING OF ASIA-PACIFIC AS A RISK-PRONE REGION

The Asia-Pacific region is arguably one of the most disaster-prone regions in the world. According to the latest World Risk Report, six Pacific Island nations and four Asian countries are among the 20 countries facing the highest disaster risk globally (Bündnis Entwicklung Hilft & IFHV, 2019). Climate-related, fast-onset hazards, such as floods, cyclones and typhoons, have claimed more lives and caused more damage over the past 20 years in countries of the Asia-Pacific than in any other world region. In addition, these countries are extremely prone to slow-onset climate-induced processes, such as sea level rise and extended droughts, as global atmospheric greenhouse gas concentrations continue to rise. Among these countries are several low-income nations, with persistent poverty in rural and coastal areas, which carries significant socio-economic risks. Yet, the devastation wrought by bushfires in southeastern Australia that burned a globally unprecedented percentage of forest biome between September 2019 and February 2020 (Boer, Resco de Dios, & Bradstock, 2020) is a stark reminder that the so-called developed countries are also becoming increasingly vulnerable to climate-related disaster risks.[1] This seems to challenge the views of mainstream disaster risk scholars who have argued that adaptive capacities of countries

> largely depend on their economic status. Generally, developed countries have higher adaptive capacities while developing and least developed countries, which are most vulnerable to climate change, need external support to build theirs. (Francisco, 2008, p. 8)

This simplistic view which also implies a dependency of 'underdeveloped' countries on support from rich, 'developed' countries has been challenged by such authors as Bankoff (2019, p. 234) who argues that Western discourses of disaster risk management accept disaster, disturbance and crisis as 'an endemic condition' of the Global South and McDonnell (2019, p. 2) who criticises 'disaster responses that see the "community" as a space to be acted upon by outsiders'. Common to these Western discourses and outsider-driven interventions in response, recovery and adaptation is a dismissal of Indigenous knowledge systems, local resilience networks and community-based adaptive capacities that exist in many 'at-risk' countries in the Asia-Pacific region.

Partially in response to such Western-centric discourses, there has been a resurgence of studies emphasising the critical role that cultural values, power relations, social norms and local knowledge play in determining resilience, recovery and adaptation at the community and household level (e.g. Fletcher et al., 2013; McDonnell, 2019; Naess & Twena, 2019; O'Brien, 2009; O'Brien & Wolf, 2010; Woroniecki et al., 2019). Numerous studies have been conducted on disaster response and recovery in the context of a specific climatic hazard event in Asia-Pacific countries (e.g. Johnston, 2014, for cyclones in Fiji; Akbar & Aldrich, 2018, for floods in Pakistan; Nguyen & Shaw, 2015, for droughts in Cambodia). Yet, to date, few studies have acknowledged the particular challenges that multi-risk environments pose for disaster risk management and climate adaptation strategies in rural and coastal communities of the Asia-Pacific region (Neef et al., 2018; Warrick, Aalbersberg, Dumaru, McNaught, & Teperman, 2017). Rural communities along the Mekong

River in Cambodia, for example, have adapted very well to seasonal floods over the past decades, but – more recently – have been forced to also adjust to increasingly frequent heatwaves, droughts and storm events (Henningsen, Pauli, & Chhom, 2020 – Chapter 7, this volume; Williams, Pauli, & Boruff, 2020 – Chapter 6, this volume; Yamamauchi, 2014). In Cambodia, additional risks are posed by non-climatic factors, such as logging, land grabbing and upstream hydropower dam construction (e.g. Grumbine, Dore, & Jianchu, 2012; Neef, Touch, & Chiengthong, 2013). Numerous coastal communities in Fiji, a South Pacific Island nation, have experienced a series of rapid-onset climatic hazards, such as floods and cyclones, while also having been subjected to slow-onset climate-associated processes, such as extended droughts and sea level rise, as well as upstream deforestation and mining over the past decade (Bennett, Neef, & Varea, 2020 – Chapter 5, this volume; Irvine, Pauli, Varea, & Boruff, 2020 – Chapter 4, this volume; Neef et al., 2018). These are only a few examples of how rural and coastal communities in the Asia-Pacific region are increasingly exposed to a multitude of climatic and non-climatic risks, which require diverse adaptation strategies and may complicate disaster recovery cycles.

DEFINITIONS AND CONCEPTS

For the purpose of this book, we adopt Aldrich's (2012, p. 3) definition of *disaster* as 'an event that suspends normal activities and threatens or causes severe, communitywide damage'. *Climate-induced disasters* encompass hydrological (e.g. floods, landslides), meteorological (e.g. storms, heatwaves) and climatological (e.g. droughts, wildfires) events (CRED & UNISDR, 2018). In line with Taylor (2015, p. 11), we object to the 'ontological division between climate and society' and the imposition of artificial 'boundaries between the assumed "natural" and "social" worlds' which represents 'climate change as an exogenous force that manifests itself in the form of external shocks to an otherwise independent society'. Hence, we acknowledge that climate and society are co-produced and mutually constitutive.

Disaster response refers to the immediate post-disaster relief efforts, which includes – for instance – search and rescue operations, mutual assistance at the community level, evacuation of affected populations to temporary shelters and provision of food and water rations. *Disaster recovery* commences when the immediate threats to human security and property have been resolved, and individuals, households and communities can start to re-establish their livelihoods and return to their pre-disaster conditions and routines (Akbar & Aldrich, 2018). The notion of *disaster recovery* does not simply refer to physical, infrastructural and economic recovery but also includes social, cultural and psychological recovery of affected individuals and communities (Aldrich, 2012; Nakagawa & Shaw, 2004; Neef & Shaw, 2013). As some of the chapters in this book will demonstrate, the speed and depth of recovery are highly uneven within and across communities and depend on a myriad of factors. These factors may include – but are not limited to – the amount of disaster damage, socio-economic conditions, demographics, the quality of governance, social capital and the amount of external aid (Aldrich, 2012; Yila, Weber, & Neef, 2013). Yet, as several studies have shown, distribution of aid does not always lead to a faster and more equitable recovery process but may engender a particular 'politics of distribution' (Ferguson, 2015, p. 10, cited by McDonnell, 2019, p. 10; see also Adams & Neef, 2019).

Resilience is a concept that has been linked closely to recovery and often described as the ability of a system (e.g. a community or a household) to absorb shocks and disturbances and to 'bounce back' and regain stability (Béné, Newsham, Davies, Ulrichs, & Godfrey-Wood, 2014; Brown, 2016). *Vulnerability* is sometimes used as an antonym of resilience, yet is more commonly described as a function of exposure, sensitivity and (lack of) adaptive capacity (e.g. Callo-Concha & Ewert, 2014; Smit & Wandel, 2006). Yet, among social scientists, there is an increasing consensus that *vulnerability* is not so much an endemic condition or innate property of a social-ecological system but rather a consequence of global and local power differentials, marginalisation of certain groups based on race, caste, class or gender, and entrenched institutional, political and material inequalities (e.g. Taylor, 2015). As Adger (2006, p. 270) puts it, 'vulnerability is driven by inadvertent or deliberate human action that reinforces self-interest and the distribution of power in addition to interacting with physical and ecological systems'.

Climate change adaptation has been defined by Smit, Burton, Klein, and Street (1999, p. 200) as 'adjustments in ecological-socio-economic systems in response to actual or expected climate stimuli, their effects or impacts'. In a similar vein – and with an added positive spin – the IPCC (2007, p. 809) defines adaptation as 'adjustment in natural or human systems in response to actual or expected climatic stimuli or their effects, which moderates harm or exploits beneficial opportunities'. Recently, scholars have drawn attention to community adaptation processes as the locus of power contestations and micropolitics, which challenges apolitical and technocratic discourses and practices (e.g. Tschakert et al., 2016; for an overview of the body of literature, see Woroniecki et al., 2019). Of particular relevance for the contributions to this volume and the concept of multi-risk environments is Pelling's (2011, p. 60) notion of 'transformative adaptation' which entails social learning processes and creative integration of local and scientific knowledge which 'can respond to the multiple scale[s] and sectors through which risk is felt and adaptations [are] undertaken'.

STRUCTURE OF THE BOOK

The remaining eight chapters of this volume explore responses to, recovery from and adaptation to climate-induced disasters in various multi-risk environments in the Asia-Pacific region. The authors of these chapters are critical of external interventions into complex social and cultural fields and call for a greater acknowledgement of local knowledge, preferences and practices in disaster risk management and climate change adaptation. They are also committed to research methodologies that are not only ethically sound but also culturally appropriate. This includes participatory methods used in the two Cambodian case studies and Pacific research methodologies (e.g. *talanoa* – a form of casual conversation and sharing stories) employed in the case studies from Solomon Islands, Fiji and Samoa.

Through an analysis of three consecutive United Nations disaster risk reduction frameworks, Chapter 2 – written by Lucy Benge and Andreas Neef – examines how disasters have been increasingly constructed as opportunities for development. The authors raise the question whether the post-disaster context is the right time for implementing development agendas given the potential for recovery to be co-opted by dominant development ideologies. The chapter explores how the flow of knowledge, expertise and technology from the Global North to the Global South has contributed to turning 'vulnerable' populations into objects to be managed and directed towards 'progress'. This involves understanding 'vulnerability' and 'underdevelopment' as labelling techniques, which are used by institutions, disaster experts and bureaucracies as a way of justifying disasters as opportunities for change. Thereby, the act of defining 'disaster' becomes a political tool for implementing particular ideas of change and progress. As an alternative, Benge and Neef examine how disasters can be used to implement dominant institutionalised ideas of progress, while also offering opportunities to disrupt status quo approaches to development.

In Chapter 3, Carl Adams and Andreas Neef examine how communities and non-governmental organisations (NGOs) in the Solomon Islands viewed the response to a severe flash flooding event in April 2014. It starts by exploring the ways in which communities interpreted and responded to the disaster, and identifies factors that assisted and constrained stakeholders in disaster response and recovery efforts. The study further investigates to what extent communities were actively involved in NGO responses and determines the factors that informed community–NGO relationships. Findings suggest that women, youth and people with disabilities were largely excluded in post-disaster decision-making processes, thereby exposing these at-risk groups to secondary disasters. The study also found that humanitarian NGOs largely overlooked ideas, knowledge and capabilities at the community level. The authors argue for greater inclusion of those affected by disaster and call for progressive improvements to disaster relief and recovery efforts based on reflexive practice.

In Chapter 4, Gracie Irvine, Natasha Pauli, Renata Varea and Bryan Boruff present findings of qualitative research conducted in three Indigenous (*iTaukei*) communities along the Ba River in Viti Levu, Fiji, with a particular focus on recent floods (2009, 2012) and Tropical Cyclone Winston (2016). Employing participatory mapping as a tool to elucidate communities' understanding of the differing impacts of multiple hazards, the authors find that communities draw on a wide range of livelihood strategies from fishing and agriculture to community-based tourism and outside work. Climate-induced hazard events vary in their impact on these livelihood strategies across the land- and seascape, imposing particular challenges on community members' adaptive capacity, local knowledge and ingenuity. The ways in which people modify their use of the various natural resources in response to the impact of climate-induced hazards demonstrate the importance of taking a broad land- and seascape approach in planning for multiple, potentially competing resource uses in multi-risk island environments.

Chapter 5 – written by Kahukura Bennett, Andreas Neef and Renata Varea – draws on local experiences and situated narratives of 2016 Tropical Cyclone

Winston in two *iTaukei* Fijian communities – the coastal village of Votua and the highland village of Navala – to provide a nuanced account of gendered responsibilities, vulnerabilities and resilience in the context of climate-induced disasters. Rather than providing a generalising and essentialising account of the role gender plays in disaster impact and recovery, the chapter presents an array of experiences that emerge as women and men negotiate opportunities to provide for their families and adapt to multiple, intersecting inequalities including the exposure to climatic threats. Surprisingly, the perception of gendered vulnerability was largely absent from respondent narratives. Roles and responsibilities were predominantly perceived as changing over time, either to a more shared sense of responsibilities or a shift from male responsibilities to female. The study concludes that conceptualising vulnerability as arising from a broad range of interacting social factors provides more in-depth insights into spaces behind unperceived vulnerability.

In Chapter 6, Mark Williams, Natasha Pauli and Bryan Boruff examine how people in four rural communities along the Mekong River in Kratie Province, Cambodia, perceive the effects of environmental change and how these perceptions influence present and future adaptation strategies. The authors found that villagers had employed complex adaptive strategies to deal with regular floods and have started to adopt changes that may help adjust to the impact of reduced rainfall and increased temperature as a result of local climatic changes. The adaptive strategies that are used by communities were wide-ranging and represented all five classes of adaptation practice as defined by Agrawal and Perrin (2008), that is, mobility, storage, diversification, communal pooling and market exchange. The study demonstrated the usefulness of combining community-based focus groups with participatory mapping as a low-cost, spatially explicit method of identifying locally relevant opportunities and challenges to climate change adaptation in small, flood-prone communities of the Lower Mekong region.

Chapter 7, written by Savuti Henningsen, Natasha Pauli and Chanchhaya Chhom, explores temporal seasonal variability in four riverine communities of Kratie Province, Cambodia, and identifies locally developed and gendered strategies to adapt to temporal changes in weather patterns. Combining historical hydrometeorological data with participatory seasonal calendars and daily routine diaries, the study finds that patterns in rainfall, flooding and drought have become more variable and less predictable, a phenomenon that will likely continue into the future. Future temporal impacts of climatic change combined with alterations in flow from the development of hydropower dams upstream are likely to hold adverse impacts for these communities, due to their strong reliance on seasonality for their agriculture-based livelihoods. Individuals and communities in the study region have developed a wide range of approaches to mitigate the adverse impacts of environmental change. This chapter reiterates the importance of incorporating both local knowledge and scientific data to gain the most accurate understanding of the impacts of environmental change in a given region.

Chapter 8 – written by Ashley Bartlett, Meg Parsons and Andreas Neef – presents an exploratory study conducted in the Pacific Island nation of Samoa into the impact of private household insurance on people's willingness to engage in community-based climate adaptation projects. The study finds that individuals whose homes were insured with natural perils insurance were more likely to express more individualistic values and attitudes than those without natural perils insurance. Insured homeowners tended to frame adaptation as a technical challenge, with insurance being part of the technical and expert-led approach to prepare for, manage and recover from extreme events. In contrast, householders without insurance perceived climate change adaptation as less of a technical and more of a social process. Correspondingly, research participants with private natural perils insurance coverage were less engaged in community-based adaptation projects compared to participants without insurance. Given the importance of household participation in community-based adaptation projects in small island developing states of the South Pacific, these exploratory findings suggest that an increased uptake of private insurance may have problematic outcomes for the adaptive capacity of the broader community.

In Chapter 9, Lucy Benge and Andreas Neef explore the discursive creation of planned relocation as a form of climate change adaptation and development in the case of Fiji. Their study critiques the way in which powerful actors – including intergovernmental agencies providing funding to support relocations – frame climate-related community relocation as 'adaptive strategies', while for affected communities these strategies feel neither voluntary in a context of limited alternatives nor adaptive, but are rather experienced as a form of loss and damage. Grounded in the discussion of the concept of *vanua* and Fijian systems of Indigenous land custodianship, the authors discuss how broader technical narratives regarding relocation as a strategy to reduce climate-related vulnerabilities need to more carefully consider the cultural, spiritual and social vulnerabilities that such approaches can heighten. The chapter also speaks to the problems of characterising relocation in overly simplistic and environmentally deterministic ways, which fail to account for the complex political and economic factors that can render some peoples more vulnerable to the impacts of natural hazard events and/or slow-onset environmental change.

We hope that these chapters will stimulate further research and critical debate among human geographers, development studies scholars, anthropologists and other social scientists in the field of disaster risk management and climate change adaptation. Some of the chapters may also inform policy making for improved post-disaster response and recovery and more inclusive community-based climate adaptation approaches.

NOTE

1. See, for example, recent research detailing: increased flooding in northwestern Europe linked with climate change between 1960 and 2010 (Blöschl et al., 2019); projected future transformational change in fire regimes in southern Australia (Boer et al., 2016) and partial attribution of the 2019–2020 Australian fires to anthropogenic climate change (van Oldenborgh et al., 2020); and increased hurricane risk in the United States (Pant & Cha, 2019).

REFERENCES

Adams, C., & Neef, A. (2019). Patrons of disaster: The role of political patronage in flood response in the Solomon Islands. *World Development Perspectives*, *15*, 100128.

Adger, W. N. (2006). Vulnerability. *Global Environmental Change*, *16*, 268–281.

Agrawal, A., & Perrin, N. (2008). *Climate adaptation, local institutions, and rural livelihoods*. Working Paper No. W081-6. International Forestry Resources and Institutions Program, University of Michigan, Ann Arbor, MI.

Akbar, M. S., & Aldrich, D. P. (2018). Social capital's role in recovery: Evidence from communities affected by the 2010 Pakistan floods. *Disasters, 42*(3), 475–497.

Aldrich, D. P. (2012). *Building resilience: Social capital in post-disaster recovery*. Chicago, IL: The University of Chicago Press.

Bankoff, G. (2019). Remaking the world in our own image: Vulnerability, resilience and adaptation as historical discourses. *Disasters, 43*(2), 221–239.

Béné, C., Newsham, A., Davies, M., Ulrichs, M., & Godfrey-Wood, R. (2014). Review article: Resilience, poverty and development. *Journal of International Development, 26*, 598–623.

Bennett, K., Neef, A., & Varea, R. (2020). Embodying resilience: Narrating gendered experiences of disasters in Fiji. In A. Neef & N. Pauli (Eds.), *Climate-induced disasters in the Asia-Pacific region: Response, recovery, adaptation* (pp. 87–112). Bingley: Emerald Publishing.

Blöschl, G., Hall, J., Viglione, A., Perdigão, R. A. P., Parajka, J., Merz, B., … Živković, N. (2019). Changing climate both increases and decreases European river floods. *Nature, 573*(7772), 108–111.

Boer, M. M., Bowman, D. M. J. S., Murphy, B. P., Cary, G. J., Cochrane, M. A., Fensham, R. J., … Bradstock, R. A. (2016). Future changes in climatic water balance determine potential for transformational shifts in Australian fire regimes. *Environmental Research Letters, 11*(6), 065002.

Boer, M. M., Resco de Dios, V., & Bradstock, R. A. (2020). Unprecedented burn area of Australian mega forest fires. *Nature Climate Change, 10*(3), 171–172.

Brown, K. (2016). *Resilience, development and global change*. London: Routledge.

Bündnis Entwicklung Hilft & IFHV (2019). *WorldRiskReport 2019*. Berlin: Bündnis Entwicklung Hilft. Retrieved from https://weltrisikobericht.de/english-2/

Callo-Concha, D., & Ewert, F. (2014) Using the concepts of resilience, vulnerability and adaptability for the assessment and analysis of agricultural systems. *Change and Adaptation in Socio-Ecological Systems, 1*(1), 1–11.

CRED & UNISDR (2018). *Economic losses, poverty & disasters – 1998–2017*. Brussels Disasters (CRED) & United Nations Office for Disaster Risk Reduction (UNISDR).

Fletcher, S. M., Thiessen, J., Gero, A., Rumsey, M., Kuruppu, N., & Willetts, J. (2013). Traditional coping strategies and disaster response: Examples from the South Pacific region. *Journal of Environmental and Public Health, 2013*, 1–9.

Francisco, H. A. (2008). Adaptation to climate change: Needs and opportunities in Southeast Asia. *ASEAN Economic Bulletin, 25*(1), 7–19.

Grumbine, R. E., Dore, J., & Jianchu, X. (2012). Mekong hydropower: Drivers of change and governance challenges. *Frontiers in Ecology and Environment, 10*(2), 91–98.

Henningsen, S., Pauli, N., & Chhom, C. (2020). Seasonal livelihoods and adaptation strategies for an uncertain environmental future: Results from participatory research in Kratie province, Cambodia. In A. Neef & N. Pauli (Eds.), *Climate-induced disasters in the Asia-Pacific region: Response, recovery, adaptation* (pp. 135–165). Bingley: Emerald Publishing.

IPCC. (2007). *Climate change 2007: Impacts, adaptation and vulnerability*. Intergovernmental Panel on Climate Change. Cambridge: Cambridge University Press.

Irvine, G., Pauli, N., Varea, R., & Boruff, B. (2020). A participatory approach to understanding the impact of multiple natural hazards in communities along the Ba River, Fiji. In A. Neef & N. Pauli (Eds.), *Climate-induced disasters in the Asia-Pacific region: Response, recovery, adaptation* (pp. 57–86). Bingley: Emerald Publishing.

Johnston, I. (2014). Disaster management and climate change adaptation: A remote island perspective. *Disaster Prevention and Management: An International Journal, 23*(2), 123–137.

McDonnell, S. (2019). Other dark sides of resilience: Politics and power in community-based efforts to strengthen resilience. *Anthropological Forum*. Advance online publication. doi:10.1080/0066 4677.2019.1647827

Naess, L. O., & Twena, M. (2019). Local adaptation governance: Examining power relations. In E. C. H. Keskitalo & B. L. Preston (Eds.), *Research handbook on climate change adaptation policy* (pp. 347–363). Cheltenham: Edward Elgar.

Nakagawa, Y., & Shaw, R. (2004). Social capital: A missing link to disaster recovery. *International Journal of Mass Emergencies and Disasters, 22*(1), 5–34.

Neef, A., & Shaw, R. (2013). Local responses to natural disasters: Issues and challenges. In A. Neef & R. Shaw (Eds.), *Risks and conflicts: Local responses to natural disasters* (pp. 1–8). Bingley: Emerald Publishing.

Neef, A., Benge, L., Boruff, B., Pauli, N., Weber, E., & Varea, R. (2018). Climate adaptation strategies in Fiji: The role of social norms and cultural values. *World Development, 107*, 125–137.

Neef, A., Touch, S., & Chiengthong, J. (2013). The politics and ethics of land concessions in rural Cambodia. *Journal of Agricultural and Environmental Ethics, 26*(6), 1085–1103.

Nguyen, H., & Shaw, R. (2015) Adaptation to droughts in Cambodia. In R. Shaw & H. Nguyen (Eds.), *Droughts in Asian monsoon region* (pp. 49–66). Bingley: Emerald.

O'Brien, K. L. (2009). Do values subjectively define the limits to climate change adaptation? In W. N. Adger, I. Lorenzoni, & K. L. O'Brien (Eds.), *Adapting to climate change: Thresholds, values, governance* (pp. 164–180). Cambridge: Cambridge University Press.

O'Brien, K. L., & Wolf, J. (2010). A values-based approach to vulnerability and adaptation to climate change. *Wiley Interdisciplinary Reviews: Climate Change, 1*(2), 232–242.

Pant, S., & Cha, E. J. (2019). Potential changes in hurricane risk profile across the United States coastal regions under climate change scenarios. *Structural Safety, 80*, 56–65.

Pelling, M. (2011). *Adaptation to climate change: From resilience to transformation*. London: Routledge.

Smit, B., & Wandel, J. (2006). Adaptation, adaptive capacity and vulnerability. *Global Environmental Change, 16*, 282–292.

Smit, B., Burton, I., Klein, R. J. T., & Street, R. (1999). The science of adaptation: A framework for assessment. *Mitigation and Adaptation Strategies for Global Change, 4*, 199–213.

Taylor, M. (2015). *The political ecology of climate change adaptation: Livelihoods, agrarian change and the conflicts of development*. London: Routledge.

Tschakert, P., Das, P. J., Pradhan, N. S., Machado, M., Lamadrid, A., Buragohain, M., & Hazarika, M. A. (2016). Micropolitics in collective learning spaces for adaptive decision-making. *Global Environmental Change, 40*, 182–194.

van Oldenborgh, G. J., Krikken, F., Lewis, S., Leach, N. J., Lehner, F., Saunders, K. R., ... Otto, F. E. L. (2020). Attribution of the Australian bushfire risk to anthropogenic climate change (preprint). *Natural Hazards and Earth System Science Discussions, 2020*, 1–46. https://doi.org/10.5194/nhess-2020-69

Warrick, O., Aalbersberg, W., Dumaru, P., McNaught, R., & Teperman, K. (2017). The 'Pacific adaptive capacity analysis framework': Guiding the assessment of adaptive capacity in Pacific Island communities. *Regional Environmental Change, 17*, 1039–1051.

Williams, M., Pauli, N., & Boruff, B. (2020). Participatory GIS and community-based adaptation to climate change and environmental hazards: A Cambodian case study. In A. Neef & N. Pauli (Eds.), *Climate-induced disasters in the Asia-Pacific region: Response, recovery, adaptation* (pp. 113–134). Bingley: Emerald Publishing.

Woroniecki, S., Krüger, R., Rau, A.-L., Preuss, M. S., Baumgartner, N., Raggers, S., ... Abson, D. (2019). The framing of power in climate change adaptation research. *Wiley Interdisciplinary Reviews: Climate Change, 2019*, e617.

Yamamauchi, K. (2014). Climate change impacts on agriculture and irrigation in the Lower Mekong Basin. *Paddy and Water Environment, 12*(S2), 227–240.

Yila, O., Weber, E., & Neef, A. (2013). The role of social capital in post-flood response and recovery among downstream communities of the Ba River, Western Viti Levu, Fiji Islands. In A. Neef & R. Shaw (Eds.), *Risks and conflicts. Local responses to natural disasters* (pp. 79–107). Bingley: Emerald Publishing.

CHAPTER 2

LINKING DISASTER RISK REDUCTION TO DEVELOPMENT: THE EVOLUTION OF 'BUILDING BACK BETTER' IN INTERNATIONAL DISASTER MANAGEMENT FRAMEWORKS

Lucy Benge and Andreas Neef

ABSTRACT

Disasters are increasingly depicted as unique opportunities to 'build back better', to make communities more 'resilient' and to address pre-existing 'vulnerabilities'. This has seen international disaster risk reduction (DRR) and recovery frameworks attempt to link short-term relief efforts with long-term development objectives while at the same time ensuring active community participation, local knowledge inclusion and ownership. This chapter looks at how 'build back better' – which became institutionalised through the 2015 Sendai Framework for Disaster Risk Reduction – attempts to reconcile normative concepts of 'better' with diverse place-based needs, interests and knowledge. Through an analysis of three United Nations DRR frameworks from 1994 to 2015, the chapter tracks how disasters have been constructed as opportunities for development, and asks whether the post-disaster context is the right time for implementing development agendas given the potential for recovery to be co-opted by dominant development ideologies.

Keywords: Building back better; disaster risk reduction; development; vulnerability; resilience; local knowledge

Climate-Induced Disasters in the Asia-Pacific Region: Response, Recovery, Adaptation
Community, Environment and Disaster Risk Management, Volume 22, 11–24
Copyright © 2021 by Emerald Publishing Limited
All rights of reproduction in any form reserved
ISSN: 2040-7262/doi:10.1108/S2040-726220200000022002

INTRODUCTION: CONSTRUCTING DISASTERS AS OPPORTUNITIES FOR DEVELOPMENT

Disasters are malleable, socially embedded events defined through the discourse of 'risk' and 'vulnerability'. Through a social constructivist lens, this chapter analyses the discursive transition towards understanding disasters as an 'opportunity for social improvement'. The chapter examines how institutionalised disaster discourse has linked disaster risk reduction (DRR) with development and how this link reinforces particular forms of knowledge and power.

In this chapter, we examine how particular constructions of disaster have come to exist and the consequence of understanding disasters in these terms. Revealing the discursive process through which policy actors in the Global North have framed disasters as 'opportunities for social change' creates space for dominant disaster management paradigms to be unpacked. In this way, we look at how disasters have been created by the socio-political space and how they can, in turn, influence its construction. This approach understands disasters as deeply political events capable of reorganising the socio-political world on multiple levels (Guggenheim, 2014).

This chapter traces how the flow of knowledge, expertise and technology from the 'developed' to the 'developing' world has contributed to turning 'vulnerable' populations into objects to be managed and directed towards 'progress'. This involves understanding 'vulnerability' and 'underdevelopment' as labelling techniques, which are used by institutions as a way of justifying disasters as opportunities for change. Disasters, Bankoff (2001, p. 29) argues, are embedded in a 'distinctly Western construction of knowledge'. This knowledge imagines geographical boundaries and borders around subjects – defining certain places as 'risky' and particular subjects as 'vulnerable'. Labelling the world in this way helps to legitimise acting on disasters as opportunities for change by influencing the way in which risk is understood and managed (Howes, 2005).

Despite a substantial body of literature depicting disasters as 'opportunities' for 'positive' change and 'better' development, there has been very little critical analysis of what these opportunities mean and whose agenda they serve. In response to this, we examine – through an analysis of the United Nations key guiding frameworks for DRR – how disasters can be used to implement dominant ideas of progress, while also offering opportunities to disrupt status quo approaches to development.

Naturalising Disaster

Ecological science, engineering and planning discourse have constructed disasters through the language of 'environmental determinism' and 'accident' (Hewitt, 1983). Consequently, disasters are often understood as unavoidable and natural 'one-off events or aberrations in the normal path of development' (Schilderman, 2004, p. 416). This approach understands disasters as problems to be dealt with by scientists, engineers and bureaucrats (Hewitt, 1983). Disasters are depicted as inevitable but capable of being managed through appropriate planning, early warning systems, seismic prediction and building codes (Howes, 2005). Understanding disasters as indiscriminate 'natural' events helps to conceal the structural inequalities which make some groups more vulnerable to the impacts of disasters. As Bassett and Fogelman (2013, p. 45) argue, this school of thinking locates risk in the hazard itself, rather than 'the underlying sources of vulnerability that exposed people to a wide range of social as well as bio-physical stressors'.

The natural hazards school approach to disaster management focusses on the reconstruction of 'normal' pre-disaster conditions through the proper management of recovery (Aldunce, Beilin, Handmer, & Howden, 2014). This approach has been criticised for reinforcing the status quo; 'namely the process of underdevelopment that produced [...] vulnerability in the first place' (Susman, O'Keefe, & Wisner, 1983, p. 279). Understanding disasters as fundamentally 'innocent' or apolitical event[s] (Cannon, 2008) may create recovery actions oriented towards 'short term relief with little linkage to long-term development' (Berke, Kartez, & Wenger, 1993, p. 94). When disasters are understood as the product of underlying social and political structural inequalities, there is a greater imperative to act on these inequalities through development-oriented actions in the recovery period. While this chapter does not deny the need to examine the social and political structures that make some groups more vulnerable to disasters, it is wary of attempts to act upon or improve these structures in the immediate aftermath of a disaster. This is in large part due to a conceptual struggle over what constitutes social improvement and who defines it, as well as a practical struggle over to how to implement these changes in contexts requiring rapid relief.

Linking Disasters to Development

Understanding disasters as socio-political events involves seeing them as both an effect of and contributor to 'underdevelopment' (O'Keefe & Westgate, 1977). Schilderman (2004) describes this as a vicious cycle which can only be overcome by addressing underlying vulnerabilities through development. In the pre-emptive phase, this involves the inclusion of disaster planning in development projects in an effort to mitigate the impact of disasters when they occur, while in the post-disaster phase, it involves including longer term development objectives in relief and recovery actions (O'Keefe & Westgate, 1977).

Linking disasters to patterns of underdevelopment involves seeing disasters as a consequence of social and political inequalities which, Susman et al. (1983, p. 267) suggest, can be traced 'to the structural imbalance between rich and poor countries'. While this attempts to recognise the *global* structures that have contributed to vulnerability, there remains a tendency to attribute disasters to maladaptive patterns of development at the *local* level (Oliver-Smith, 1996). Attributing disasters to inequitable local social structures or corrupt national development strategies helps to legitimise international relief efforts which use the post-disaster moment as an opportunity to develop 'better' local-level social and political systems. Understanding disasters as a consequence of underdevelopment creates disaster management strategies which attempt to address vulnerability through efforts to 'build back better'.

Fan (2013, p. 1) describes 'building back better' as 'the latest iteration of a long-standing concern to link immediate relief with longer-term processes of [...] development'. The concept of 'building back better' emerged following the 2004 Indian

Ocean earthquake and tsunami with the intent of ensuring the recovery process achieved 'more than just restoring what was there before' (former US President Bill Clinton, as cited in Fan, 2013, p. 1). In its narrow sense, 'building back better' refers to the rebuilding of physical infrastructures with the imperative of ensuring communities are 'better prepared to face the next disaster' (Srivastava & Shaw, 2015, p. 26). In its more holistic form, 'building back better' articulates the process of 'helping society achieve much broader development goals' (Haigh & Amaratunga, 2011, p. 9). Attempts to 'build back better' can therefore be understood as involving the reconstruction of physically safer communities which are also 'fairer, stronger and more peaceful than they had been before the disaster' (Fan, 2013, p. 1).

With the inclusion of social and political change within the rhetoric of 'building back better', there is an imperative to examine whose idea of 'better' is being implemented. Using disasters as an opportunity to enact social change risks perpetuating a form of imperialism in which powerful external stakeholders determine the metrics of 'recovery' and 'progress'. Palliyaguru and Amaratunga (2011, p. 268) suggest that 'it is common for affected communities to demand a return to normalcy almost immediately, although experts often recognise that disaster is an opportunity to "build back better".'

Practical attempts to 'build back better' after disasters are complicated by diverse ideas, values and interests surrounding what it means to enact 'better' development. This complexity is heightened in the post-disaster moment by the introduction of multiple actors and the collapse of pre-existing social systems – creating the potential for expert ideals to be privileged over local voices. Fan (2013) suggests that the post-disaster context may not be the right time to act upon long-term development problems given the difficulty of reconciling the need to 'build back quickly' with the desire to 'build back better'. Kim and Olshansky (2014, p. 289) articulate this as a 'trade-off between "speed and deliberation", between restoration of what was lost and building back better, stronger, greener, and more equitably'.

AN ANALYSIS OF GLOBAL DISASTER RISK MANAGEMENT FRAMEWORKS

In this section, we examine the discourse of three consecutive United Nations disaster mitigation, relief and recovery frameworks produced out of the World Conferences on Disaster Mitigation from 1994 to 2015. We look at how a particular disaster knowledge has been produced and how effort has been made to reconcile science-based concepts of vulnerability and risk with local knowledge and community participation. Through this analysis, we trace the gradual development of the 'build back better' concept and begin to unpack how this concept has been justified as the latest objective of disaster recovery.

The Yokohama Strategy and Plan of Action for a Safer World (1994)

The Yokohama Strategy (1994) was developed in a context of rapidly expanding global interdependence, calling for cooperation and coordination at an international level to integrate disaster prevention into development assistance. It aimed to foster a global partnership based on 'common interests and shared responsibility', while at the same time emphasising the need for a 'greater insight into individual and collective perception of development and risk' (UNDHA, 1994, p. 4). The Yokohama Strategy attempted to improve risk awareness in vulnerable communities through appropriate education, training and technical support and to use participation as a way of incorporating traditional knowledge into mainstream scientific measures of prevention and risk management (UNDHA, 1994, p. 12).

Constructing a Culture of Prevention

The Yokohama Strategy was based around the reduction of vulnerability and the construction of a 'global culture of prevention' (UNDHA 1994, p. 10), through the introduction of DRR into development goals. Emphasising the shift from reaction to prevention, the Yokohama Strategy endeavoured to shift the focus 'from disaster management to disaster risk management' (Manyena, O'Brien, O'Keefe, & Rose, 2011, p. 422). This approach focussed on the reduction of 'risk' before disasters occurred, thus keeping risk reduction objectives separate from those of recovery. Rather than integrating the goals of DRR into the recovery phase, the Yokohama Strategy focussed on sustainable development and vulnerability reduction *before* disasters occurred in order to mitigate the need for relief later.

Despite the emphasis on pre-disaster vulnerability reduction, the Yokohama Strategy continued to reinforce the natural hazards school approach to risk, understanding disasters as fundamentally 'natural' events 'beyond human control', and human suffering as something to be managed through the application of technical assistance and preparedness planning (UNDHA, 1994, p. 9). In this way, the Yokohama Strategy contributed to the discursive construction of vulnerable communities – 'the poor and socially disadvantaged [...] in developing countries' who have the capacity to adapt into 'resilient safety cultures' (UNDHA, 1994, p. 4). 'Vulnerability reduction' required appropriate preventative planning and the enforcement of 'safety standards and rules' (UNDHA, 1994, p. 14). This approach understood 'vulnerability' as the *physical* exposure to a 'natural hazard', thus understanding disasters as largely apolitical events capable of being acted upon in the preventive moment through science-based, 'good practice' (UNDHA, 1994).

Reconciling Local and Scientific Knowledge

The Yokohama Strategy argued that 'preventative measures are most effective when they involve participation at all levels' (UNDHA, 1994, p. 8). Despite this, the Yokohama Strategy's attempt to acknowledge local knowledge and risk perception was in tension with its need for measurable objective standards of risk. The Strategy suggested that 'vulnerable countries should be enabled to [...] share traditional methods to reduce the impact of natural disaster, supplemented and reinforced by access to modern scientific and technical knowledge' (UNDHA, 1994, p. 9). This approach understood vulnerability reduction as requiring the 'application of proper design', 'risk assessment', the 'transfer of technology' and the application of 'appropriate education and training' (UNDHA, 1994, p. 8).

Consequently, *traditional* local risk reduction approaches were acknowledged in so far as they could be 'propagat[ed] ... as part of development activities' (UNDHA, 1994, p. 11). The Yokohama Strategy's attempt to construct a global 'culture of prevention' suggested that local culture must adapt in order to cooperate with the construction of a 'safer world' (UNDHA, 1994, p. 11). This reinforced an institutionalised idea of safety and common interest over diverse context-specific knowledge, values and interests.

Shying Away from Global Accountability

The Yokohama Strategy argued that 'disaster prevention and preparedness should be considered integral aspects of development policy' (UNDHA, 1994, p. 8). The Strategy further recognised that:

> some patterns of consumption, production and development have the potential for increasing the vulnerability to natural disaster .... However, sustainable development can contribute to reduction of this vulnerability, if planned and managed in a way to ameliorate the social and economic conditions of the affected groups and communities. (UNDHA, 1994, p. 8)

The Strategy placed a strong emphasis on the need to 'strengthen the resilience and self-confidence of local communities' and to adopt a 'policy of self-reliance'. This had the effect of focussing on *local*-level action at the expense of examining the action required *globally*. While at the national level, developing countries were encouraged to recognise the link between their own development patterns and their vulnerability to disasters, at the international level, the focus was on correcting the patterns of development *within* developing nations rather than addressing the global drivers of inequality and underdevelopment.

The Hyogo Framework for Action 2005–2015

The Hyogo Framework for Action (2005) built upon the Yokohama Strategy (1994) looking for ways to enhance 'resilience' at the *local* level. This Framework expanded the emphasis on DRR into the recovery phase itself, breaking down the distinction between short-term relief and long-term development objectives. Disasters were understood by the Hyogo Framework as transitional 'windows of opportunity', requiring the 'sharing of good practices, knowledge and technical support' in an effort to promote sustainable, self-directed, physical, social and economic recovery (UNISDR, 2005, p. 17).

The Emergence of a New Discourse: Constructing Global Resilience

A key priority of the Hyogo Framework was to 'use knowledge innovation and education to build a culture of safety and resilience at all levels' (UNISDR, 2005, p. 6). The shift towards the discourse of resilience indicated a move towards a neoliberal rationality in which risk reduction is an exercise of personal responsibility and autonomy. Manyena et al. (2011, p. 418) describe how the emergence of resilience 'shifted the focus to self-reliance as a counter to vulnerability'.

Resilience was defined by the Hyogo Framework as the capacity of communities to

adapt, by resisting or changing in order to reach and maintain an acceptable level of functioning [...]. This is determined by the degree to which the social system is capable of organising itself to increase [...] capacity for learning from past disasters for better future protection and to improve risk reduction measures. (UNISDR, 2005, p. 4)

With the shift towards the discourse of resilience, the Hyogo Framework was also able to shift accountability, making disasters the consequence of an underfunctioning *local*-level system rather than inequitable global power structures, thus 'clouding the issue of responsibility' (Gillard, 2016, p. 15). Resilience continued to be defined by the Hyogo Framework through a science-based metric in which 'generic, realistic and measurable indicators' were used to assess the resilience of disaster prone, developing countries and their progress towards 'internationally agreed development goals' (UNISDR, 2005, p. 17). Resilience, despite its attempt to promote local capacity, is benchmarked by the Hyogo Framework in relation to institutional expert standards of risk and progress rather than grounded in nuanced, diverse local knowledge.

The 'Window of Opportunity'
The Hyogo Framework introduced the concept of disasters as 'windows of opportunity' for sustainable development and the building of community resilience (UNISDR, 2005, p. 5). While the Yokohama Strategy focussed on linking DRR measures with development programming *before* disasters occurred, the Hyogo Framework took this a step further, looking at how the post-disaster period could also be utilised as an opportunity for implementing sustainable development practice.

The recovery period, in the Hyogo Framework, was seen as an opportunity to 'reduce disaster risk in the long-term through the sharing of expertise' (UNISDR, 2005, p. 11), in particular around land-use planning, building codes and livelihood diversification. This process of knowledge sharing is often bound up with political and geographical power structures which encourage 'North–South and South–South cooperation' (UNISDR, 2005, p. 18), to the exclusion of a 'South' to 'North' knowledge transfer. The post-disaster context, when seen as an opportunity to bring about long-term change helps to legitimise external interventions and knowledge transfers in the aftermath of disaster events. Larsen, Calgaro, and Thomalla (2011) provide evidence from recovery efforts to demonstrate how 'resilience building measures during recovery, disaster preparedness, and early warning system development, rarely address the underlying causes of vulnerability and trajectories of social inequality in disaster prone societies' (p. 482). Using the example of the 2004 Indian Ocean tsunami in Sri Lanka, they show how the policy decision to create a no-build coastal buffer zone after the tsunami led to the 'resettlement or eviction from prior, legal or de facto, property with subsequent negative consequences for livelihoods' (Larsen et al., 2011, p. 482).

The Hyogo Framework attempts to mitigate the negative effects of decisions made in the aftermath of disasters by emphasising the importance of participation at all levels. Larsen et al. (2011, p. 483) point also to the challenge of achieving this due to the 'chaotic and sometimes competitive nature of humanitarian relief and post-disaster recovery ... limited differentiation of beneficiaries needs', and significantly the multitude of 'agencies and organisations with different mandates and agendas'. This makes the task of reaching consensus on acceptable levels of risk and the development of strategies to reduce those risks in the aftermath of disasters all the more fraught. Furthermore, the Hyogo Framework suggests that the starting point for reducing disaster risk and creating a culture of resilience lies in 'knowledge of the hazards and the physical, social, economic and environmental vulnerabilities to disasters that most societies face' (UNISDR, 2005, p. 7).

Creating consensus among international, national and community stakeholders on what these vulnerabilities consist of and what the desirable state of 'resilience' ought to look like during the disaster recovery period is likely to be impended by imbalances in power. For example, despite the introduction of new planning guidelines and building codes for beach-front hotels in Thailand following the Indian Ocean tsunami, 'lack of financial and human capacity to enforce new regulations coupled with widespread corruption and nepotism amongst government officials [...] resulted in failed implementation' (Larsen et al., 2011, p. 482). Despite the challenges of linking disaster recovery with long-term development objectives, the rhetoric of 'disasters as opportunities' continued into the 2015–2030 Sendai Framework, which saw the institutionalisation of the 'building back better' concept.

The Sendai Framework for Disaster Risk Reduction 2015–2030

The 2015 Sendai Framework for Disaster Risk Reduction demonstrates the gradual discursive shift that has taken place since 1994 – from preventative attempts to reduce 'vulnerability', towards 'resilience-building' and the breakdown of the distinction between DRR and development. The Sendai Framework expands on this, building stronger, more complex links between ideas of risk, vulnerability, progress and development. It does this through recognition of multiple underlying social, economic and political risk factors and an understanding of risk as context-specific. This framework sees the mainstreaming of DRR into development in both the pre-emptive and post-disaster context, understanding DRR as involving action on underlying 'risk drivers' including poverty and inequality (UNISDR, 2015, p. 10).

A People-Centred Approach

The Sendai Framework (2015) attempts to reconcile the tension between external scientific standards of risk with the demand for genuine local participation and traditional knowledge inclusion. It moves beyond the recognition of multiple risk factors, towards an understanding of how risk affects particular groups in different ways. This people-centred approach understands risk as relative to individual capacity and understands DRR as the process through which individuals expand their capacity to avoid, adapt and recover from disasters. In this context, international support for developing countries must be 'tailored to the needs and priorities as identified by them [the subjects of development]' (UNISDR, 2015, p. 36).

The Sendai Framework argues that the

extent to which developing countries are able to effectively enhance and implement national disaster risk reduction policies and measures in the context of their respective circumstances and capabilities, can be further enhanced through the provision of sustainable international cooperation. (UNISDR, 2015, p. 13)

This approach attempts to marry international cooperation with respect for local autonomy, yet continues to perpetuate uncertainty as to how a standardised metric of risk can be implemented in the context of diverse cultural values, livelihoods and needs. Institutional attempts to recognise risk as contextually situated and individually relative continue to be limited by the bureaucratic need to measure progress through a generic metric of risk reduction.

'Building Back Better': A New Paradigm
Priority 4 of the Sendai Framework calls for '[e]nhancing disaster preparedness for effective response and to "Build Back Better" in recovery, rehabilitation and reconstruction' (UNISDR, 2015, p. 14). Building back better, according to the Sendai Framework, involves: 'integrated and inclusive economic, structural, legal, social, health, cultural, educational, environmental, technological, political and institutional measures that prevent and reduce hazard exposure and vulnerability to disaster' (UNISDR, 2015, p. 12). This involves the reduction of risk through improved physical and social structures. However, given the scale and multiplicity of underlying risks – as well as differences in how risks are perceived – the feasibility of 'building back better' in the post-disaster context still remains highly uncertain. In an effort to reduce the social, economic, political and environmental causes of disaster, 'building back better' has become another way of talking about development objectives, while using the post-disaster environment as a way of legitimising or pushing through changes which might not be possible under ordinary conditions.

'Building back better' is complicated not only by multiple underlying risk factors but also by diverse interpretations of risk. Local risk perception continues to be discussed relative to 'actual risk' – typically understood as the purview of engineers and scientists (Oliver-Smith, 1996). While the Sendai Framework recognises how disasters affect people in different ways, the risk continues to be acted upon through top-down solutions which call upon 'principles of universal design and the standardisation of building materials' (UNISDR, 2015, p. 19). This perpetuates a reality in which science-based knowledge sits outside of cultural values and where ideas of 'better' are assumed self-evident. 'Building back better' becomes a way of enacting global development standards rather than addressing localised, context-specific needs and interests.

The Role of Local Knowledge: Reframing Familiar Challenges
The Sendai Framework's attempt to recognise diverse conceptions of risk, vulnerability and improvement is undermined by its continued emphasis on strengthening the 'technical and scientific capacity to capitalise on and consolidate existing knowledge' (UNISDR, 2015, p. 15). Again, this demonstrates the privileging of

science over local interests and the attempt to incorporate local knowledge into the mainstream disaster management paradigm. Despite the attempt to acknowledge local needs and values, there remains a strong sense that local knowledge is being symbolically appropriated by science as a way of legitimising development interventions.

In the more than 20 years between the adoption of the Yokohama Strategy and the promulgation of the Sendai Framework, we can observe a discursive transition in thinking about local knowledge and its interaction with standardised, international disaster management strategies. Despite this narrative shift, the challenges identified in the Yokohama Strategy and Hyogo Framework continue to play out in the Sendai Framework. Initially used in 1994 as a way of justifying international intervention, 'local knowledge' and attempts at 'active participation' were kept separate from the main goals of technological management and planning. With the Hyogo Framework in 2005, we saw a move towards the integration of 'local' and 'technological' knowledge in an attempt to bring about a 'cultural shift' towards resilience. Finally, the 2015 Sendai Framework demonstrates the most holistic attempt at including localised needs and knowledge in the design of risk reduction strategies, through recognition of 'risk' as contextually specific. Yet, despite this shift, the Sendai Framework continues to perpetuate a distinction between 'global objective science' and 'local subjective knowledge', thus contributing to the de-legitimisation of local conceptions of risk, vulnerability and development. As Larsen et al. (2011, p. 489) argue, more needs to be done to acknowledge and incorporate 'the processes through which legitimate visions of resilience are generated' – and, we argue, legitimate visions of risk, vulnerability and desirable development.

DISCUSSION: DISASTERS AS AN OPPORTUNITY FOR ALTERNATIVES

In this discussion, we return to the question of whether disasters should be used as opportunities to enact long-term social change and look at how 'opportunity' has been defined by those in positions of power, as well as how local knowledge can help to challenge normative ideas of progress and betterment.

Normative approaches to DRR suggest that what is needed is a more in-depth understanding of natural hazards and better integration of disaster knowledge into the wider efforts of sustainable development (White, Kates, & Burton, 2001). This assumes the existence of an objective 'disaster knowledge' based on materially tangible risks which can be assessed and managed. In an attempt to make normative approaches to risk reduction and recovery more inclusive of diverse risk perceptions, this chapter argues for the conceptual expansion of risk and development narratives and an awareness of how these ideas are contextually determined.

A key aspect of the original 'building back better' concept – established following the 2004 Indian Ocean tsunami – was that 'recovery should be driven by the community and that all operations require the consultation and participation of locals' (Mannakkara & Wilkinson, 2014, p. 334). Local participation, ownership, empowerment and Indigenous knowledge inclusion have been introduced by the Sendai Framework as a way of complementing expert-orientated approaches to DRR. Yet, in practice, attempts at inclusion have often led to the drawing of boundaries around the 'local', the failure to recognise power structures at all levels and the co-option of traditional knowledge into dominant forms of risk management. Cooke and Kothari (2001, p. 12) argue that participation has become a technique used by development professionals to conceal political motivations and to clean up local knowledge, marginalising 'that which might challenge the status quo'. Consequently, participation can be used as a technique of control; a way of representing opportunities to make them appear locally constituted and empowering despite the continued privileging of so-called expert knowledge.

Situating Risk

Attempts at addressing disaster risk have focussed on the construction of responsible, physically resilient, cultures. This has often occurred with little recognition of the autonomy involved in decisions around which risks are acceptable to live with. Cannon (2008, p. 354) draws attention to how people 'trade-off the risks they face with the benefit of their livelihood and [...] their desire to live in a place they are accustomed to'. Deciding which risks are acceptable to live with involves expanding the capability of people to make genuine choices in situations where physical exposure to risk must be weighed against risk to culture and tradition. Without understanding how risks are weighted in different cultural contexts, DRR strategies may emphasise physical risk avoidance at the expense of protecting culture, history and identity. This is particularly evident in post-disaster reconstruction processes – such as those following the 2004 Indian Ocean tsunami – where many coastal communities in Thailand, Indonesia and Sri Lanka were made to leave their ancestral land through the creation of 'no-build zones'. This was often justified as a way of enabling communities to rebuild in physically safer – and hence seemingly 'better'– locations. In many cases, this led to the loss of traditional livelihoods, traditional building practices and historical relationships with the land (Attavanich et al., 2015). The physical safety of the new sites was thus undermined by the new risks posed to livelihoods and well-being.

This reiterates the need for risk reduction and recovery strategies to account for multiple underlying physical, economic *and* sociocultural risk factors, as well as an awareness of how these risks are weighted, understood and managed at the community level. Definitions of 'building back better' are dependent upon how risk and vulnerability are understood in relation to progress and resilience. Attempts to 'build back better' should therefore ensure people are able to decide for themselves which risks they are willing to live with and which they demand action upon.

Doing Development Differently

'Building back better' is complicated by the diversity of interests, needs and forms of knowledge involved in determining what 'better' might look like. Despite the conceptual challenges of reconstructing 'better' physical and social structures, disasters may offer an opportunity to disrupt pre-existing power structures and patterns of development (Guggenheim, 2014). Gunder (2008) suggests that disasters provide opportunities for creative potential and alternative socio-political worlds, while Oliver-Smith (1996, p. 310) argues that disasters can act as catalysts for 'political solidarity, activism, new agendas, and [...] new power relations'. By disrupting the taken-for-granted social fabric, disasters create an opportunity for new development discourses to emerge – not necessarily for doing development 'better', but certainly for change and innovation by doing development 'differently' (Aldunce et al., 2014). In this way, disasters have the potential to disrupt the dominant development paradigm, drawing attention to how previous patterns of development contributed to inequality, vulnerability and ultimately disaster.

Attempts at 'building back better' are limited by the difficulty of reconciling multiple, contested and continually shifting ideas of 'better'. Emphasis should therefore be placed on ensuring that groups with the least political autonomy are able to contribute to determining the direction of disaster reconstruction and recovery. This involves more than the generalised inclusion of 'local knowledge' through symbolic attempts at 'participation'. Instead, it requires understanding how local ideas of improvement are shaped by differences in which risks are deemed acceptable to live with. Attempts at 'building back better' should be flexible enough to accommodate people's own descriptions of vulnerability, risk and improvement. This can help to resist a permanent, positivist, scientific reality in which disasters are acted upon and managed by experts alone.

CONCLUSION

This chapter has looked at how disasters have been created and acted upon as problems of 'underdevelopment'. We have argued that there is a need for recovery and risk reduction efforts to become aware of nuanced social contexts rather than attempting to fit these into a standardised model of disaster risk management. Attempts to 'build back better' continue to perpetuate an approach in which people are treated as statistics to be 'moved up and down the charts of progress' (Escobar, 1995, p. 44). Turning disaster recovery efforts into opportunities for long-term development is complicated by the numerous social, cultural, economic, environmental and political impacts of disasters, coupled with the diverse ways in which these impacts are understood and acted upon. Consequently, attempts to 'build back better' are likely to perpetuate a particular idea of improvement – often emphasising the need for *local*-level change at the expense of *global* accountability.

The difficulty of utilising disasters' opportunities to 'build back better' is both conceptual and practical, contending with issues of how to define 'better' and how to enact it in circumstances requiring rapid relief. In this chapter, we have focussed largely on the conceptual issue, demonstrating how particular ideas of vulnerability and improvement have been institutionalised at the expense of recognising these concepts as contextually relative. This suggests a need for dialogue between diverse values and interests so that normative ideas of 'better' can be resisted and reconstructed through the introduction of alternative concepts of change and progress. Disasters might, in this way, create an opportunity for diverse understandings of risk to be placed in conversation – helping to break down the hegemonic narratives that have constructed parts of the world as vulnerable, underdeveloped and at risk.

REFERENCES

Aldunce, P., Beilin, R., Handmer, J., & Howden. M. (2014). Framing disaster resilience: The implications of the diverse conceptualisation of "bouncing back". *Disaster Prevention and Management*, 23(3), 252–270.

Attavanich, M., Neef, A., Kobayashi, H., & Tachakitkachorn, T. (2015). Change of livelihoods and living conditions after the 2004 Indian Ocean Tsunami: The case of the post-disaster rehabilitation of the Moklen Community in Tungwa Village, Southern Thailand. In R. Shaw (Ed.), *Recovery from the Indian Ocean Tsunami: A Ten-Year Journey* (pp. 471–486). Tokyo, Heidelberg, New York, Dordrecht, London: Springer Publishers.

Bankoff, G. (2001). Rendering the world unsafe: 'Vulnerability' as Western discourse. *Disasters*, 25(1), 19–35.

Bassett, T. J., & Fogelman, C. (2013). Déjà vu or something new? The adaptation concept in the climate change literature. *Geoforum*, 48, 42–53.

Berke, R. P., Kartez, J., & Wenger, D. (1993). Recovery after disaster: Achieving sustainable development, mitigation and equity. *Disasters*, 17(2), 93–109.

Cannon, T. (2008). Vulnerability, "innocent" disasters and the imperative of cultural understanding. *Disaster Prevention and Management*, 17(3), 350–357.

Cooke, B., & Kothari, U. (2001). The case for participation as tyranny. In B. Cooke & U. Kothari (Eds.), *Participation: The new tyranny?* (pp. 1–15). London: Zed Books.

Escobar, A. (1995). *Encountering development. The making and unmaking of the Third World*. Princeton, NJ: Princeton University Press.

Fan, L. (2013). *Disaster as opportunity? Building back better in Aceh, Myanmar and Haiti*. HPG Working Paper. Overseas Development Institute, London.

Furedi, F. (2007). The changing meaning of disaster. *Area*, 39(4), 482–489.

Gillard, R. (2016). Questioning the diffusion of resilience discourses in pursuit of transformational change. *Global Environmental Politics*, 16(1), 13–20.

Guggenheim, M. (2014). Introduction: Disasters as politics – Politics as disasters. *The Sociological Review*, 62(S1), 1–16.

Gunder, M. (2008). Ideologies of certainty in a risky reality: Beyond the hauntology of planning. *Planning Theory*, 7(2), 186–206.

Haigh, R., & Amaratunga, D. (2011). *Post-disaster reconstruction of the built environment: Rebuilding for resilience*. Oxford: Wiley-Blackwell.

Hewitt, K. (1983). The idea of calamity in a technocratic age. In K. Hewitt (Ed.), *Interpretations of calamity* (pp. 3–32). Boston, MA: Allen & Unwin Inc.

Howes, M. (2005). *Politics and the environment. Risk and the role of government and industry*. London: Earthscan.

Kim, K., & Olshansky, R. B. (2014). The theory and practice of building back better. *Journal of the American Planning Association*, 80(4), 289–292.

Larsen, R. K., Calgaro, E., & Thomalla, F. (2011). Governing resilience building in Thailand's tourism-dependent coastal communities: Conceptualising stakeholder agency in social-ecological systems. *Global Environmental Change*, 21, 481–491.

Mannakkara, S., & Wilkinson, S. (2014). Re-conceptualising "building back better" to improve post-disaster recovery. *International Journal of Managing Projects in Business*, 7(3), 327–341.

Manyena, B. S., O'Brien, G., O'Keefe, P., & Rose, J. (2011). Disaster resilience: A bounce back or bounce forward ability? *Local Environment*, 16(5), 417–424.

O'Keefe, P., & Westgate, K. (1977). Preventative planning for disasters. *Long Range Planning*, 10(3), 25–29.

Oliver-Smith, A. (1996). Anthropological research on hazards and disasters. *Annual Review of Anthropology*, 25, 303–328.

Palliyaguru, R., & Amaratunga, D. (2011). Linking reconstruction to sustainable socio-economic development. In D. Amaratunga & R. Haigh (Eds.), *Post-disaster reconstruction of the built environment: Rebuilding for resilience* (pp. 268–286). Oxford: Wiley-Blackwell.

Schilderman, T. (2004). Adapting traditional shelter for disaster mitigation and reconstruction: Experiences with community-based approaches. *Building Research & Information, 32*(5), 414–426.

Srivastava, N., & Shaw, R. (2015). Institutional and legal arrangement and its impact on urban issues in post Indian Ocean tsunami. In R. Shaw (Ed.), *Recovery from the Indian Ocean tsunami: A ten-year journey* (pp. 17–27). Tokyo: Springer.

Susman, P., O'Keefe, P., & Wisner, B. (1983). Global disasters, a radical interpretation. In K. Hewitt (Ed.), *Interpretations of calamity* (pp. 263–283). Boston, MA: Allen & Unwin Inc.

UNDHA. (1994, May). Yokohama strategy and plan of action for a safer world: Guidelines for natural disaster prevention, preparedness and mitigation. Paper presented at the World Conference on Natural Disaster Reduction, United Nations Department of Humanitarian Affairs (UNDHA), Geneva, Switzerland.

UNISDR. (2005, January). Hyogo framework for action 2005–2015: Building the resilience of nations and communities to disasters. Paper presented at the World Conference on Disaster Reduction, United Nations Inter-Agency Secretariat of the International Strategy for Disaster Reduction (UNISDR), Geneva, Switzerland.

UNISDR. (2015). *Sendai framework for disaster risk reduction 2015–2030*. Geneva: United Nations Office for Disaster Risk Reduction (UNISDR).

White, F. G., Kates, R. W., & Burton, I. (2001). Knowing better and losing even more: The use of knowledge in hazards management. *Environmental Hazards, 3*, 81–92.

CHAPTER 3

INTERSECTIONS OF COMMUNITY RESPONSES AND HUMANITARIAN INTERVENTIONS IN THE AFTERMATH OF THE 2014 FLOODS IN SOLOMON ISLANDS

Carl Adams and Andreas Neef

ABSTRACT

This chapter presents an exploration of the ways in which humanitarian non-government organisations (NGOs) and communities affected by the 2014 floods in Solomon Islands interpreted and responded to the disaster, identifying factors that assisted and constrained stakeholders in disaster response and recovery. The research investigates the extent to which communities were consulted and participated in NGO responses, and the factors which informed community–NGO relationships. A qualitative case study approach was used, employing interviews, focus groups and document analysis, guided by a reflexive discourse analysis and narrative inquiry approach, which places the focus of the study on the experiences of participants. Communities played very limited roles in NGO responses, especially non-dominant or marginalised sectors of society, such as youth, women and people with disabilities. Failure to respond appropriately to the differentiated needs of affected populations can exacerbate their risk of experiencing secondary disaster. The authors argue that there is a need to improve the inclusiveness of responses to disaster, engaging women, youth and people with disabilities in decision making in order to respond more appropriately to their needs.

Climate-Induced Disasters in the Asia-Pacific Region: Response, Recovery, Adaptation
Community, Environment and Disaster Risk Management, Volume 22, 25–55
Copyright © 2021 by Emerald Publishing Limited
All rights of reproduction in any form reserved
ISSN: 2040-7262/doi:10.1108/S2040-726220200000022009

Keywords: Flood events; disaster response; community participation; humanitarian interventions; discourse analysis; narrative inquiry; Solomon Islands

INTRODUCTION

Solomon Islands has experienced a number of disasters which remain large on the national psyche due to their scale and devastation. People's lived experience of past disasters can have a profound impact on the way they perceive and respond to future disasters. This study focusses on the April 2014 flash flooding, which the United Nations Office for the Coordination of Humanitarian Affairs (UNOCHA, 2014) termed the 'worst flooding in the history of the Solomon Islands'. Three large-scale past disasters had impacted on communities who participated in this study, prior to the April 2014 flash floods, namely an earthquake, a cyclone and flooding. Radford and Blong (1991) conducted a survey of 200 natural disasters in Solomon Islands, finding that damage from tropical cyclones exceeded that of earthquakes by a factor of five. Their research showed that Guadalcanal, Makira and Malaita provinces have suffered the most damage historically, and also projected that tropical cyclones, earthquakes and volcanoes would be the most significant hazards going forward (Radford & Blong, 1991).

The aim of this study is to investigate community participation and non-governmental organisation (NGO) responses to the April 2014 floods in Solomon Islands. To support this objective, the study is guided by the following questions:

- In what ways did flood-affected communities and NGOs respond to the disaster?
- What do impacted communities think of how NGOs responded to the April 2014 floods and to what extent were they consulted or participated in these responses?
- What factors enhanced or constrained organisations in their disaster responses, and why?

The study approaches these questions with a reflexive discourse analysis and narrative inquiry approach, which places the focus on the experiences of participants, giving franchise to their realities and the meaning, which they attribute to their lived experiences. This approach was selected for its practical and epistemological relevance for both Solomon Islands context and the research objectives as it places the focus on the experiences of participants, giving franchise to their realities and the meaning which they attribute to their myriad of lived experiences (Trahar, 2006). Since colonial times, Solomon Islanders have been spoken for and about by others, but rarely have their own understandings and experiences been shared in their own voices in the literature (Fairbairn-Dunlop & Coxon, 2014; Narokobi, 1983).

COMMUNITIES AND HUMANITARIAN AGENCIES IN DISASTER RESPONSE: A BRIEF REVIEW

Communities in Disaster Response

Community participation is widely discussed in disaster response, but the nature and extent of participation are contentious. Masaki (2007) contended that people tend to be constrained to act as 'users and choosers' of externally devised programmes, and instead called for them to become 'makers and shakers', of projects and policy decisions which affect them (p. 125). The role that populations affected by disaster play in relief efforts is usually under-analysed, and observers often posit them as 'populations in need' (Krause, 2014, p. 39). In light of this, it is important to delineate the term 'participation', to determine how NGOs and communities see the extent of their engagement with one another. In the past, discourse on 'participation' has largely concerned itself with the processes of disaster response – through design, implementation and evaluation phases of a project (Masaki, 2007). In its crudest form, participation has been reduced to 'an instrument to ensure people's acceptance of [NGO] projects, and to solicit their labour contributions' (Masaki, 2007, p. 118).

Disaster-affected populations are 'not naturally beneficiaries', although they 'appear as such through the eyes of the relief agency' (Krause, 2014, p. 64). Moreover, the presumption of linear processes and orderly structures, conditions upon which many participatory methods are predicated, often do not exist. Therefore, the conclusions determined from participatory tools and processes, when compounded by lag-time in decision making, may lead policy makers to 'impose policies incongruent with local circumstances' (Masaki, 2007, p. 127). This can also be true of organisations responding to disasters. The situation on the ground is often fluid, and by the time conclusions are derived from data, the circumstances have likely evolved, challenging the relevance of data collected from affected communities. Therefore, participation may not necessarily correlate with the appropriateness of response.

Disaster is gendered in the discourse that is employed to articulate, study and theorise disasters – who receives what training, the work that is funded and published, and 'who is the "we" in disaster practice' (Enarson & Marrow, 1998, p. 13). It has been widely discussed in the literature that women face greater risks and are disadvantaged in times of disaster (cf. Bennett, Neef, & Varea, 2020 – Chapter 5, this Volume). There has also been discussion of how organisations respond (or do not respond), to gendered needs, an important theme of Chapter 5. There is less literature about women's agency and a lack of recognition that 'women are active throughout the disaster management cycle: in mitigation, prevention, preparedness, emergency response and recovery' (Ariyabandu, 2005, p. 11). Women are and always have been engaged in varied and diverse ways in disaster response. Furthermore, when disasters strike, community members, including women, generally respond as emergency workers, rendering assistance well before the arrival of relief agencies, government and the media (Yila, Weber, & Neef, 2013).

Women frequently face a double impact of disasters due to the compounding effect of often unequal gender relations. In times of disaster, women's subordinate power position often deprives them of decision making and influence. Enarson and Marrow (1998) illustrate that women are often denied leadership positions in emergency management and face increases in domestic violence following disaster, and their work is often devalued. Where gender is discussed, it is often limited to contrasting

> the behaviour of men and women in terms of risk perception or warning response with little concern given to explaining the differences within and between genders or why such differences might exist at all. (Enarson & Marrow, 1998, p. 31)

Responding organisations' interactions with gender have the ability to challenge or reinforce, either explicitly or implicitly, gendered patterns of domination and subordination.

NGO responses to disaster often 'neglect the particular needs of women, and sometimes even contribute to diminishing their status'; furthermore, tension periods, such as those following disaster, 'occasionally contribute to reinforcing the inferior status of women within their own communities' (Pirotte, Husson, & Grunewald, 1999, pp. 97–98). Following a disaster, established identities may be perceived to be threatened or in flux, particularly as men struggle to reassert the control and dominant position that they had before – which may manifest itself in a rise in domestic violence, restrictions placed on women and other socially harmful negative coping mechanisms (Pirotte et al., 1999).

In strongly patriarchal societies, men often control access to resources and make decisions regarding how they are distributed and used, both at the household and community level. Women often do not have land tenure or other assets and have poor access to education and training (Pirotte et al., 1999). Women-headed households and women from racial or ethnic minorities are particularly vulnerable to poverty and face greater exposure to the risks presented by disasters (Enarson & Marrow, 1998). They are often under-represented in positions of influence in decision making at the local and national levels, which places them at a disadvantage when the nature of aid is decided and distributed (Pirotte et al., 1999).

Post-Disaster Response by Humanitarian Organisations

Literature relating to the ways which humanitarian organisations approach disaster response tends to focus on three thematic areas – conceptualisation of disaster response, organisational structure and broader issues of power, which include interpersonal relations and gender (Ariyabandu, 2005; Krause, 2014; Pirotte et al., 1999). Foremost in the literature on approaching disaster response has been the ways in which organisations interpret disasters.

Pirotte et al. (1999) argued that the United Nations Development Programme interpreted disasters as 'temporary interruptions in the development process', conceptualising an 'emergency-to-development' continuum (p. 20). They suggested that this view is damaging as it seeks not to understand crises, but is reactionary from an organisation justifying the diversion of resources from development to emergency response purposes. This can be damaging insofar as the response that follows may weaken the adaptive capacity of the affected population and foster long-term dependence (Pirotte et al., 1999). Yet, over the past 20 years, with climate change progressing at a more rapid pace, we have developed an understanding that disasters become recurring issues in many parts of the Asia-Pacific that require constant adaptation and frequent recovery (e.g. Neef et al., 2018).

The structure of organisations involved in disaster response is a key determinant of how they interpret and respond to disasters. Responses to disasters are usually characterised by being unsystematic and coming from 'highly centralised, top-down, inflexible bureaucracies', where communities are rarely involved with the making of decisions which affect them (Ariyabandu, 2005, p. 35). This view may be applicable to a generalised experience; however, it is important to acknowledge the diversity of agents responding in times of disaster – from individual and kinship networks, religious institutions, NGO, governmental and multilateral agencies. While there may exist some common characteristics of organisations involved in disaster response, it is important to understand and appreciate the differences within and among organisations.

Krause (2014) discussed the dual effect of the 'project' as a unit of helping people and fundraising for NGOs – 'agencies raise funds to do projects, but they can also do projects to raise funds' (p. 47). Only by raising funds can an organisation survive, to serve its purpose of providing humanitarian or development support. There are obviously strategic imperatives which determine the course of action NGOs take in disaster response. Beristain (2006) proposed that this may cause a disjuncture between NGO management who are likely to be more aware of organisational strategy when providing resources; as opposed to aid workers on the ground, who are more attuned and sensitive to the priorities and needs of affected populations.

In the event of a disaster, there is often a dichotomy of power and resources between affected communities and responding organisations, including NGOs. Aid workers have power over affected populations insofar as agencies control access to resources and services, and aid workers make decisions pertaining to the distribution of those resources (Krause, 2014). Beristain (2006) argued that the 'implicit presumptions' of those who have knowledge or power while communities are in a dependent state 'suggest an attitude of superiority' (p. 85). More broadly, the idealisation of the affected population and aid can create attitudes of paternalism and belittle the agency and abilities of the population. This can also be seen through the representation and articulation of disaster survivors through patronising or disparaging terms such as 'passive', 'victim' or 'helpless' (Beristain, 2006, p. 112). NGOs often identify populations 'by what they lack: their needs are emphasised, while their political aspirations or conflicts are de-emphasised' (Beristain, 2006, p. 50). While this is patronising, it also reflects the de-politicisation of development and humanitarian interventions. The representation of disasters by NGOs to their respective supporter bases is often oversimplified, treating disaster as a stand-alone event, disengaged from the contexts which inevitably determined the extent of the impact of a disaster and the response that follows.

Situating Disaster in the Cultural Context of the Solomon Islands

Situated in the South-West Pacific Ocean, bordering Papua New Guinea to the west, Vanuatu to the south-east and Australia to the south, Solomon Islands is an archipelago comprised of over 900 islands. Solomon Islands is often noted for its diversity – of cultures, languages, polities and geography. It is home to a population of more than 500,000 according to the 2009 census, and over 90 Indigenous languages and dialects are spoken within its borders (Bennett, 1987). Contemporary Solomon Islands is divided into nine provinces, comprising a predominantly Melanesian population, with a minority of Polynesian and Micronesian groups. McDonald (2003) describes 'each island in the Solomons is effectively its own world with its own unique tribal groundings and fabric of languages, customs and beliefs' (pp. 59–60). Appreciating this diversity, national-level generalisations or characterisations predictably negate the multiplicity of histories and identities therein.

Solomon Islands' formal economy is dominated by extractive industries (mining, logging and fishing), and the country depends significantly on overseas development assistance. While the extractive industries remain the primary revenue generators, the country has been unable to substantially capitalise on its economic potential due to limited in-country value addition and porous regulatory enforcement (Moore, 2004). Over the last few decades, logging and mining have reached unsustainable levels, destroying the natural environment and exacerbating land disputes (Braithwaite, 2010; Moore, 2004). This has increased the country's susceptibility to climate-related hazards.

If 'every Pacific society has a framework of knowledge that is systematically gathered and formulated within a paradigm of general truths and principles', then *kastom* is this framework in Solomon Islands (HRC, 2004, p. 11, in Fraenkel, 2004). Encompassing both traditions and customs, *kastom* also has more epistemological connotations – determining the ways in which societies 'create meaning, structure, and construct reality' (Taufe'ulungaki, 2000, p. 11, in Fraenkel, 2004). It is, therefore, unsurprising that *kastom* is a central feature of identity politics in Solomon Islands. Cultural knowledge, values and practices are transmitted through stories and everyday living, forming what Subramani (1993) described as 'Oceania's library' of oral cultures (cited in Fairbairn-Dunlop & Coxon, 2014, p. 109). *Kastom* has been connected with representing and protecting the interests and independence of Indigenous communities; bringing people together in new ways, and emphasising local solutions and knowledge (Fraenkel, 2004; Timmer, 2008).

METHODOLOGICAL FRAMEWORK

Research Approach: Narrative Inquiry and Discourse Analysis

After days of heavy rain in early April 2014, Solomon Islands was struck by severe flooding, culminating in the loss of 22 lives and the destruction or damage of the livelihoods of over 52,000 people. The flooding claimed casualties and caused significant infrastructure damage, crop destruction, psychosocial trauma, as well as health and shelter issues. During the crisis, evacuation centres housed around

10,000 people, and upwards of 75% of Guadalcanal Province's food gardens were destroyed. In the two months following the floods, an outbreak of rotavirus spread across Solomon Islands, causing the deaths of at least 18 children and infecting in excess of 1,000 people (UNOCHA, 2014).

A wide range of government and non-government agencies predominantly focussed on responding to populations who were displaced within the immediate Honiara vicinity. Rural communities were difficult to access in the days and weeks following the flooding but were where at least 40,000 of the estimated 52,000 affected population resided.

Designed as a case study of three distinct communities in Guadalcanal one year after the flooding occurred, the research sought to reveal community members' perspectives of the disaster response, through reflecting on their own lived experiences of the events. The study focussed on one urban settlement in Central Honiara, one peri urban settlement on the outskirts on Honiara and one rural community.

This research engages both narrative inquiry and discourse analysis as the methodological framework underpinning the study. Narrative analyses premise that narrative is the dominant method by which people construct knowledge and create meaning. It places the focus on the experiences of participants, giving franchise to their realities and the meaning which they attribute to their myriad of lived experiences (Trahar, 2006). Narrative analysis has played an important role in feminist and Indigenous movements as it gives currency to the voices of marginalised groups who are under-represented or excluded from dominant discourses, allowing them to tell their story in their own voice (Fox, 2006; Trahar, 2006). In the context of this research, a narrative approach would posit that reforms to organisational responses to disasters are unlikely to be successful if the perceptions, experiences and subjectivities of all stakeholders are not understood (Cortazzi & Jin, 2006).

The combination of discursive analysis and narrative inquiry in this framework places focus on research participants' own stories, situated within their broader material and discursive context. Fittingly, both discursive and narrative approaches recognise that narrative significantly differs across political, social, cultural and temporal contexts, with variations including place, time, the position of participant(s) and researcher, and the topic of discussion (Cortazzi & Jin, 2006). This variability influences and informs the research, and thus, strong reflexivity is important to situate the findings of the research. Chase (2005, p. 657) characterises narratives as 'situated interactive performances', which are subject to change based on the circumstances of the researcher.

This research seeks to ground narrative and discursive approaches in Pacific epistemologies, with the aim of supporting and validating participants' expression. Vaioleti (2006) has suggested that 'if researching ethically is about respecting human dignity, then it is critical that the process is culturally appropriate for the participants' (p. 29). Pacific countries have a myriad of cultures whose ways of being and knowledge are diverse, both in lived experiences and epistemologies. Thus, research methods developed in a Western context may not be appropriate for Solomon Islands and risk asserting hegemonic control over participants (Vaioleti, 2006). Fairbairn-Dunlop and Coxon (2014) stressed the importance of understanding Pacific knowledge systems and their influence on the 'framing, implementation and application of research findings' (p. 17).

In Solomon Islands, knowledge sharing is generally an informal and relational process, often articulated as '*stori*', referring to both an object and a process. *Stori* is a narrative inquiry method which places participants in a knowledge-sharing setting with which they are familiar. The concept of *talanoa* is found in many Pacific languages and closely resembles *stori* in nature and function (Fairbairn-Dunlop & Coxon, 2014). *Talanoa* is purposive dialogue, which begins with presenting a topic and broad themes to open discussion, without specifying an end point. It is led by participants who explore and discuss topics and issues they identify with (Fairbairn-Dunlop & Coxon, 2014; Vaioleti, 2006). The combining of relational and narrative approaches with the use of Solomon Island Pidgin (*pijin*) language helped to demonstrate an informal research practice which was positively received by participants; as it allowed sharing, as opposed to an inter-rogation of experiences.

Fieldwork: Semi-structured Interviews and Focus Groups

Semi-structured interviews were conducted by the first author with 23 individuals, representing 17 NGO, governmental, multilateral and civil society organisations in Solomon Islands. Participants were selected purposefully, having a managerial role in their organisation's response to the disaster, and participation in interviews was voluntary. It is notable that of 23 participants, 15 were Solomon Island nationals, and 8 were expatriates, predominantly from Australia, United Kingdom and New Zealand. Participants were offered either confidentiality for their personal identity and that of their respective organisations, or to have their details published. Likewise, interviews were audio-recorded only with the consent of the interviewee. Semi-structured interviews were guided by a brief list of open-ended questions to foster discussion, but were predominantly steered by the interviewee who focussed on topics they considered most pertinent or were within their area of experience (O'Leary, 2009). The interview code keys for the semi-structured interviews are presented in Table 3.1.

Focus groups were conducted to understand the perspectives of communities impacted by the floods. In each of the three communities, four focus groups were held – one for women, one for men, one for male youth and one for female youth. Experiences of NGO response were likely to vary according to gender and age, and separate focus groups provided a space for participants to speak more openly about

Table 3.1.   Interview Categories.

Stakeholder Category	Code
High commissions	A
Government ministries	B
Multilateral agency	C
Non-government organisation	D
Community	E
Civil society organisation	F

their experiences, in gender- and age-disaggregated environments. Audio recordings were taken in each focus group, with two exceptions, as participants did not unanimously agree to use the voice recorder. In these cases, detailed notes were taken by the researcher and research assistants both during and after the focus group.

Two female and one male research assistants, aged between 25 and 35, were engaged to assist the first author with facilitating focus groups. Female research assistants were particularly important for facilitating the women's focus groups, as it allowed for discussion concerning gendered issues which would not typically be addressed in the presence of a male. All three research assistants were youth workers and had prior experience in conducting focus groups following Pacific methodological approaches of *talanoa* and *stori*. They were valuable cultural interpreters and effective at observing and recording what was said and what was not said, including focus group dynamics and non-verbal communication within the groups. They brought a depth of cultural awareness that supported the researcher to have an improved understanding of the nuances of what was being communicated.

FINDINGS I: COMMUNITIES AND NGOS IN DISASTER RESPONSE

This section explores the perspectives of members of the three case study communities which were impacted by the April 2014 floods, with a view to better understand the roles they played in the disaster response and recovery. It also presents findings concerning the effectiveness of the disaster response from organisational stakeholders who were interviewed in this study. This section looks at how NGOs interacted with communities and responded to their varied needs, from the perspectives of organisations and community members. Thereafter, the ways in which communities responded to the disaster independently of NGOs are presented and discussed.

Community Responses to the Disaster

The three case study communities in this study were engaged in disaster response far beyond the scope of their participation in NGO responses. Their roles in response were extensive and wide-ranging. Focus group participants described partaking in rescue and emergency response, evacuation, clean-up and repair, early crop harvesting, prevention and mitigation. This section presents the roles that community members undertook in response to the disaster, from the perspective of focus group participants in the three case study communities.

Located at the mouth of the Mataniko River on its western bank, the settlement at Lord Howe witnessed some of the most dramatic events of the disaster. During torrential rain on 3 April 2014, the Mataniko River burst its banks, washing away the bridge at Chinatown and sweeping houses, buildings and people downstream. In the flood, 22 people lost their lives and further lives were taken as a result of post-disaster conditions. Residents from Lord Howe settlement were among the first responders who attempted to rescue people from the swollen river. Some youth also tried precariously to retrieve goods from shipping containers which had been swept down the river. The male youth focus group in Lord Howe settlement reflected on the combined efforts of attempting to rescue people from the river and evacuating their own community which was at risk from the floodwaters:

> During the flood we helped by carrying and shifting belongings from people living under the houses to the upper floor; and also trying to rescue men, women and children who were floating down the river.

Equally, the settlement at Lunga is low-lying and flood-prone. The female youth focus group in the community reported how one of the men from their community rescued a woman from a neighbouring settlement who had been left behind in the rush to evacuate:

> One man from this community helped to save a woman from another settlement near the river. They were in a rush to escape from the place and they forgot the woman so the man from here went and rescued her.

The women's focus group in Lord Howe settlement reflected on evacuation, but also highlighted longer term options of returning to their home province, or accessing land which is less marginal and vulnerable to the impacts of disasters:

> If a disaster happens again, we know what to do – find a safe place to evacuate to or go back home (*laugh*). If not, we will go further inland to higher ground of Guadalcanal Province (*laughter*). Or marry someone from Guadalcanal so that we own land (*all laughed*).

While the women responded jovially, they highlighted the issue of access to land in Honiara, which was identified as a key challenge by many stakeholder agencies. Land in Guadalcanal Province is held under customary ownership. The vast majority of freehold land in Solomon Islands is concentrated in Honiara. However, the Honiara town boundaries are very limited, and this has resulted in high demand and high prices for land. This has pushed land ownership out of reach for many from other provinces (such as those residing in Lord Howe settlement), who in many cases have informally settled on marginal land around Honiara.

Given its location at the mouth of the Mataniko River, Lord Howe settlement was littered with debris following the flooding. Male youth from the community described the clean-up and repair efforts of their community, acknowledging the roles of different sectors of the community:

> After the flood, men, women and all youth helped in clearing the logs and the debris from the flood and the cleaning up the community. We helped the mothers set up their homes and brought their belongings back from the evacuation centre.

Community members in Aruligo made an effort to recover and sell root crops from their silted food gardens. This is an example of the role of affected communities in safeguarding their livelihoods and planning for the following months until a new harvest. The men's focus group explained the rationale behind their actions:

> We harvested all the crops in our gardens and sold them for cheaper prices so we had money to sustain our living while we waited for the disaster to finish before we started planting again. In some cases, the gardens were not ready for harvest but we had to harvest them because if we left the crops they would rot.

The women and male youth focus groups in Lord Howe settlement reflected on preparation and mitigation measures that the community has taken or is planning to take. Notably, each group outlined a different solution to the same issue of protecting the community from flooding. One woman in the women's focus group explained the importance of the sago palms along the riverbank in protecting the settlement:

We are planting more of the sago palm trees along the river bank to protect us because I witnessed how those sago palms protected us from the waves and the flood. I planted a lot beside my house and also along the river bank. I see the importance of that tree, so when someone came and asked to cut one down, I told them the story of the flood – no one is allowed to cut them down. I told other families within our settlement to also plant this tree beside their houses and beside the river so that if there is another flood, we will all hang on to it (*all laughed*).

The women's focus group also noted that some households have rebuilt their houses higher above the ground than previously. They discussed that if there was persistent rain, they would begin to prepare their belongings in case of evacuation, and some would go and stay with relatives.

The three communities in this study responded to the flooding in different ways; determined in part by the impact of the disaster, the context of their community and past experiences of disaster.

Views in Communities about Responding Agencies

Conducting Assessments: An Implied Obligation to Assist?

Following the flash flooding, NGOs, Red Cross and the National Disaster Management Office (NDMO) mobilised to undertake impact and rapid needs assessments of affected areas. All three case study communities were determined to be affected areas, but were not impacted severely and were prioritised accordingly. Focus group participants discussed the organisations which conducted assessments in their community, sharing disapproval of organisations that did not follow up with providing assistance. Participants inferred that assessments generated expectations that assistance will follow and created distrust when these expectations were not realised. Where communities did not receive assistance from an agency following an assessment, participants determined that agencies used that information for their own fundraising purposes and they gained nothing in return. A village elder from the Aruligo men's focus group discussion shared:

For the agencies that came and did assessments but did not assist us, we do not want them to return in time of disaster and do the same again. Otherwise, we will refuse to cooperate with their survey in our community .... They made us feel better with their promises and then left and made money with our names.

The feeling of distrust was compounded by the conduct of rapid needs assessments at the household level was discussed at the Flash Flooding Lessons Learned Workshop, held from 6–8 October 2014. On the one hand, household-level assessments facilitated broader engagement between agencies and affected communities. On the other hand, they were widely identified as too time-consuming and micro-level for the purpose of making broad assessments concerning the impact and deciding the locations, scale and nature of assistance to provide. Lunga settlement received assistance only from church and family members following the floods. A participant in the women's focus group discussion shared views similar to the village elder's in Aruligo, stating:

> A group that may have been from the NDMO did damage assessments and submitted their reports but we do not know what happened afterwards. We joked about that, saying 'you came and wrote for your own benefit'.

All three case study communities held the idea of agencies making a 'promise' to return, or community members believing that agencies would return to their community with assistance. It is unclear whether these commitments were explicit or implicit. In Aruligo, both the men's and women's focus groups shared that there is a need for responding agencies to come and visit the community themselves in order to better understand the impacts of the disaster. A woman explained:

> [...] if we do the assessment, we only share our own thoughts. We think they should come and witness the real situation.

Separately to the women's discussion, the men in Aruligo shared the same concern, advising that agency staff made inaccurate assumptions that they were unaffected and still had food. One participant explained:

> When the NDMO officers saw that people from our village went to the market to sell our [salvaged] crops, they thought we were not affected by the floods. They thought we still had food, not realising that those were our last remaining crops which we were trying to convert into cash in order to sustain ourselves.

The outward appearance of food security due to selling crops in the market masked the food insecurity that was experienced in the three months following the floods. Some community members could not salvage any crops to sell for cash and relied on others in the community for assistance. The misconceptions held by agencies involved in the response would have been challenged had decision makers visited the community, as explained above by a woman in the community.

Breadth of NGO Consultation

In Lord Howe settlement, all four focus groups (men, women, male youth and female youth) shared a common view that responding agencies insufficiently consulted with the communities. This is unique compared to Lunga settlement and Aruligo, where youth discussed not being consulted, but men and women shared that they were consulted to some extent.

A commonality across all four focus groups in Lord Howe settlement was the desire to be included and listened to when agencies consult the community following a disaster. Men from Lord Howe settlement collaboratively shared their story of the assessments in their community. They took issue with the attitudes of agency staff or volunteers who conducted assessments, identifying it as an impediment to wider consultation and collecting of accurate information:

> We had heard only the names of most agencies that visited, but never saw or talked to them. Some agencies came here but could not take the smell of the dead and debris, so [they] left, and we do not know what report they took with them. They were unfriendly and were selective about who they chose to talk to. Furthermore, they were very cheeky in the way they look and walk about our settlement, which was disrespectful toward us.

The men's focus group in Lord Howe settlement also pointed to their lack of inclusion in decision making:

> We would like them to come and talk to us about anything during the disaster and allow us to be part of the team which distributes assistance.

The exclusion of women and youth from decision making in disasters was consistently raised by participants who considered that it reinforced their subordinate social and economic status within their communities. It is notable that in both focus groups, community elders and leaders were described as the decision makers, not men more broadly.

Evidence from stakeholder interviews suggests that many of those conducting assessments in communities were volunteers who lacked experience in disaster response, leading to poor quality of assessments in many cases (Interviews B2 and C2). In some cases, inexperienced volunteers conducting assessments could cause offence which may be especially pronounced following a stressful and traumatic disaster event.

Homogenous Notions of Heterogeneous Communities

During a visit for focus group discussions in Aruligo, the research team inquired about an uninstalled water tank, supplied by a responding NGO. Participants in the men's focus group discussion explained that it has not been installed because they could not agree from whose roof the tank will harvest water. The position of the tank was of concern, as only residents living close to the tank would benefit, commented one participant. Therefore, nobody in the community had installed the tank, as it would create unequal access to water. Another participant suggested that it would be more suitable if assistance catered for individual families, as the community is structured around households.

While visiting food gardens in Aruligo which had been impacted by the disaster, the village chief elaborated on earlier comments in the focus group about the water tank. He argued that many outsiders and – to an extent – locals as well see Guales (people from Guadalcanal) as a singular, homogenous group, which negates the diversity and differences therein. He described his community as different to others in the area, having been relocated to the area in 1977 from the Weathercoast (on the other side of Guadalcanal). The chief's critique mirrors concerns raised by Litonjua (2012) who observed the homogenising of groups in development practice. Also, Gibson-Graham (2005) widely elaborated on this subject and advocated the need to de-essentialise development, recognise local diversity and respond appropriately.

Lunga settlement received the least external assistance out of the three case study communities. The April 2014 flash floods were the fourth flooding event that the community had experienced since 2009, and residents described it as the worst. The settlement is a small and close-knit Gilbertese (I-Kiribati) community comprised of eight households, with each containing three or four families. A participant in the men's focus group described outside assistance:

> We have faced four flood disasters and have never received assistance from any NGOs. We depend only on our relatives living in town and each other for recovery. We do not depend on assistance from others because we do not trust them.

Participants in the female youth focus group discussion attributed their recovery to the settlement's small size and common culture shared by residents, which fostered a strong sense of social cohesion. The settlement was moderately impacted by the floods, with residents losing food gardens, kitchens, fruit trees, church, meeting house and a few houses. Participants in all focus groups in Lunga settlement attributed their recovery to their kinship networks, past experience and culture – which they felt made them resilient and resolute people.

NGOs and Their Volunteers: Relationships of Reciprocity?

NGOs and Their Volunteers: Relationships of Reciprocity?
The women's focus group in Lord Howe settlement discussed their volunteer work for NGOs and argued that these NGOs should assist the community in return following a disaster. The presence of client/patron relationships in politics is discussed in Adams and Neef (2019) who compared Members of Parliament to distant *big-men* who were considered to be the most bankable avenues for the provision of services and resources (cf. Morgan, 2005). Client/patron relationships also appear to exist between NGOs and communities, as volunteering is seen to increase the likelihood of an NGO providing assistance to their community (Cox, 2009).

Organisational stakeholders interviewed shared that NGOs prioritise responding to communities which they have existing linkages and relationships with, such as current/past projects, or staff/volunteers residing (e.g. Interviews D4 and B3). When an NGO does not respond to communities where its volunteers reside, they may be seen to have violated social obligations of reciprocity.

The women's focus group in Lord Howe settlement problematised NGOs' non-provision of assistance to communities where their volunteers and staff reside and discussed a number of implications that would arise as a result. Focus group participants argued that NGOs should have prioritised responding to the home communities of their volunteers. They indicated that volunteer efforts should be reciprocated by the provision of assistance when the community was impacted by disaster.

Several women from the community who volunteered for a responding NGO collaboratively discussed their interactions with the NGO and their expectations:

> One woman from the Lord Howe settlement who works for [responding NGO] went to their office and asked for water tanks, that is how we got one here. We asked for water tanks prior to the floods because we were volunteers with the agency, but none was ever given to us. They promised to give us nine taps after the flood and until now we have not received any taps – so we no longer put our hopes and trust in [the responding NGO].

Evidently, volunteers expected tangible assistance from the NGO in exchange for their volunteer work and were disappointed when their expectations were not fulfilled. In this case, they asked for assistance prior to the floods, stating that they were volunteers. Following the floods, when expectations were unfulfilled, the NGO lost its clients' confidence.

Community Participation in NGO Responses to Disaster

The role that communities have in disaster response from the perspectives of NGOs is threefold: provision of labour, good assessments and sharing of local knowledge. In a participant interview, Sophie Boucaut, Pacific Programmes Manager with Save the Children, described community members' role in her agency's response:

> In a lot of the work we do, like building and cleaning out wells – there's an element of community engagement required. To support not just physically cleaning out of wells, but also if you want that well to be maintained in the future, there needs to be community buy-in from the beginning .... Mobilising communities in the first few weeks of a response can be challenging if you haven't worked there before because there may be limited pre-existing relationships .... It is also important to engage groups whose voices may be heard less, for example, people with disabilities – to make sure that wells are within reach and they're not up a cobbled staircase.

In this case, labour contributions by community members were located as an important part of ensuring community buy-in and sufficient training for maintenance of the wells. Boucaut's reference to seeking out the voices of marginalised groups, such as people with disabilities, is significant, given that less than one-third of organisational stakeholders discussed the position of people with disabilities in interviews. She suggested that participation can take varied forms, one of which is household assessments, through which:

> You are really seeking programmatic recommendations from the communities themselves. But also triangulating that data with data from other sources, from the NDMO, from other agencies as well who are doing their assessments or joint assessments with us. So that's what informs higher, overarching programme decisions.

Genuine participation through household assessments was described as a challenge by Ola Fou Solomon Islands Director Elisha Pitanoe. He argued that while communities should be thoroughly consulted in the designing of a proposal, the process needs to be conducted quickly due to deadlines of donor stakeholders. On the other hand, Benjamin Afuga of Forum Solomon Islands made the point that 'Solomon Islanders want to see material things – they don't like assessments'. There is a notable distinction between the term 'assessment' and 'consultation' in interview and focus group responses. Consultation was held almost unanimously to be positive and generative, whereas 'assessment' was commonly considered bureaucratic and extractive. Peter Weston, Programme Quality Manager at World Vision, contemplated the importance of community participation through consultation:

> As NGOs, we pride ourselves on being community-based and responsive. In the early days, we manifest that with focus groups, key informant interviews and follow up .... The more I see the results of, and community responses to, highly consultative development approaches (action learning kind of approaches); the more I see actions by communities of losing interest, building frustration. We NGOs can get into the mindset of 'we want to make sure we're fulfilling their aspirations, we need to keep going back and having reflections together about the progress, and then more reflections about the progress'. I think sometimes we are guilty of taking it too far to the extreme. I guess it's our ideological bend that we need to keep asking questions and checking in.

This response was distinct from all but one other interviewee. Most agency stakeholders interviewed reflected an implicit presumption that consultation and good disaster response are closely correlated. The only other interviewee who expressed somewhat comparable views was a high commission staff member (Interview A1), who explained how the Transport Division of the Ministry of Infrastructure received criticism for lack of participation in various cluster meetings, while their priority was securing the damaged Mataniko Bridge. The interviewee commended the Transport Division for their conduct – as the Mataniko Bridge was the last remaining bridge connecting the airport and industrial area with the port and commercial district of Honiara. If the bridge had washed out, as the Chinatown Bridge upstream did, the implications would have been extreme. Thus, consultation should not precede astute decision making.

Interviewees from several NGOs acknowledged that community members' participation in NGO responses to disaster is limited and pointed to their work in recovery and community development as being more participatory. As the focus of this study is on responses to the disaster, participation was viewed in the context of the six-month response phase following the disaster. One NGO involved in livelihoods response engaged older people in the communities where they responded to share their traditional knowledge about resilient cropping (Interview D7). Several other agencies provided implements such as tools which rural communities could use to recover their food gardens, through their own labour.

Community members in the focus groups perceived that NGOs prioritised responding to communities where they had existing relationships, as well as based on the situation (needs, impact). A majority of non-NGO interviewees described NGOs as having good relations with the communities where they responded. However, Benjamin Afuga of Forum Solomon Islands International recognised that 'some individuals from organisations were not liked so would not be welcome back in communities'. Similarly, in their response, Ola Fou field officers observed that community members resisted providing their names for the response, as previously 'people have come in and said "we will help you" and then left' (Ola Fou Interview).

The disorder and confusion which characterised the first week following the floods have been noted by most stakeholder organisation interviewees. Many interviewees recalled that it took time for operations to ramp up, and there was a limited amount that could be done due to heavy rain continuing until 6th April (the Mataniko River burst its banks on 3rd April) (e.g. Interviews A1, A2 and D6). Following this, the coordination of the response had visible challenges in the first few weeks:

> I think because Solomons hasn't necessarily dealt with responses like this year after year, the coordination aspect of that was sometimes very confusing in the first few weeks. I think cluster meetings were being scheduled at the same time and the clusters weren't necessarily communicating information like 'are you going to use this room, or are we going to use this room'. (Sophie Boucaut, Save the Children)

Honiara had not experienced a large-scale disaster since Cyclone Namu in 1986, so for many NGO staff, it was the first disaster they had both experienced and responded to. This poses an interesting dynamic, where staff were responding as both insiders to the disaster experience and outsiders of the communities with which they were working. Community participation in NGO responses to the flooding was characterised by participation in household surveys, provision of labour in projects, some sharing of knowledge and the use of assistance provided by NGOs to recover livelihoods. The extent of participation in NGO responses as described by stakeholders interviewed suggests that community members were little involved in the design process, beyond providing input through household assessments. Ultimately, however, permission for NGOs to carry out activities in communities must be obtained from community gatekeepers, who have the power to decide which activities an NGO can and cannot do in the community.

FINDINGS II: TARGETING AND INCLUSIVENESS OF NGO RESPONSES

This section explores the inclusiveness of NGO responses with regard to youth, people with disabilities and gender. It seeks to disaggregate the disaster response and identify specific challenges that may have been experienced by groups whose voices are heard to lesser extents in dominant disaster discourses. While this section is divided thematically, it is acknowledged that there is much interconnectedness between each theme.

Youth: A Silenced Majority

The absence of youth involvement in NGO responses to disaster was raised by both male and female youth focus groups in Lord Howe settlement and Aruligo – the two communities which received assistance from NGOs following the flooding. These groups expressed discontent overall and considered that their voices were not listened to by responding NGOs. Participants shared that they felt excluded from consultation and implementation, and that assistance provided did not sufficiently address their specific and differentiated needs as youth. This correlates with the response from an interviewee from the Ministry of Women, Youth, Children and Family (MWYCF), who argued that there is currently very little targeting of youth, beyond the establishment of child-friendly spaces. The protection cluster was restricted by a lack of funds, and needs assessments did not specifically target youth, the interviewee suggested.

The female youth focus group in Lord Howe settlement shared that agencies conducting needs assessments met only with community leaders and elders. They emphasised that they want their voices to be heard and have the opportunity to contribute to decisions that are made concerning their settlement.

> We want our voice to be heard when it comes to decision making in our settlement. When people came to talk with us, they only met with our leaders and elders. We also want to contribute to decisions concerning our settlement. (Lord Howe Settlement female youth FGD)

The male youth focus group expressed an eagerness to be involved in the team that collects data and distributes assistance; explaining 'we want to help with distributing the assistance because we were always left out'.

> Agencies should identify our needs as youth, and also the children. The response catered only for the elders and we were not part of it ... they seem to rush and have no time to talk; collecting unreliable information as a result .... They were not friendly nor comforting in time of disaster. (Lord Howe Settlement male youth FGD)

In the male youth focus group at Aruligo, debate on the place of youth and NGO responses was robust, as participants interjected one another, responding:

> We were not happy with the way they approached our community because they only talked to the elders – we too have our needs and want to share ... they did not care for the youth ... because they did nothing for us in the community .... What is the use of coming and collecting data only to do nothing with it? It would be better for them not to come at all because we can still survive even if they don't come and assist us.

When youth focus groups were asked how NGO responses would be different if they were more involved, they cited improving accountability, equity in distribution and sufficient relief supplies for a full household. There was also a general impression that responding agencies cannot understand all needs and determine an appropriate response while simultaneously excluding everyone except elders and leaders in the community. Community and organisational stakeholders have widely reflected on the politicisation of relief supplies distributions (cf. Adams & Neef, 2019), which contributed to undermining accountability and equity. Organisational stakeholders considered the size of households and recognised that households were under-reported where more than one nuclear family lived under one roof. As a result, some families especially female-headed households were essentially invisible. In many cases, youth may have reported these issues; as it was their live experience, they experienced the negative consequence of patterns of inclusion and exclusion following the disaster.

Further issues relating to youth were presented 'off the record' by youth participants in focus groups or organisational interviewees – their specific stories and any identifying characteristics have been cautiously omitted from this chapter. However, the issues that they identified and alluded to have been discussed in the following sections on gender, violence and psychosocial trauma, through evidencing 'on-record' interviews and secondary data.

On the Margins: Disaster for People with Disabilities

There were no assessments or particular attention given to people with disabilities, elderly people or pregnant women in the response; groups that are particularly at risk following a disaster. In many cases, their ability to quickly evacuate, adapt and survive in inferior living conditions (such as evacuation centres) may be limited. Coupled with this, some may have lost essential medications in the disaster or may not be able to meet their dietary or sanitary requirements with the relief supplies distributed. Three key issues emerged from interviews and focus group discussions – the challenges of evacuating people with disabilities, their lack of voice and inclusion in responses and the absence of supporting infrastructure for people with disabilities.

Lord Howe settlement was one of the two case study communities which were flooded and had to evacuate, and the only one where people with disabilities resided. The two male focus groups discussed evacuating the settlement:

> Everyone was in a state of fear and panic. A few sick people decided to stay even though they knew it was dangerous to stay, they could not move themselves because of the rain and lack of transport. (Lord Howe Settlement male youth FGD)

> During the flood when things got worse, a lot of us especially the women, children, those with disabilities, and the elderly people were evacuated. We helped rescue them to a church where we went and asked for help. (Lord Howe Settlement men's FGD)

The male youth focus group recognised that the challenges of evacuation were compounded by the heavy rain and lack of transport. The youth focus group was comprised of residents from the side of the settlement closest to the Mataniko River, which had more difficulty evacuating as floodwaters encroached on the settlement. The men's focus group was constituted of residents from the western side of the settlement, less exposed to the river and floodwaters, but more prone to sea storm surges. This highlights the challenges of evacuation for people with impaired mobility – that on one side of the settlement, all were evacuated, and on the other side, some people remained due to their difficulty evacuating.

The barriers for those with disabilities were addressed by less than one-third of organisational participants interviewed. Those who addressed the subject advocated that the voices of people with disabilities need to be heard and that infrastructure needs to improve to support them. A public servant at the MWYCF noted that disability will be an increasing priority for the ministry in the coming years. One NGO stakeholder considered:

> These people's voices need to be heard. What is our part and what can we do? ... Do you think that everyone's able? That's making a generalisation. How can you push a wheelchair to evacuate when there are no flat paths? People get left [behind]. (Interview D5)

The interviewee identified the issue raised in the Lord Howe settlement men's focus group of people being left behind in communities during the evacuation. The interviewee chastised dominant social attitudes which hold that people with disabilities belong to the confines of the home. Fiji was alluded to as an example of more disability-friendly infrastructure, such as flat sidewalks which have enabled people with disabilities to be more active, integrated and productive community members. Julian Tung, Programme Manager at Save the Children, discussed challenges in building more disability-friendly infrastructure after the disaster:

> The infrastructure was broken to begin with. We were all constrained by budget and tight project timeframes to bring infrastructure to an ideal level, so in many cases, it was about repairing to how it was before. For example, there was no budget to rebuild schools with ramps. There are also social implications, as those with disabilities don't usually go to school, so we were also contending with that. (Julian Tung, Save the Children)

The literature has noted that people with disabilities are often under-represented in positions of decision making, determining how disasters are responded to (e.g. Pirotte et al., 1999; Enarson & Marrow, 1998). As both a cause and consequence of this, disability rights are not always identified and prioritised in mainstream discourses within NGO disaster responses. A civil servant acknowledged the poor condition of urban infrastructure but expressed an even greater concern at the government's repatriation programme of sending people to a village environment where infrastructure is even more inadequate (Interview B3). He questioned how people would be able to take care of family members who are elderly or have a disability, suggesting that they would become an additional burden, which they are not supposed to be.

Gender: Structural and Practical Issues

Most interview stakeholders discussed gender to varied extents, and understandings of what gender means, and its applicability in disaster response varied widely. Gender was often conflated with 'vulnerable groups', which encompassed children, people with disabilities, elderly persons, pregnant women and at times everyone except adult men. Interview participants predominantly reflected on the practical implications of gender. They identified the need to consult women in disaster response, acknowledging the presence of women-headed households and widows, and the need for non-food item kits (NFI kits) to better address the needs of women. Participants also identified gender-based violence – both physical and sexual – as an issue. Interviewees reported that there was no assessment of domestic violence following the disaster, but many added that rates of violence against women had increased, based on the anecdotal evidence they had. Two factors are important to acknowledge here; first, as a male researcher, female interviewees may not have felt comfortable discussing particular female needs and issues with the first-named author Second, 19 out of 23 of interview participants were male. This is significant as it indicates the immense gender imbalance at the decision-making management level of organisations which responded to the disaster, given that the person interviewed was generally nominated by the organisation for the interview on the basis of being the most involved staff member in overseeing their organisation's response. It also suggests that the people interviewed may not be privy to information regarding women's needs and issues.

Gender has only entered policy and planning dialogues in the last decade in Solomon Islands, and people are still trying to make sense of it, advised one civil servant (Interview B3). An interviewee from MWCYFA recognised the importance of gender in the response, but also the government's need to manage expectations, highlighting one NGO that was very assertive on gender and human rights issues. This particular NGO was described as challenging to work with by several stakeholders, and its rights-based approach was considered counter-productive at times, as people viewed it as an imposition of Western values. One multilateral stakeholder elaborated:

> [NGO name] can be quite pushy on protection issues which NDMO is not comfortable with. They have been on the red-hot spot on that one …. They need to respect the cultural sensitivities which they mostly bypass. [The] Ministry of Women, Youth and Children have been upset with that – their concern is that it doesn't cause more tension. (Interview C1)

Considering gender without inflaming tensions was described by Julian Tung of Save the Children, who emphasised respecting cultural hierarchy, but therein finding ways to consult with women. A government interviewee agreed, suggesting that by consulting women, responding agencies can better understand their different needs (Interview B3). He said that the government was supportive, but conceded that consultation could have been done better. Consulting women in the response was commonly situated as a means to an end – to find out discrete needs women may have. Unsurprisingly, a more holistic view of gender was espoused by two women interviewees, who related protection issues and access to relief distributions.

One woman interviewed explained that in the evacuation centres, toilets were not gender-segregated, and this led to incidents of tension or conflict (Interview D5). This was a safety concern for women but was likely overlooked by the male-dominated disaster response managers who – with the benefit of hindsight – may have differently prioritised such concerns. Another woman interviewed explained that those conducting distributions often bypassed widows, single mothers and people with disabilities in distributions; presuming men were household heads in all cases (Interview C1). Both of these issues expose women to greater levels of risk and contribute to reinforcing their inferior social position.

The distribution of NFI kits insufficiently addressed gendered needs. Far too few sanitary pads were included in dignity kits, in an underestimation of both women's needs and household size. Further, sanitary pads were distributed through women-friendly spaces in dignity kits and not part of standard hygiene kits. One interviewee suggested that relief distributions are only purposed for life-saving emergency relief staples and that people should use their own resources to cover their additional needs (Interview B2). What this view fails to acknowledge, however, is cases where people lost their possessions in the flood, including money. An NGO interviewee identified that household assessments did not count babies or elderly people, which is important in order to tailor NFI kits appropriately (Interview D5). In a similar vein, a public servant at MWYCF suggested that NFI kits should be reviewed to ensure their appropriateness for women.

FINDINGS III: FACTORS THAT ENHANCE OR CONSTRAIN AGENCIES IN DISASTER RESPONSE

The timeliness and effectiveness with which agencies can respond to disaster have direct implications for affected communities. This section outlines and reflects on the key factors which assisted and constrained agencies in their responses to the disaster. It identifies difficulties concerning newly arrived expatriate staff, encounters with community dependency and opportunism, and the challenge of organisational re-gearing from community development work to disaster response.

Expatriates: Not 'Whites in Shining Armour'

Insufficient Contextual Experience

The influx of expatriate staff following a disaster, many of whom have little or no experience or familiarity with the context and institutional arrangements in Solomon Islands, was raised as problematic by a range of agency stakeholders. While 'expatriates' do not constitute a singular, indistinct category, interviewees often discussed 'expatriates' as a category, unless they provided specific details. Interviewees drew distinctions between expatriate staff already in-country at the time of the disaster and those who arrived subsequently. A staff member of a high commission in Honiara described the presence of newly arrived expatriate staff engaging in the humanitarian cluster system, where disaster response activities are coordinated through thematic 'sectors':

> The cluster system is very different in Solomon Islands. Expatriate staff came in without Melanesian experience. I saw instances, such as in the nutrition cluster where one expat stood up and said 'how can you only be distributing rice and tuna. That's not a balanced diet', without paying regard to the fact that those are staple foods in Solomon Islands. (Interview A1)

Interviewees from a multilateral agency and NGOs shared this concern and suggested that it takes time for expatriates to adapt to the context and understand the institutional arrangements already in place. They suggested that with time expatriates have an improved understanding of the context; however, during the response, it was largely the newly arrived expatriates who were involved in the cluster meetings:

> It takes a little bit of time for expatriates to understand the context and the arrangements which are already in place. But for those who already understand, having experienced cluster systems elsewhere – they quickly adapted, and tried their best to understand our system works. They then worked very well supporting those cluster systems in their work. (Interview C1)

> I think with the time in the country, expatriates became better versed with the situation in Solomon Islands. Existing expatriates were better than those who were coming in. However, it was the new arrivals who were attending the meetings ... they would just discuss, discuss, discuss – they threw their ideas and then left, without always reaching a conclusion. (Ola Fou Interview)

Interviewees from a range of sectors emphasised the importance of expatriates understanding and respecting existing arrangements and valuing the context experience of in-country staff of respective agencies. Loti Yates, NDMO Director, argued that incoming staff often talked about themselves as 'experts', and referred to their experiences elsewhere, discrediting existing arrangements and trying to dominate in the meetings. This is a familiar issue which has been widely elaborated in development literature – specifically, that Western assumptions of expertise and superiority frequently accompany aid and development interventions (e.g. Pieterse, 2001; Sidaway, 2007). The basis for discrediting existing arrangements by newly arrived expatriates appears tenuous, or pre-emptive at best, reflecting expatriates' preconceptions of what disaster response should look like.

Roles and Responsibilities

Concern was highlighted by five interviewees over a need to clearly define the roles of incoming expatriates. The key areas of concern were with expatriate staff becoming implementers and asserting themselves or dominating in coordination meetings. These concerns were described by NDMO Director Loti Yates and a multilateral agency staff member:

> We need to understand the role of supporting staff – whether they are coming in as technical support, additional resource, or whatever their role may be. (Loti Yates, NDMO)

> Who do they report to, are they here to advise, to provide support? They come in as technical support, and then you see them as implementers as well. In my view, they should be providing advice, or working on high-level issues – not working on the ground as actual responders. (Interview C2)

The perceived dominance of incoming expatriate staff was identified as an issue by several participants. There was a perception that with little or no experience in Solomon Islands, some expatriates were inappropriate or unsuitable for responding to the disaster. On the other hand, two organisations explained that they only recruit expatriates for sectors in which they lack expertise. In both cases, their organisation's structures and processes are standardised throughout the world so it is relatively straightforward for someone from overseas to arrive and fit in, with the addition of understanding the context. A multilateral agency manager described their experience:

> [NGO name] have been challenging to work with. I think one issue is that they brought in *pala-gis* (white people) who came in and took over a lot of work from the local staff. If they had just left it to the local staff, the local staff would understand the context. However, they came in and try and take charge, and sort of ruined it for everyone else. (C2 Interview)

The perceived seniority of expatriates and their relationships with others inform the ways that they are seen to dominate in meetings and impinge on the roles of local staff. Where expatriates dominate the discussion in meetings or seek to be involved in all areas of a response, this may be viewed by national staff as asserting neocolonial control. It may also suggest attitudes of superiority, whereby expatriates consider themselves to be bearers of relevant knowledge, and that what they have to say is of greater importance than what others in attendance do. Supposed patronising attitudes were unsurprisingly not well received by local disaster relief staff.

'This Is Solomon Islands': Touting Experience Is Not Appreciated

One of the most frequently cited characteristics of incoming expatriates following the disaster was their tendency to refer to their experiences in disaster response elsewhere. This may reflect expatriates' common identity as 'outsiders' or 'recently arrived'; or it could reflect the prevalence of certain behaviours among expatriates which has led them to be labelled as a singular group. There was one expatriate who was referred to by a number of participants, as discussed by interviewees in the following text:

> One man came along from [NGO name], an expat. He described himself as a camp management expert. He was sitting in the wrong cluster, and criticising, rather than using his so-called 'expertise' constructively. (Interview B2)

> This man from [NGO name], was a specialist in evacuation camps. He came to every meeting and talked about his experience in Pakistan, his experience in wherever. I was already stressed out, so I said: 'you say Pakistan one more time, and I am going to throw you out of the chair' .... He was like 'In Pakistan we do...' I got so pi**ed, like 'Pakistan is totally different from us'. In Pakistan you may be dealing with millions of people, here you are dealing with thousands of people, but the needs and context are totally different. That's what a lot of these expats do when they come in. Every time there is a meeting, I get very sick of it – they refer back to their experiences 'in my experience in Africa, in my experience in Asia' – this is Solomons, it's different. (Interview C2)

As well intentioned as they may have been, expatriates' references to disasters in dissimilar contexts was not well received. The raising of these experiences appears to be seen by local staff as pretentious, bearing little relevance to the current disaster, and an attempt to boast credentials. A participant from a Government Ministry shared that he sometimes wished the airport had remained closed for longer after the floods, then they would not have 'all of these bloody so-called "experts" coming in here and telling us how to do our jobs' (Interview B2). In an interview with staff from Ola Fou, the need for expatriates to listen first and then share their knowledge and experiences as appropriate to the situation was emphasised:

> Many of them had been in Haiti and always talked about their time in Haiti after the earthquake. One of the locals stood up and said 'this is a different situation to what you are saying, we appreciate your experience – listen first, then get the information you need'. We respect organisations that came into the country, with the vast experiences that they have. However, what they don't understand is that what works in Southeast Asia might not work in Solomon Islands. (Ola Fou Interview)

These excerpts suggest that there is a time and place for expatriates to share their experiences from other contexts, but that they should listen first to see how their expertise and experience can be best applied to the situation at hand.

Dependency and Opportunism: Two Sides of the Same Coin

Internally displaced persons who sheltered in temporary evacuation centres following the floods were discussed by all except two interviewees. The presence of proportionately large numbers of people seeking shelter exceeded public areas available to be used for evacuation centres, and as a result, schools were used to shelter those displaced. All interviewees who commented on the evacuation centres added that the number of people who had lost all their possessions was far fewer than the number of people in the evacuation centres. Benjamin Afuga of Forum Solomon Islands International observed:

> There were genuine victims and opportunists – how do you qualify someone for the evacuation centre? In the evacuation centres, people were getting three meals a day. (Benjamin Afuga, FSII)

Disasters in an urban setting such as Honiara are dynamic and complex in nature due to the diversity of residents. A multilateral stakeholder (Interview C1) argued that the levels of expectations in urban settings were higher as working-class people tend to think they deserve more than rural people. An interviewee from a high commission noted that donor governments and NGOs were publicly reporting on the amounts they had raised or contributed (Interview A1). However, donor governments channelled funds through NGOs and both reported on the amounts – effectively reporting the same funds twice. People affected by the disaster quantified the amount of aid they believed they should be receiving by adding up the amounts reported by various stakeholders, and then essentially dividing by the number of people in evacuation centres and other affected populations. This was problematic insofar as when the government moved to close the evacuation centres, people were refusing to leave until they received the assistance which they believed they were entitled to.

In discussing increasing levels of dependency, interviewees often referred to the evacuation centres as an example. NDMO Director Loti Yates alluded to both dependency in the evacuation centres and the wider challenge of access to land which informed the NDMOs response:

With all of these people staying in the evacuation centres, it was reinforcing dependency. Many were squatters on government land, so we couldn't give materials and authorise building in these marginal areas. It would also be unfair to give land to squatters over public servants. The land issue is a big one in Honiara. (Loti Yates, NDMO Interview)

While there is a diversity of experiences and circumstances among people in evacuation centres, an alternative conceptualisation could suggest that while people appear in a state of dependency to agencies responding, rather, they may be exercising their agency and taking advantage of the resources available to them. Elisha Pitanoe of Ola Fou Solomon Islands described opportunism and the government's response:

Initially, the evacuation centres were only for the people who had been victimised by the flash floods .... People were using this as an opportunity to serve their own interests – and I know that this is something that we will continue to struggle with, because it is people's own attitude, their mindset. The government knows that many who were there were not victims of the flash floods. Those who were truly victimised by the flash floods did not get what they were supposed to, they were pushed back – that's another big challenge. (Ola Fou Interview)

Evacuation centres can be described as locations of both dependency and opportunism. The ways in which disasters are experienced, along with the resources, skills and social position of those affected, are highly contingent on the contexts in which they occur. Accordingly, material distributions in evacuation centres may have differing undesirable consequences on different groups of people – such as fostering increased dependency, leading to opportunism or undermining resilience.

Transitioning between Community Development and Disaster Response

Distinct differences exist between the nature and practices of community development and disaster response. NGOs who participated in this study predominantly worked in various sectors of community development and responded to disasters as the need and opportunity presented itself. In this study, participating NGOs suspended their community development work in Honiara and Guadalcanal and diverted resources into disaster response purposes, with an understanding that community development work would be picked up and continued after the response.

A multilateral stakeholder and NDMO Director Loti Yates elaborated on the challenges many NGOs were faced with re-gearing their organisations for disaster response and the implications that had:

A lot of NGOs are not emergency response oriented or disaster response oriented. They are more focused on programmes that support communities. But when a disaster happened everyone had to chip in, and some had no experience with working in disaster situations. They have good intentions, but they were very much taking a reactive approach, rather than a proactive approach. (Interview C2)

While many NGOs are large in size, they have perhaps only one or two staff working in the humanitarian space on an ongoing basis. They re-divert their resources from ongoing community development projects, into disaster response and recovery. Because many of them do not specialise in disaster response, the quality of the response and assessments were often quite bad. Many NGOs did not understand the language of the standard operating procedures (SOPs). (Loti Yates, NDMO)

A manager from a Government Ministry involved in the response made similar observations but acknowledged that NGOs were the fastest to respond, ahead of the Solomon Island Government (SIG) response (Interview B2). Another multilateral stakeholder elaborated that the SIG is often the third partner to respond, following NGOs and donor governments (Interview C1). Red Cross had large responsibilities in the response for assessments and displaced people, yet were limited in their capacity immediately following the floods as their own offices had been flooded (Anna Reid, NZ High Commission). Peter Weston, Programme Quality Manager at World Vision, described the challenges he witnessed in transitioning into disaster response:

> Initially, it was chaotic. For the first week. No matter how organised you are, no matter where in the world, it's always chaotic .... For an organisation like World Vision, we're 90 per cent community development, but at the same time, we're also the country's largest emergency responder.

Due to the fluid situation on the ground, the time available for NGO staff to make key decisions, and the level of information on which those decisions are based is often substantially less than in community development work. Most stakeholders have characterised the first one to two weeks following the disaster as unsystematic, disorderly and messy, which was reflected in almost every discussion on coordination. It was a period of NGOs re-gearing for disaster response, but also one of assessing the scale of the disaster and trying to fill information gaps. As the disaster impacted Honiara, there was an additional factor that staff of stakeholder agencies were themselves impacted, and understandably had concerns for the welfare of their own kin and livelihoods.

DISCUSSION

This section discusses the implications of the findings and their applications. Disaster response specialists and academics alike have recognised the importance of ensuring that marginalised sectors of society are included and not exposed to further risk. Enarson and Marrow (1998) have placed importance on discerning 'who is the "we" in disaster practice' (p. 13). Who are disaster responders, and who are those being assisted? Literature has widely discussed the under-representation of women in positions of influence and decision making, which is affirmed in the findings of this research (Ariyabandu, 2005; Enarson & Marrow, 1998; Pirotte et al., 1999). However, there is much less literature on the position of other sectors of society, which the findings of this study indicated were often excluded from consultation and implementation, and their voices marginalised.

The Intersectionality of Exclusion: Avoiding Secondary Disaster

NGO responses to disaster often neglect the particular needs of marginalised groups, at a time when these groups face increased exposure to risks resulting from disaster (Pirotte et al., 1999). Focus group findings in this study indicated that women, young people and people with disabilities were often not consulted by responding stakeholders following the disaster. Findings suggest that NGO responses did not specifically cater to the differentiated needs of community members.

Much of the literature that elaborates on women's exclusion in disaster response has broader applicability to other groups and can help to understand the intersectionality of exclusion and marginalisation by different and overlapping groups. Mohanty (1988) was highly critical of homogenising of women into singular pre-constituted groups, as it conceals the complex interplay of factors that influence lived experiences. Similarly, the conflating of 'young people', 'people with disabilities' or 'men' as singular identities overlooks the high degree of heterogeneity within each. This was abetted in this study by the use of focus group discussions to generate community-level data.

It is noteworthy that all research participants utilised social groupings to identify and explain experiences and attributes that were widespread among each group. This study employs groupings such as 'women', 'men', 'young people' and 'people with disabilities' for the purpose of discussing trends. However, in doing so, it moves beyond commonplace representations in literature and practice that situate 'affected communities' as undifferentiated in their needs and capacities, united in their having been affected by disaster (Krause, 2014).

Focus group discussions in the three case study communities found that no women, youth or people with disabilities were consulted or represented in decision-making processes. At the stakeholder agency level, of a total 23 people interviewed from management levels within their respective organisations, only four were women. Acknowledging that interviewees represented the decision-making level in disaster response, women were significantly under-represented. If national and expatriate staff were distinguished, the disparity is higher, with only two female national staff. It may be the case that women were more highly represented at the operational and field level (the findings do not detail this). Yet it is important to note that most decisions are made at the managerial level of organisations, the level dominated by men.

Marginalised sectors of society frequently encounter increased exposure to risks following disaster (Enarson & Marrow, 2000; Pirotte et al., 1999). Following the April 2014 floods, there were reported increases in physical and sexual abuse against women, children and people with disabilities (Enarson & Marrow, 2000; Pirotte et al., 1999). Moreover, it was individuals from these groups who faced the negative implications of responses to the disaster that did not tailor to their differentiated needs. The challenges to this are systemic – if these groups were not well integrated into dominant discourses in non-emergency times, they are unlikely to be integrated in a high-pressure period following a disaster.

Improving male managers' understandings of the needs, capabilities and priorities of non-dominant groups may contribute to improved decision making and leadership in these areas. However, it remains an insufficient substitute for increased representation of marginalised groups at decision-making levels within organisations who can more accurately and comprehensively represent the nuances of the groups they identify with. Improved representation of non-dominant groups at levels of influence and decision making would help ensure disaster responses are congruous to the differentiated needs of those affected, as opposed to standardised to the needs of dominant groups (Masaki, 2007; Pirotte et al., 1999).

Needs which are not addressed in responses to disaster may expose at-risk groups to secondary disaster. Pirotte et al. (1999) discussed how established identities may be perceived to be threatened or in flux following a disaster, which may compound the already high levels of stress and anxiety experienced and manifest in outbursts of violence. Stakeholders interviewed in this study reflected that the design of responses, particularly evacuation centres, did not manage or mitigate these risks well. Women and children were exposed to avoidable risks in evacuation centres, and gender-segregated toilets, private bathing areas, sufficient lighting and security would have significantly reduced the incidence of physical and sexual violence. The majority of evacuation centres were established in schools, and all were ad hoc facilities not designed or suitable for housing evacuees.

The failure to count infants, elderly people or accurately assess household size in needs assessments inevitably had negative implications. People with disabilities, elderly, pregnant mothers and babies often have heightened health risks and diminished capacity to subsist and recover without assistance. Similarly, poorer households were disproportionately comprised of more families living under the same roof and were counted as a single household and distributed a single allocation of relief supplies. Some items in NFI kits, such as sanitary pads, were already scarce based on assumptions of average household size, and for larger households, scarcity of these items would be even more pronounced.

(In)visible Agents: Communities in Disaster Response

This study has sought to present the active and diverse ways in which people affected by disaster reacted and responded to their situation. The findings detail the limited involvement of case study communities in NGO responses to the disaster. The participation of communities in NGO responses largely mirrored what Masaki (2007) considered were 'users and choosers' of externally devised interventions (p. 125). The research findings indicated that all sectors of the community were actively engaged in responding to the disaster and recovering their communities. However, it was clear that formal inclusion and consultation in NGO responses to the disaster were limited to community leaders – elders, religious leaders or *bigmen*.

Published literature and findings from stakeholder agency interviews have widely reflected on the exclusion of communities or groups within communities from consultation and participation in formal responses to disaster. The ways in which community members respond to disaster themselves were seldom discussed, underscoring the view that their agency is frequently unrecognised or under-recognised. Ariyabandu (2005, p. 11) argued that women are active 'in mitigation, prevention, preparedness, emergency response and recovery'. The findings show that young people are also actively involved in disaster response – from assisting in evacuating their communities and attempting rescues from the floodwaters to recovery and rebuilding after the floodwaters receded. Yila et al. (2013) highlighted the importance of social capital and networks in disaster response, describing them as 'social insurance' that mobilises response and recovery (p. 82). These comprise significant yet under-analysed contributions to response and recovery.

Beristain (2006) argued that NGOs need to adopt models of understanding that are more complete. He described how NGOs often idealise affected communities, emphasise their needs and (perhaps inadvertently) foster patronising and disparaging representations of their agency. NGOs frequently adopt a deficiency view of disaster-impacted communities, identifying what they lack in order to validate their responses (Beristain, 2006; Krause, 2014). In all three case study communities, participants discussed not being consulted, and their ideas, knowledge and capabilities overlooked. Ultimately, it is responding agencies which determine how resources are distributed. Time constraints restricted thorough consultation and co-design of interventions, and in many cases, community members were limited to providing programmatic recommendations through household assessments.

Among NGO staff, it is perhaps field officers who are the most attuned and sensitive to the needs and priorities of affected communities. Beristain (2006) described a disjuncture between NGO management and field staff, the former with decision-making power and the latter having greater interaction with and understanding of affected communities. The process of communicating the realities on the ground through needs assessments, the data of which are then reviewed and decided upon by managers has the potential to impose inappropriate disaster responses. Equally, the use of metadata to devise programmatic responses can risk overlooking power dynamics within communities and between communities which may influence distribution – who benefits or is excluded from a response.

CONCLUSION

Just as lived experiences are heterogeneous, so too are responses to disaster. Being both contextual and dynamic, disaster response cannot be understood as a singular or universal process. Responses that may work in one context and point in time may not be appropriate in a different time or context. While context critically informs disaster impacts and how those impacts are experienced, international discourses also play a key role in informing and shaping disaster response in this globally connected world. Thus, this study has attempted to ground international theory in Solomon Islands contextual realities and practical applications.

The findings were inevitably influenced by the timing of the fieldwork, which was conducted one year after the disaster. During this time, national elections resulted in a change of government, and Tropical Cyclones Pam and Raquel impacted the country. For many still recovering from the floods, the disaster was not an event that occurred on 3 April 2014, but rather a process within which vulnerabilities had been created long before, and impacts persist long after the floodwaters receded. Further research could look deeper into the intersectionality of power relations and inclusion/exclusion in disaster response activities. This would be beneficial for improving understanding of how those affected experience and respond to disasters.

Locating the varied discourses of stakeholders was a key theme throughout this study, through which patterns of intersectionality of inclusion and exclusion of people in disaster response became evident. In highlighting the voices of participants, the aim was to better understand the perspectives, motivations and subjectivities present in disaster response as the first step towards bridging gaps between stakeholders and between international theory and practice. This chapter argues for the greater inclusion of those affected by disaster in order to improve disaster planning, response and recovery, based on considerate and reflexive practice.

ACKNOWLEDGEMENTS

We are grateful to all research participants for generously sharing their perspectives and experiences. We thank the research assistants, Elisa Matahia, Patricia Kennedy and Jerry Tamonge, for their support in coordinating and facilitating the fieldwork. The financial support of the New Zealand Ministry of Foreign Affairs and Trade through the provision of the New Zealand Aid Programme Post-Graduate Field Research Award is gratefully acknowledged.

REFERENCES

Adams, C., & Neef, A. (2019). Patrons of disaster: The role of political patronage in flood response in the Solomon Islands. *World Development Perspectives, 15,* 100128.

Ariyabandu, M. M. (2005). Addressing gender issues in humanitarian practice: Tsunami recovery. In All India Disaster Mitigation Institute (Ed.), *Special issue for international day for disaster risk reduction* (pp. 8–9). Geneva: United Nations International Strategy for Disaster Reduction (UNISDR).

Bennett, J. A. (1987). *Wealth of the Solomons: A history of a Pacific archipelago, 1800–1978.* Honolulu, HI: University of Hawaii Press.

Beristain, C. M. (2006). *Humanitarian aid work: A critical approach.* Philadelphia, PA: University of Pennsylvania Press.

Braithwaite, J. (2010). *Pillars and shadows: Statebuilding as peacebuilding in Solomon Islands.* Canberra: ANU E Press, Australian National University.

Chase, S. E. (2005). Narrative inquiry: Multiple lenses, approaches, voices. In N. K. Denzin & Y. S. Lincoln (Eds.), *The Sage handbook of qualitative research* (3rd ed., pp. 651–679). Thousand Oaks, CA: Sage Publications.

Cortazzi, M., & Jin, L. (2006). Asking questions, sharing stories and identity construction: Sociocultural issues in narrative research. In S. Trahar (Ed.), *Narrative research on learning comparative and international perspectives* (pp. 27–46). Oxford: Symposium Books.

Cox, J. (2009). Active citizenship or passive clientelism? Accountability and development in Solomon Islands. *Development in Practice, 19*(8), 964–980.

Enarson, E. P., & Morrow, B. H. (1998). *The gendered terrain of disaster: Through women's eyes.* Miami, FL: IHC.

Fairbairn-Dunlop, P., & Coxon, E. (2014). *Talanoa: Building a Pasifika research culture.* Auckland: Dunmore Publishing.

Fox, C. (2006). Stories within stories: Dissolving the boundaries in narrative research and analysis. In S. Trahar (Ed.), *Narrative research on learning comparative and international perspectives* (pp. 47–59). Oxford: Symposium Books.

Fraenkel, J. (2004). *The manipulation of custom: From uprising to intervention in the Solomon Islands.* Wellington: Victoria University Press.

Gibson-Graham, J. K. (2005). Surplus possibilities: Post-development and community economies. *Singapore Journal of Tropical Geography, 26*(1), 4–26.

Krause, M. (2014). *The good project: Humanitarian relief NGOs and the fragmentation of reason.* Chicago, IL: University of Chicago Press.

Litonjua, M. (2012). Third World/Global South: From modernization, to dependency/liberation, to post-development. *Journal of Third World Studies, 29*(1), 29–56.

Masaki, K. (2007). *Power, participation, and policy: The "emancipatory" evolution of the "elite-controlled" policy process.* Lanham: Lexington Books.

McDonald, R. (2003). *Money makes you crazy: Custom and change in the Solomon Islands.* Dunedin: University of Otago Press.

Mohanty, C. T. (1988). Under Western eyes: Feminist scholarship and colonial discourses. *Feminist Review, 30*, 61–88.

Moore, C. (2004). *Happy isles in crisis: The historical causes for a failing state in Solomon Islands, 1998–2004.* Canberra: Asia Pacific Press.

Morgan, M. (2005). *Cultures of dominance: Institutional and cultural influences on parliamentary politics in Melanesia* (State, Society and Governance in Melanesia (Series); 2005/2). Canberra: Australian National University.

Narokobi, B. (1983). *The Melanesian way.* Boroko: Institute of Papua New Guinea Studies, The University of the South Pacific.

Neef, A., Benge, L., Boruff, N., Pauli, N., Weber, E., & Varea, R. (2018). Climate change adaptation strategies in Fiji: The role of social norms and cultural values. *World Development, 107*, 125–137.

O'Leary, Z. (2009). *The essential guide to doing research.* London: Sage Publications.

Pieterse, J. (2001). *Development theory* (1st ed.). Thousand Oaks, CA: Sage Publications.

Pirotte, C., Husson, B., & Grunewald, F. (1999). *Responding to emergencies or fostering development? The dilemmas of humanitarian aid.* London: Zed Books.

Radford, D. A., & Blong, R. J. (1991). *Solomon Islands final report: Natural hazards and risk assessment in the Solomon Islands.* Sydney: Macquarie University.

Sidaway, J. (2007). Spaces of post-development. *Progress in Human Geography, 31*(3), 345–361.

Timmer, J. (2008). *Kastom* and theocracy: A reflection on governance from the uttermost part of the world. In S. Dinnen & S. Firth (Eds.), *Politics and state building in Solomon Islands* (pp. 194–210). Canberra: Australia National University E Press, Asia Pacific Press.

Trahar, S. (2006). Introduction. The contribution of narrative research to comparative and international education: An editor's story. In S. Trahar (Ed.), *Narrative research on learning comparative and international perspectives* (pp. 1–23). Oxford: Symposium Books.

UNOCHA (United Nations Office for the Coordination of Humanitarian Affairs). (2014). Solomon Islands: Worst flooding in history. Retrieved from http://www.unocha.org/top-stories/all-stories/solomon-islands-worst-flooding-history

Vaioleti, T. E. (2006). *Talanoa* research methodology: A developing position on Pacific research. *Waikato Journal of Education, 12*, 21–34.

Yila, O., Weber, E., & Neef, A. (2013). The role of social capital in post-flood response and recovery among downstream communities of the Ba River, Western Viti Levu, Fiji Islands. In A. Neef & R. Shaw (Eds.), *Risks and conflicts: Local responses to natural disasters.* Community, Environment and Disaster Risk Management (Vol. 14, pp. 79–107). Bingley: Emerald Group Publishing Limited.

CHAPTER 4

A PARTICIPATORY APPROACH TO UNDERSTANDING THE IMPACT OF MULTIPLE NATURAL HAZARDS IN COMMUNITIES ALONG THE BA RIVER, FIJI

Gracie Irvine, Natasha Pauli, Renata Varea and Bryan Boruff

ABSTRACT

The Ba River catchment and delta on the island of Viti Levu, Fiji, supports a wealth of livelihoods and is populated by diverse communities who are living with an increased frequency and intensity of hydro-meteorological hazards (floods, cyclones and droughts). Participatory mapping as part of focus group discussions is a tool that can be used to elucidate communities' understanding of the differing impacts of multiple hazards, as well as the strategies used to prepare and respond to different hazards. In this chapter, the authors present the results of qualitative research undertaken with members of three communities along the Ba River, from the Nausori highlands to the coastal mangroves, with a particular focus on recent floods (2009, 2012) and Tropical Cyclone Winston (2016). The communities draw on a wide range of livelihood strategies from fishing and agriculture to tourism and outside work. Natural hazard events vary in their impact on these livelihood strategies across the landscape and seascape, so that community members can adjust their activities accordingly. The temporal 'signatures' of ongoing impacts are also variable across communities and resources. The results suggest that taking a broad, landscape (and seascape) approach to understanding how communities draw livelihoods is valuable in informing effective and inclusive

Climate-Induced Disasters in the Asia-Pacific Region: Response, Recovery, Adaptation
Community, Environment and Disaster Risk Management, Volume 22, 57–86
Copyright © 2021 by Emerald Publishing Limited
All rights of reproduction in any form reserved
ISSN: 2040-7262/doi:10.1108/S2040-726220200000022003

adaptation strategies for environmental change. Furthermore, documenting how the landscape is used in a mapped output may be a valuable tool for future social impact assessment for resource extraction activities.

Keywords: Participatory mapping; multiple hazards; livelihoods; local knowledge; environmental change; Fiji

INTRODUCTION

Historically, approaches to understanding natural hazards have tended to focus on exposure, vulnerability and risk related to individual hazards, such as flooding, earthquakes or landslides. Over the last two decades, there has been increasing recognition that many regions are exposed to risk from more than one hazard, and that for effective disaster preparedness and recovery, planning should take into account the presence of and interaction among multiple hazards (Gallina et al., 2016; Hagenlocher, Renaud, Haas, & Sebesvari, 2018; UNISDR, 2015). At the same time, approaches to multiple hazard research have so far tended towards a relatively static view and have largely not taken into account how climate change may affect exposure and vulnerability to multiple hazards (Gallina et al., 2016). Further, multiple hazard research has often employed quantitative methods to model and map cumulative impacts and interactions among hazards (e.g. Ashraful Islam, Mitra, Dewan, & Akhter, 2016; Hagenlocher et al., 2018), with relatively less emphasis on the use of qualitative methods to develop a deeper understanding of human views on managing multiple risks.

Some landforms and regions of the world are particularly exposed to multiple natural hazards. Coastal regions and deltas have been highlighted as environments that are exposed to a variety of interrelated hazards such as flooding, coastal erosion, tsunamis, saline intrusion and storms as well as being heavily populated (Ashraful Islam et al., 2016; Hagenlocher et al., 2018; Hoque, Ahmed, Pradhan, & Roy, 2019). Small island states, and the Pacific region in particular, are also regarded as regions that are exposed to multiple hazards (Giardino, Nederhoff, & Vousdoukas, 2018; Kelman, 2017; Noy & Edmonds, 2016). Many Pacific small island states lie within the tropical cyclone belt and may be affected by the passage of several cyclones per year, with the magnitude and frequency of cyclones and tropical storms projected to increase with climate change (Jin, Boucharel, & Lin, 2014). Other acute hazards faced by Pacific nations include earthquakes and tsunamis. For the period 1990–2012, the burden of disaster in terms of deaths, people affected, reduced life expectancy and economic damages was assessed as more acute in the Pacific region than in other small island regions such as the Caribbean (Noy, 2015).

In addition to rapid-onset events such as cyclones, the Pacific islands are vulnerable to gradual-onset events associated with climate change, including sea level rise. Settlements are often concentrated in coastal regions, increasing exposure to rising seas, saline intrusion of groundwater and mangrove encroachment (Gravelle & Mimura, 2008) with heavy reliance on marine and agricultural resources found in the coastal zones. Sea level rise is associated with increased erosion, inundation and storm surges, all of which will threaten local resources, coastal settlements and infrastructure (Piguet & Laczko, 2014). Moreover, changes to rainfall patterns and saltwater intrusion threaten water resources on small islands, including those in the Pacific. Additionally, climate change may increase the occurrence and strength of drought periods (Kuleshov et al., 2014; McGree et al., 2019). While the physical exposure of Pacific nations has been widely discussed in climate change literature, there has been less acknowledgement of the varied ways in which Pacific nations and communities are addressing and adapting to climate change (McLeod et al., 2019). Pacific Islanders have adapted to natural fluctuations in climate and environmental hazard over centuries (McNamara & Prasad, 2014; Nunn, 2007). Pacific Island leaders have been instrumental in international climate negotiations, pressing for ambitious global targets, and Pacific communities have played a leading role in action on climate at a local level (McLeod et al., 2019). The strong kinship ties and social structures evident in many Pacific cultures can hold advantages for building resilience to climate change-related hazards and aiding in post-disaster recovery (Armour, 2010; Kelman, 2017).

Qualitative Approaches to Understanding the Impact of Multiple Hazards

Many of the existing studies of multiple hazard exposure, risk and vulnerability have taken markedly numerical approaches, such as developing composite indicators, quantitative models of hazard interactions, or employing quantitative geospatial methods (Asare-Kyei, Kloos, & Renaud, 2015; Ashraful Islam et al., 2016; Hagenlocher et al., 2018; Hoque et al., 2019; Tilloy, Malamuda, Winter, & Joly-Laugel, 2019). Qualitative and participatory approaches can contribute to understanding how communities perceive and adapt to living with multiple risks. While there are a multitude of examples of participatory approaches to mapping singular natural hazards such as flooding (Brandt et al. 2019; Ceccato, Giannini, & Giupponi, 2011; Kienberger, 2014; Tauzer et al., 2019), there are comparatively few qualitative, spatially explicit studies examining local communities' experience of and adaptation to multiple hydro-meteorological hazards under conditions of environmental change. The relative lack of qualitative research on this topic exists despite the fact that physical exposure to multiple natural hazards requires people and communities to develop complex, heterogeneous knowledge to navigate a changing environment. Such rich knowledge is not well captured by indices and may indeed lead to the development of a cultural landscape shaped by resource management practices that reduce hazard risk (Reichel & Frömming, 2014).

Spatially explicit approaches use maps or other means of representing space (as in participatory mapping) to document how hazards and risks manifest across a landscape. Several authors have used qualitative methods to capture local understandings of multiple hazards without the concurrent use of a spatially explicit approach. Examples include Hiwasaki, Luna, Syamsidik, and Shaw's (2014) description of local knowledge of disaster risk reduction in the Philippines, Indonesia and Timor-Leste, and the development of indicators to represent local perceptions of multiple hazards in Uganda (Sullivan-Wiley & Short Gianotti, 2017) and West Africa (Asare-Kyei et al., 2015). Rampengan, Law, Gaillard, Boedhihartono, and Sayer (2016) used participatory mapping as a discussion tool for understanding local perceptions of multiple hazards in North Sulawesi, but did not publish spatially explicit results such as maps of hazard impacts or livelihood impacts.

The published research using participatory geospatial approaches to understand multiple hazards demonstrates the potential of visualising community perceptions of vulnerability, risk and exposure for use in collaborative decision-making with authorities. Some examples include mapping of local perceptions on: flood and landslide risk in Grenada (Canevari-Luzardo, Bastide, Choutet, & Liverman, 2017); flood and tsunami risk in a coastal Chilean town (Cubelos et al., 2019); landslide and avalanche risk in a mountainous region of Switzerland (Reichel & Frömming, 2014); and salinity and flood risk in the Mekong Delta in Vietnam (Yen, Son, Tung, Amjath-Babu, & Sebastian, 2019). The authors of these papers emphasised co-developed mapping products that could be used to aid in decision-making at a variety of spatial scales from detailed household scale (Canevari-Luzardo et al., 2017), town scale (Cubelos et al., 2019), watershed scale (Reichel & Frömming, 2014) and up to sub-catchment scale (Huang & London, 2016; Yen et al., 2019). In all cases, considerable time, repeated visits, trust and rapport were needed to develop the final mapping products, including time for validation and further discussion of initial maps with community members. Often, local communities held a wealth of information that was well aligned with 'expert' modelling. For example, Cubelos et al. (2019) highlighted that knowledge of historic tsunami events had been passed down orally through generations, and although these events were rare, the community's spatial understanding of tsunami exposure and vulnerability was similar to that described by scientific modelling.

Local Knowledge for Adaptation to Environmental Change

The value of local knowledge[1] for both disaster risk reduction and effective climate change adaptation is becoming increasingly recognised (Dube & Munsaka, 2018; Hiwasaki et al., 2014; Lebel, 2013; Mercer, Dominey-Howes, Kelman, & Lloyd, 2007; Walshe & Nunn, 2012). Indigenous knowledge, passed down through generations, can provide a unique, unrivalled and culturally respected source of information communicating details of the past that cannot be obtained by monitoring or modelling (Janif et al., 2016). In addition to providing valuable, contextual information in data-scarce regions, the acknowledgement and incorporation of local knowledge in disaster risk reduction and climate change adaptation plans can help to increase effectiveness, inclusivity and local ownership. The participatory process of discussing local knowledge can also aid in identifying contested knowledge and potential conflicts between recommended adaptation strategies, local priorities and cultural values (Lebel, 2013).

A deep understanding of environmental relationships and change has been the foundation for Pacific peoples' successful settlement and society on islands that are subject to multiple hazards. McNamara and Prasad (2014) outline the various techniques used in the Pacific to predict extreme weather, asserting that the continued existence of Indigenous communities in the Pacific is testament to their preparation, resilience and adaptation to change. For instance, Indigenous *iTaukei* Fijian communities recognise changes in vegetation such as excessive breadfruit production and changes in the curl of the *vudi* (plantain) plant leaf as indicators of upcoming severe weather. These physiological changes in plants indicate a period of extreme heat, favourable to the formation of tropical cyclones (Janif et al., 2016). Weather predictions based on local knowledge are widely accepted by the community and motivate preparation activities to reduce the impact of adverse weather (Janif et al., 2016; McNamara & Prasad, 2014).

Local knowledge alone may not provide sufficient capacity to cope with the adverse effects of future extreme weather (McNamara & Prasad, 2014), particularly as knowledge is lost due to cultural change, or undermined due to changing environmental conditions. Rapid climate change calls for an interdisciplinary approach, incorporating both scientific and Indigenous knowledge (de Andrade & Szlafsztein, 2015). The involvement of all local stakeholders in the evaluation, planning and implementation of mitigation strategies increases the likelihood of adaptation initiatives being sustained by the community (Janif et al., 2016).

Research Objectives

The research presented here fills a gap in the available literature concerning the use of qualitative, spatially based methods to understand local responses to multiple natural hazards in a Pacific Island context. In this chapter, we present qualitative research on community perceptions of flooding, cyclones, erosion and drought using a case study from the Ba River catchment, on the island of Viti Levu, Fiji. The overall aim of the research is to ascertain whether participatory mapping techniques can be used as an effective means of linking livelihoods with the impact of hydro-meteorological hazards. Specifically, the objectives of the research were to: (1) understand the impacts of recent climate-related hazards on the local environment and associated livelihoods; (2) outline heterogeneity across livelihoods and within landscapes in terms of the impacts and adaptive responses associated with multiple environmental hazards; and (3) explore the extent to which local knowledge aids in preparing for and responding to multiple climate-related hazards. We provide recommendations for adaptation planning and management, and show how participatory approaches to understanding landscape and livelihood relationships can reach beyond adaptation planning and disaster risk reduction, and be potentially useful for social impact assessment and resource management.

Fiji and the Ba River Catchment: Living with Floods, Cyclones and Drought

The archipelago of the South Pacific nation of Fiji comprises 332 islands; 70% of the population reside on the nation's largest island, Viti Levu. Fiji has a tropical marine climate with two distinct seasons: the dry season from May to October and the wet season from November to April (PICCAP, 2005). Agriculture accounts for 13.5% of Fiji's GDP (2017 estimate), with 44% of the Fijian labour force are engaged in the primary production sector (2011 estimate) with major products including sugarcane, cassava, livestock and fish (CIA, 2017). Fiji is a multicultural society, with 57% of the population identifying as *iTaukei* (Indigenous Fijian) and 37% as Fijian of Indian descent. *iTaukei* Fijians have customary rights to land and sea.

Fiji's geographic location within the southern tropical Pacific makes it physically exposed to extreme weather, including the effects of tropical cyclones, storms and depressions (CDKN, 2014). Several recent extreme weather events have caused extensive damage in Fiji (Table 4.1), with the impact of these events compounded by the location of some villages in remote and rugged areas, together with heavily populated low-lying coastal regions that are exposed to cyclones, storm surges and flood events (Gravelle & Mimura, 2008).

Table 4.1. Selected Severe Extreme Weather Events and Associated Damage in Fiji (1993–2018).

Event	Date	Cause	Damage	Sources
Flooding	April 2018	Rainfall from Tropical Cyclone Josie (Category 1) and Severe Tropical Cyclone Keni (Category 3), one week apart	• Five fatalities, one missing person • US$3 million damages • 12,000 people evacuated • 77,140 people affected • 800 homes affected on Kadavu	CARE Australia (2018); Radio New Zealand (2018)
Cyclone Winston	February 2016	Landfall of Severe Tropical Cyclone (Category 5)	• 42 fatalities, 126 people injured • US$500 million damages • 40,000 homes damaged or destroyed • Over 51,000 people displaced	UNOCHA (2016)
Flooding	January–February 2012	Heavy rain caused by tropical disturbance	• Eight fatalities • US$17 million damages • 4,000 people evacuated	Chaudhury (2012)
Flooding	January 2009	Monsoonal trough and South Pacific Convergence Zone (SPCZ) over Fiji combined with intense rainfall	• 11 fatalities (6 children) • 9,000 people displaced • US$81 million damages	McGree, Yeo, and Devi (2010) and UNICEF (2009)
Flooding	January 1999	Trough stayed over Viti Levu for 12 hours causing strong winds, heavy rain	• Six fatalities • US$10 million damages	McGree et al. (2010)
Drought	~June 1997 to ~October 1998	El Niño event with SPCZ absent from Fiji islands across two dry seasons and intervening wet season	• National disaster declared September 1998 • Estimated US$46 million damages • Over 200,000 people needed basic food for survival • 377,000 people required emergency water supply	Rhee and Yang (2018), Terry and Raj (2002) and Feresi et al. (2000)
Cyclone Kina	December 1993	Severe Tropical Cyclone (Category 4)	• Nine fatalities • US$87 million damages	McGree et al. (2010)

Meteorological droughts in Fiji are connected with variability and interactions among the El Niño Southern Oscillation (ENSO), Pacific Decadal Oscillation and the SPCZ, with the western region of Fiji (including the western side of Viti Levu) having experienced drier conditions since the 1950s compared with earlier decades (Rhee & Yang, 2018). Fiji has experienced a number of severe droughts since 1940, with the 1997–1998 ENSO-related drought event having severe impacts across two dry seasons and the intermediate wet season (Feresi et al., 2000).

The Ba River catchment in north-western Viti Levu, within Ba Province, was chosen as the study site for this research, having been impacted by floods in 2009 and 2012, and by Cyclone Winston in 2016. The town of Ba and many villages along the floodplain of the Ba River suffered damage during flood events in 2009 and 2012, and were again affected by flooding in April 2018. The population of Ba Province is susceptible to natural hazards in part due to relatively high poverty levels (Yila, Weber, & Neef, 2013), as well as the impact of global and local change. Using global climate models, Hay (2006) report that the frequency of heavy rainfall events of greater than 400 mm is increasing for Viti Levu; prior to 1965 such events occurred approximately once every 190 years, but by 2100 such an event can be expected approximately every 25 years. Furthermore, tropical cyclone frequency in the eastern Pacific is also expected to increase (Jin et al., 2014).

Residents of the Ba River floodplain are likely to experience increased impacts associated with heavy rainfall events over the coming decades, due to the intersection of climate and land-use change. Under projected climate change, streamflow from the steeply sloping upper Ba catchment is expected to increase in magnitude and frequency (Qamese, 2015). Replacement of forest and shrublands with croplands has increased within the catchment over the last three decades, resulting in an increase in overland flow during rainfall events (Dadhich & Nadaoka, 2014). Impacts from increased run-off include sedimentation smothering agricultural land and changing the course of the river channel (Simpson, 2016), as well as coastal impacts such as increased algae cover and degraded reefs due to increased volumes of sediments and nutrients (Dadhich & Nadaoka, 2012). An additional concern for the lower Ba catchment is mining of magnetite-rich iron sands from sediments of the Ba River delta, which commenced in 2019 (Chambers, 2019). Concerns over the potential impact of mining activities on mangrove ecosystems have been raised by community members, particularly as these areas are important locations for fishing and gathering shellfish (reported in the press by Rawalai, 2019; Srinivasan, 2020, and others).

METHODS

Study Site

The research focussed on three villages along the Ba River, encompassing the lower catchment (*iTaukei* villages of Nawaqarua and Votua within the District of Nailaga, Ba Province) and the upper catchment (*iTaukei* village of Navala in the Qaliyalatini District, Ba Province) (see Fig. 4.1 for a location map). The three villages are largely reliant on natural resources, although the resources drawn on differ for all three villages. Overview information on the three villages is provided in Table 4.2.

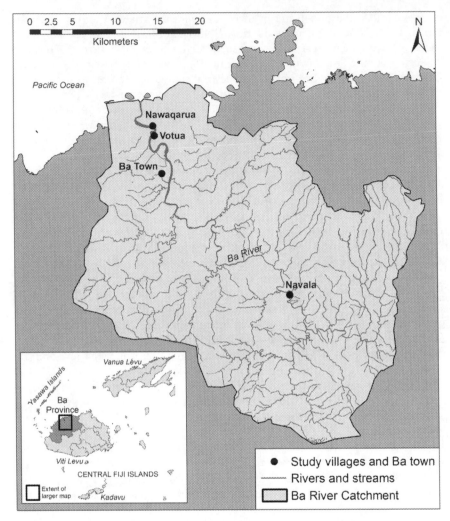

Fig. 4.1. Location of Study Villages. *Source*: Authors' own.

Nawaqarua and Votua villages are close to the mouth of the Ba River, and marine and mangrove resources feature strongly in terms of local livelihoods. Both villages are exposed to storm surges, riverbank erosion, flooding and meteorological drought. More than 100 houses were severely damaged across the two villages during the passage of Cyclone Winston in 2016, and around 50 were destroyed. During the time of research, many families who had lost their homes in Cyclone Winston were still waiting on rebuilding. The Fijian government granted FJD7,000 for homes that were completely destroyed, FJD3,000 to partially destroyed buildings and FJD1,500 for homes with lost roofs. The grants could only be redeemed in the form of vouchers for building supplies, with no money provided for labour costs, resulting in a slow process of rebuilding based largely on voluntary labour and self-building.

Table 4.2. Characteristics of the Three Study Villages.

Village	Pop'n	Major Livelihood Sources	Other Information
Nawaqarua	~250	Agriculture, fishing (fish, prawns, crabs, mussels), livestock rearing	Nawaqarua was founded in 1920 by six families to ease growing population pressure in nearby Votua (Neef et al., 2018). The village is located immediately adjacent to extensive mangroves at the Ba river mouth
Votua	~650	Agriculture, leasing of land for sugarcane plantations, to Fijians of Indian origin, and *iTaukei* Fijians, farm labour, work in Ba town, fishing (fish, prawns, crabs and mussels)	Votua controls the largest *qoliqoli* (customary fishing grounds) in Fiji and in the past has received license fees from outsiders using their fishing grounds
Navala	~800	Agriculture (including *yaqona/kava*), fishing (fish and eels), livestock rearing, foraging for wild plants, hunting (pigs), tourism (visitor fees and handicrafts)	Navala is the only community in Viti Levu in which the traditional *bure* (dwelling built from timber, pandanus and other natural materials) predominates. At the time of the research, the village did not have electricity (it now does)

Navala village is located in the rugged Nausori highlands in the upper Ba catchment. Community members draw on agriculture, livestock rearing, hunting and cultivation of the lucrative *yaqona* shrub (Piperaceae: *Piper methysticum*), the powdered dried roots of which are used as the basis for *kava*, a culturally important beverage in much of the South Pacific. Navala's architecture is distinctive, as the only community in Viti Levu in which traditional dwellings (the *bure*, built from a variety of natural materials including timber, bamboo and thatch) still predominate. Although Navala village is situated on high ground above the river, heavy rainfall events can lead to short-term submersion of the main access road and bridge to the village. In Navala, 30 houses were severely damaged and 32 were destroyed by Cyclone Winston, including both non-traditional houses and *bures* (iTaukei Institute of Language and Culture and Ministry of Itaukei Affairs, 2016; Miyaji, Fujieda, Waqalevu, & Kobayashi, 2017).[2] Much of the highlands region is susceptible to landslides in part due to the large-scale removal of native forest and vegetation cover.

Research Design and Data Collection

A multi-method, qualitative approach was considered appropriate for this research. The research drew primarily on participatory mapping with community members, participant observation, village walks and boat rides (conducted over three weeks in November and December of 2016). The research was also informed by one-on-one interviews undertaken during the same time period in 2016 (see Bennett, Neef, & Varea, 2020, Chapter 5, this volume) and a final presentation of the research to community members at the conclusion of the research project in September 2019. Conversations were undertaken in a mixture of English and Fijian depending on the context and the participants. Fijian language sessions and interviews were translated by three local research assistants.

Access to the three communities was facilitated through involvement in an international consortium of researchers with prior experience in the area (see Bennett et al., 2020, Chapter 5, this volume; Neef et al., 2018), and negotiated with the Ba Provincial Council, the *yavusa* (tribal) chiefs and *turaga-ni-koro* (village headmen). Cultural protocols observed by the research team included the formal presentation of *sevusevu* (a ceremonial gift) to the village leaders, in this case a bundle of dried roots of *yaqona*, as well as a formal introduction to the research and the members of the research team to the community (as described by Neef et al., 2018).

The primary method of data collection involved participatory mapping within 13 focus groups of 3–9 people each. This interactive technique has the capability to promote direct engagement of relevant stakeholders particularly on risks, perceptions and vulnerability (Preston, Yuen, & Westaway, 2011). Focus groups increase the likelihood of participants taking control and are particularly applicable when there is an uneven power dynamic within communities (Morgan, 1997). In our research, having members of the focus group draw responses to questions on transparent overlays superimposed on printouts of satellite imagery centred on the village was used to facilitate conversations around local views on livelihoods, natural hazards and impacts of climate-related events. Question themes were developed, loosely following those provided by Nakalevu (2006) and Williams, Pauli, and Boruff (2020, Chapter 6, this volume). Discussion was encouraged around the themes of environment and livelihoods; hazards and impacts; vulnerability; adaptation and reducing impacts; and coping and resilience. Participants were assured that lines drawn on maps were not going to be used for any 'official' purposes or interpreted as definite boundaries of ownership or otherwise.

Conducting mapping using satellite images demands little in the way of resources, but can be considered as a relatively reliable means of communicating information if representations are well understood by participants and researchers (Gaillard, Hore, & Cadag, 2015). We trialled the use of topographic base maps as an alternative form of spatial representation; however, A0-size satellite images at 1:6,000 scale proved the most popular during focus groups. Satellite imagery at a more detailed scale (1:2,500) was provided but not preferred, as these maps did not depict sufficient area of importance to participants. Indeed, even 1:6,000 scale maps did not adequately represent offshore fishing grounds (important to Nawaqarua and Votua) nor all lands used for hunting, *yaqona* plantations, timber and foraging (Navala).

Participants in the mapping focus groups were invited via village authorities, or by word-of-mouth or invitation, once the researchers had arrived in the community. Sessions generally took place in public areas such as community halls or in the open air. Focus groups were divided into adult and youths (Table 4.3). Adults were further divided by gender (with the exception of one mixed-gender group in Navala), given the highly patriarchal nature of *iTaukei* society, and the likelihood that women may speak less in a mixed-gender group (Arksey, 1996). As Fijian communities have great respect for elders, the potential for a similar effect on young adults was realised. One mixed-gender youth focus group was conducted in each of the two larger villages (Votua and Navala). The number of sessions in each community was roughly proportional to the total population.

Table 4.3.   Composition of Participatory Mapping Focus Groups in the
Study Villages.

Village	Men	Women	Mixed Gender	Youth	Total
Navala	**2** (5, 6)	**2** (7, 6)	**1** (6)	**1** (8)	**6** (38)
Votua	**2** (4, 5)	**2** (4, 3)	0	**1** (4)	**5** (20)
Nawaqarua	**1** (7)	**1** (9)	0	0	**2** (16)
Total focus groups and participants					**13** (74)

Note: Numbers in bold refer to the total number of focus groups. Numbers in brackets indicate the number of participants in each focus group, with numbers separated by commas indicating participants in each of multiple focus groups in that category.

During the time spent in the three communities (2 days in Nawaqarua and 5–6 days in each of Votua and Navala), notes and photographs from all research activities were collated and contributed to the analysis. Mobile participatory mapping was also undertaken using the software platform Mappt (Takor Group, 2016), which was used to annotate imagery using a tablet computer. Individual interviews on the broad theme of food security with 32 women (Bennett et al., 2020, Chapter 5, this volume) were drawn on to augment and interpret data collected through other avenues. Finally, the results of the research were presented to and discussed with community members from Nawaqarua and Votua during a research dissemination workshop in September 2019 in Ba town. Feedback and comments from the workshop were used to inform parts of the Discussion for this chapter.

The research embraced the *talanoa* technique, which is widely understood in Fiji and much of the Pacific as a means of discussing issues in a transparent, inclusive and free-flowing manner. *Talanoa* is regarded as a culturally appropriate research method within the Fijian context, and a means by which communities can take ownership of their knowledge, their ideas and how these are interpreted in the research process (Meo-Sewabu, 2014). Using the *talanoa* technique for gaining insight into local understanding recognises that asking a specific question may not result in the interviewee disclosing the desired information (Fa'avae, Jones, & Manu'atu, 2016), and instead focusses on developing rapport, having conversations that flow in a natural, semi-structured way, and without the use of a strict question guide. Audio recordings were not made of mapping sessions nor interviews; instead, notes were taken during focus group discussions and interviews by at least one researcher, leaving at least one member of the team free to concentrate on the conversation at hand. Following the conclusion of each session, team members met to discuss, corroborate and finalise notes. Observations and notes from walks, boat rides and other interactions within the community were noted down as soon as feasible.

Analysis

Analysis of notes from participatory mapping sessions and other sources was carried out using a simple coding method, developed according to key themes identified during the sessions (Payne & Payne, 2004). Key themes and sub-themes were highlighted during the coding process and related to the research questions.

Participatory maps were digitised by transferring key information from each map using Google Earth Pro (Google LLC, 2019), with final maps produced in ArcMap (ESRI, 2014) through a compilation of features drawn by all participants in each location. Participatory mapping was intended as a medium for exploration and explanation of key issues for participants, and as such, the maps produced are intended only for illustrative purposes rather than as a key diagnostic tool for where to direct resources or to identify which areas are under severe threat from hydro-meteorological hazards. This clarification is particularly important, as some features that are significant to local people may not have been mapped, and the boundaries of features that were mapped were treated as 'fuzzy' edges which have been reproduced using words rather than shapes on the final livelihood/hazard maps.

FINDINGS

The findings section focusses strongly on details related to the first two objectives of this research, namely: to understand how livelihoods in the study areas are impacted by climate-related hazards through documenting patterns of resource use, and to take a spatially explicit view of the heterogeneity of landscapes and livelihoods, reflecting on how hazard impacts manifest across space and time. Information pertaining to the third objective of how local knowledge is used to prepare for hazards is also included in this section. The findings pertinent to the research objectives are presented first for the coastal villages of Nawaqarua and Votua, and second for the upland village of Navala.

Nawaqarua and Votua

The villages of Nawaqarua and Votua are located in relatively close proximity on the lower reaches of the Ba River. The participatory mapping sessions for both of these villages (two from the smaller village of Nawaqarua and five from Votua) have been combined into one drawing, depicted in Fig. 4.2. Votua remains the larger village, holding a majority in decisions pertaining to land allocation for farming and leasing, and access to the very large traditional fishing grounds (*qoliqoli*), which reach to the Yasawas (see Fig. 4.1, inset).

Residents of Votua and Nawaqarua draw their livelihoods from fishing, agriculture, labour and off-farm work (for many young people and professionals, this occurs in Ba Town). The most lucrative fishery is for *qari*, the green mangrove crab (*Scylla paramamosain*). *Qari* are caught by men and women, although from different habitats, with men able to dive and women restricted to collecting crabs from the mangroves; participants highlighted that the latter habitat is more difficult to navigate with the result that men may catch more *qari* relative to effort. *Qari* are sold at the market directly or to a middleman. During the wet season and during periods of flooding, women cannot catch *qari* due to limited access to mangrove habitat, and instead catch smaller, less lucrative *kuka* (black mangrove crab – *Metopograpsus messor*). *Mana* (mud lobster – *Thalassina anomala*) and *uraura* (mangrove prawn – *Palaemon concinnus*) are also collected from mangrove

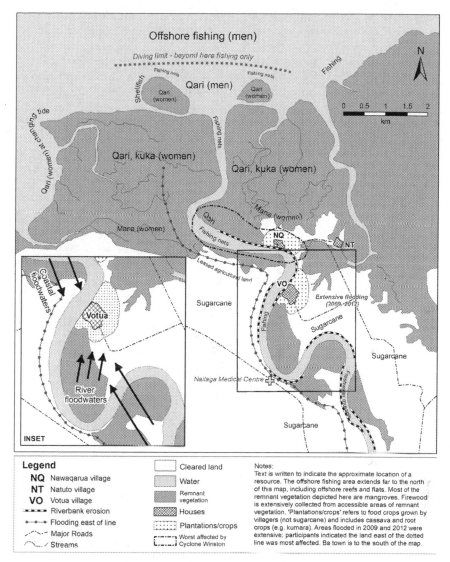

Fig. 4.2. Representation of Resources Used to Support Livelihoods Around Nawaqarua and Votua Villages, and Acute Impacts of Recent Natural Hazards. The map represents a conceptual collation of information provided in seven participatory mapping sessions in Nawaqarua and Votua villages. 'Fishing' encompasses a diverse range of fish and crustaceans, caught using nets, diving and other methods (see text for further details). Text and lines have been placed on the map to approximate locations indicated by participants. It should not be implied that the location of the words or lines/boundaries represents the precise location, nor all locations for each resource or activity. Inset map depicts participants' representation of the path of floodwaters towards Votua village during recent (2009, 2012) floods. Source: Authors' own.

habitats. Nets may be used to catch prawns in waterways. Shellfish including cockles and clams (*kaikoso, qeqe, kai*) are collected from mudflats exposed during low tide and further upstream from the riverbanks.

Crops for home consumption and some sale are grown in the fields immediately surrounding the villages in plantations. Cassava is a staple crop, and *kumara* alongside a wide variety of vegetables and tree crops including plantain, coconut, breadfruit and mango are also grown. A number of sugarcane fields are owned by Votua village and leased for income; villagers also work as paid labour in sugarcane plantations and other forms of agriculture. When there is a downturn in agricultural yield or labour, community members are still able to gain income from fishing activities.

Both villages suffered severe impacts due to the floods of 2009 and 2012 and during the passage of Cyclone Winston. In Nawaqarua, 7 homes were destroyed and 17 damaged during the cyclone, while in Votua, 18 houses were destroyed and a further 92 damaged. The two villages and their home gardens and crop plots were entirely inundated during recent flooding events, with the exception of the community centre at Nawaqarua, which has been built on higher ground set further back from the river. The community centre acted as the evacuation point for the 2012 flood and 2016 cyclone for Nawaqarua and the nearby settlement of Natuto (location is shown in Fig. 4.2). The floods of 2009 were more severe than those of 2012, reaching greater flood heights and with a longer period of inundation. In 2009, community members recall that there were three flood surges, the first when the water came down from the upper Ba River, and the other two due to high tides, so that floodwaters approached Votua village in particular from two opposing directions. The pathways of approaching floodwaters are depicted in the inset map to Fig. 4.2, with details of the temporal dimensions of multiple hazards provided in Table 4.4.

Participatory mapping sessions revealed that recent floods and cyclones had extensive impacts on marine and freshwater resources, in addition to having severe impacts on crops and livestock. During floods, *qari* are flushed out of mangroves and are no longer available for women to collect; they can still be collected by men while diving although the waters are laden with sediment. The debris left in the Ba River and offshore from floods and cyclones created hazards for fishers and their nets, reducing access to estuarine and nearshore fishing grounds and resulting in a reduced catch. Changes in water quality due to higher levels of suspended sediment following flooding also led to reduced fish abundance. Some fisheries recovered quickly (within days) once the sediment settled, while others (such as *kai*, freshwater clams: *Batissa violacea*) were heavily depleted for months and took a whole year to recover. With most crops destroyed or heavily damaged following the cyclone and flood, marine and freshwater resources take on additional importance as a source of income and sustenance.

Community members were alerted to the imminent approach of Cyclone Winston and floods through warnings issued on radio and directly by local leaders going from house to house. A wealth of local knowledge exists around whether flooding or cyclones are imminent. For flooding, several days of heavy rain indicate

Table 4.4. Impacts of Multiple Natural Hazards Near the Villages of Nawaqarua and Votua.

	Cyclonic Winds (Cyclone Winston)	Flooding (Esp. 2009, 2012)	Drought (Seasonal)
Immediate impacts	• Multiple homes destroyed and damaged in Nawaqarua and Votua • Crops (cassava) badly impacted • Mangroves damaged, leaves stripped and branches broken off • Tree crops (banana, cassava) damaged • Sugarcane damaged • Shellfish smothered by sediment • Stunned fish caught in mangroves, could be easily collected	• Nawaqarua village flooded except for community hall. Votua village flooded, second storey of school was evacuation centre • Extensive flooding on the eastern side of Ba River • Crops (cassava) destroyed • Silt deposited in agricultural fields • Multiple homes destroyed and damaged • Houses flooded; silt deposits left behind • Tree crops (coconut, mango, breadfruit) not affected • Livestock lost (cattle, pigs; goats were mostly saved by being put on roofs) • Sugarcane flooded • Stunned prawns and crabs easier to collect in mangroves	*Slow-onset hazard*
Short-Term impacts (< 1 month)	• Water supply disrupted • Electricity supply disrupted • Road access to Ba blocked, need to take a more expensive boat • Debris from broken mangroves and trees in the river; affected access to fishing grounds; reduced fish catch and income • Root crops more expensive to buy	• Road access to Ba blocked, needed to take a boat (road is cheaper) • Storm surge after initial flood stranded some people outside of the village, could not return • Dwellings and belongings damaged; silt had to be removed • Water supply disrupted; tankers brought in and some rainwater collection • Electricity supply disrupted • Rations of flour and rice provided • Reduced fish catch nearshore due to poor water quality; male fishers must travel further offshore to fish • Debris in water reduces access to fishing grounds and increases the difficulty of catching fish (nets snag) • *Qari* crabs washed out from mangroves; women cannot catch them and instead catch a less lucrative crab species • Shellfish greatly depleted, covered in sediment • Root crops planted as these are fast maturing • Debris in sugarcane fields made harvesting more difficult and could not be finished before mills closed; once collected debris could be sold	*Slow-onset hazard*

Table 4.4.   (*Continued*)

	Cyclonic Winds (Cyclone Winston)	Flooding (Esp. 2009, 2012)	Drought (Seasonal)
Medium–term impacts (1–12 months)	• Electricity supply cut for many months • Debris in the river affected access to fishing grounds; reduced fish catch and income • Root crops more expensive to buy • Change in diet to more rice and flour as cassava not available • Families and individuals must make other accommodation arrangements while houses repaired and rebuilt	• Electricity and/or water may still be disrupted • Families and individuals must make other accommodation arrangements while houses repaired and rebuilt • Cassava crops replanted after 2–3 months • Agricultural fields rejuvenated by nutrients in flood sediments (Votua), improved crop growth • Change in diet to more rice and flour as cassava not available • Freshwater mussels reduced, recovered slowly over one year	• Cassava takes longer to grow and harvest, becomes hard • Yield drops for root crops • Reduced sugarcane yield • Water rationing • Fishing not affected
Longer term impacts (>1 year)	• Trees (e.g. coconut) cut down within the village to reduce the risk of flying debris during cyclones • Reduced income means some women have left cooperative as they could not afford membership due to impacts from Cyclone Winston. Cooperative provides microfinance (including for small business) and acts as a safety net	• Some homeowners have added a second storey to reduce the impact of flood • Reluctance to replace lost livestock due to potential for further flooding and loss • River becoming wider and shallower; agricultural land lost to bank erosion • *Bures* no longer built in the village (Votua), cannot withstand floods • Periodic dredging was undertaken to theoretically reduce flood risk; dredging reduces fish catch for about one month	• Increased temperature makes conditions less suitable for some crops (e.g. root crops such as *kumara,* taro)
Hazard interactions	• Drought occurred following Cyclone Winston, compounding the issue of crop loss with slow crop growth • Ba River morphology changing, in part due to flooding, resulting in riverbank erosion and accretion. Bank erosion has led to loss of some houses and agricultural land • Following flooding, fruit from trees still available as food source (coconut, mango, breadfruit) while all root, ground crops destroyed. Following the cyclone, fear that trees could be lethal debris during future cyclones meant some trees were cut down, which could impact food availability after future floods		

that flooding is likely, and families prepare their homes by storing and moving belongings to higher elevations. Marks of past flood heights are recorded on homes. Elders in Votua highlighted several sources of local knowledge that indicate severe cyclonic activity is likely. These included: seabirds flying inland; birds making nests under verandahs and bees constructing hives at ground level; a particular orientation of leaves and new shoots on *vudi* (plantain) trees; and excessive fruit production (such as breadfruits and oranges). However, the direction from which Cyclone Winston arrived was unusual; villagers were not prepared for the cyclone to come from the east, as previously only the western side of the island was directly affected by cyclones.

Navala

A combined map representing livelihoods and hazard impacts within and around the village of Navala is presented in Fig. 4.3. Villagers from Navala utilise the surrounding landscape for diverse purposes, with a degree of spatial zonation increasing with distance from the village. In Fig. 4.3, we have drawn an approximate representation of how these livelihoods are distributed across the landscape, based on input from all six participatory mapping sessions, augmented with observations and other notes from conversations with local people.

The central zone (within a 250 m radius of the village centre) contains houses, the school, places of worship, home gardens (including an array of vegetables and fruit trees), and poultry (chickens and ducks). Between ∼250 and 1,000 m from the village centre, food crops are grown within plantations (with the chief crop consisting of cassava, with *kumara* and plantain as additional important crops), the village's main water sources are found, goats are reared, and firewood and wild chillies, spices (including *haldi*/turmeric) and yams are foraged. Within this zone, fishing is prohibited for a period of time during the year to allow fish to breed and restock. Between ∼1,000 and 2,000 m, fishing becomes important (including for tilapia, mullet and eels), livestock are grazed, and spring water-fed wetlands (natural soaks – also known as damplands – where the soil remains wet) are found at the base of escarpments. These damplands (Fig. 4.3) provide important resources often collected and used by women including taro, *duruka* (*Saccharum edule* – a species of sugarcane grass with an edible stalk), pandanus (used for weaving mats, handicrafts and in *bure* construction), *ota* (fiddlehead fern *Matteuccia struthiopteris*) and *ota karisi* (watercress – *Rorippa nasturtium-aquaticum*). Beyond ∼2,000 m from the centre, *yaqona* is cultivated, and hunting is undertaken for wild pigs. *Bure* thatch materials are found within this zone, with many of the hardwood trees used for *bure* poles (including the *vesi* tree, *Intsia bijuga*) cut from further upstream, beyond ∼4,000 m from the village. Beyond the dimensions of the map shown in Fig. 4.3, commodities including *yaqona*, fish, livestock and produce are sold at markets in Ba, Lautoka and other centres. Youths may pick up supplementary work cutting sugarcane on the coastal plain during harvest time.

During sessions in Navala, the impacts of destruction from the winds of Cyclone Winston (2016), flooding from Cyclone Kina (1993) and a significant

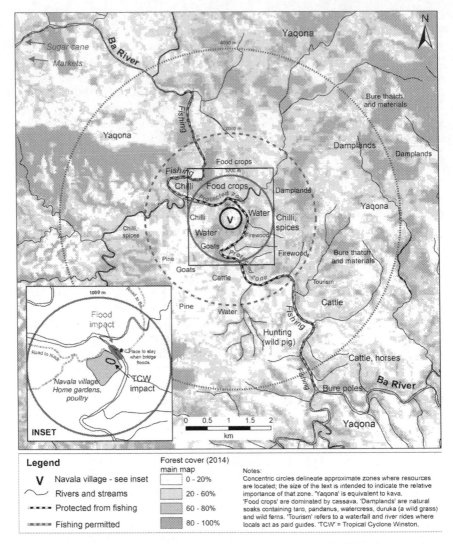

Fig. 4.3. Representation of Resources Used to Support Livelihoods Around Navala Village, and Acute Impacts of Recent Natural Hazards. The map represents a conceptual collation of information provided in six participatory mapping sessions in Navala village. Words representing important resources have been placed on the map to approximate locations and distances from the village for these resources; it should not be implied that the location of the words represents the precise location, nor all locations for each resource or activity. Concentric zones have been used to give a sense of the relative distance from the village within which livelihoods are drawn. *Source*: Authors' own.

Table 4.5. Impacts of Multiple Natural Hazards Near the Village of Navala.

	Cyclonic Winds (Cyclone Winston)	Flooding of Riverbank (Torrential Rain)	Drought (Seasonal)
Immediate impacts	• Homes destroyed and damaged (many were older *bures*) • Kitchens (located outside) destroyed • Home gardens damaged • Poultry died • Shrub food crops damaged or destroyed (chiefly cassava) • Productive trees damaged (banana, breadfruit) • Root crops (*kumara*, taro) undamaged • Mature *yaqona* crops destroyed; immature crops survived	• Low-lying crops damaged • Houses near river may be flooded • Reduced fish abundance • Bridge flooded, transport affected	*Slow-onset hazard*
Short-term impacts (< 1 month)	• Increased fishing difficulty due to debris • Salvageable crops (cassava, banana, chillies, lemons) quickly harvested and sold at the market to purchase rice and flour • Fast-growing crops planted (*kumara*) • Piped water supply disrupted • Firewood easier to collect from damaged forests	• Increased fishing difficulty due to debris • Piped water supply contaminated by sedimentation • Road access to the village may be hampered	*Slow-onset hazard* • Water may be stored by households if dry conditions apparent
Medium-term impacts (1–12 months)	• Change in diet emphasis to rice and flour as no cassava available (takes eight months to mature), reliance on supplied food rations • *Bure* destroyed during Cyclone Winston could not be rebuilt until the end of the wet season; annual, communal process following the official meeting – *vesi* logs are cut and floated down the river when the water flow is high • Less work available for youth to cut sugarcane as crops affected by Cyclone Winston	Flooding rarely lasts more than a couple of days	• Wetlands and associated resources affected (dry up) • Crops affected that cannot be irrigated (*yaqona*) • Piped water supply rationed • Reduced fruit production • Home gardens can be watered • Cassava production can withstand drought • Reduced supply of natural housing materials for *bure* • Lower river flow makes transport (timber, produce) downriver more difficult • Livestock can drink from the river

Table 4.5. (*Continued*)

	Cyclonic Winds (Cyclone Winston)	Flooding of Riverbank (Torrential Rain)	Drought (Seasonal)
Longer Term Impacts (> 1 year)	• *Yaqona* takes three years to mature before [destructive] harvesting possible. Important income source for Navala. Higher prices for *yaqona*/*kava* throughout Pacific due to drop in supply • Reparation to extensive dwelling damage takes time; more 'modern' houses constructed in village to replace bures	Flooding rarely lasts more than a couple of days	• Concerns expressed over how to grow water-hungry crops (e.g. taro)
Hazard interactions	• Drought occurred following Cyclone Winston, slowing growth of new crops and adding further delays to local production following crop destruction and rapid harvesting of salvageable crops • Breadfruit damaged during Cyclone Winston, giving less fruit, and drought caused slower maturation of available fruit • Riverbank erosion noted during trips to cut timber for *bure* poles: flooding may exacerbate erosion, removing tree roots contributes to erosion • Cassava was extensively damaged by cyclonic winds, prompting consideration of growing more low-growing root crops that are less susceptible to wind. However, cassava can cope with drought/dry conditions		

drought in 1988 were the most frequently mentioned hydro-meteorological events. A hazard impact map for the village of Navala is provided as an inset in Fig. 4.3, depicting the section of the village that was hardest hit by Cyclone Winston, and the areas near the river impacted by flash flooding. In addition, large swathes of the landscape and watercourses surrounding Navala were affected by Cyclone Winston in particular and by drought more generally. The various impacts of cyclonic winds, flash flooding and seasonal drought are summarised in Table 4.5, together with some of the key interactions among hazards.

The residents of Navala are accustomed to infrequent flash flooding where the river breaks its banks following torrential rainfall events; these are often associated with tropical storms and cyclones where the main impacts are in areas distant from Navala. Following Cyclone Kina, numerous respondents said that the bridge across the Ba River was flooded for eight hours. There exists a perception that the weather is getting hotter and droughts are of concern, with some consideration given in discussions as to how livelihoods might be affected or change with increased warmer weather. Some participants were unconcerned with potential crop failure due to lack of water, maintaining that it would be possible to supplement crops with foraged foods such as wild yams. Participants mentioned that the vegetables grown around houses are relatively drought-proof, as these can be watered and there are natural springs near the village that can be used to supply water if the piped water supply is interrupted for any reason.

While floods and droughts are within the community's long experience, for Navala, the passage of a cyclone was novel, as this part of Fiji has rarely been in the direct path of tropical cyclones. Several participants in the mapping session expressed concerns about strong winds and worried that cyclones would become more frequent. Many villagers were unprepared for the advent of Cyclone Winston, with some not taking heed of warnings from local leaders and others taking shelter in the school with bare essentials only (such as sleeping mats and tinned food) and no cooking equipment. The elderly and sick were identified as particularly vulnerable due to limited mobility. Cyclone Winston caused extensive damage to shrub and tree crops, including cassava, *yaqona* and fruit trees. In the immediate aftermath of the cyclone, community members quickly harvested whatever food crops could be salvaged (including cassava, chillies, lemons and bananas) and took these to market in order to purchase rice and flour; supplies of these provisions lasted for about one month, with further provisions of rice, flour and sugar supplied as aid to the villages in the months that followed. Following Cyclone Winston, there was an extended dry period, which compounded the damage caused by the cyclone, with crops taking longer to mature. The dietary staple of cassava was replaced by rice and flour for many months.

DISCUSSION

This research employed participatory mapping as a technique to explore the spatial and temporal dimensions of multiple hazards in three communities adjacent to the Ba River in Fiji. Conceptual maps illustrating the links between livelihoods and hazard impacts were developed based on the responses of mapping participants.

The qualitative techniques used resulted in a set of mapped outputs that differ from both those provided by quantitative, data-driven geospatial techniques for assessing vulnerability at broad spatial scales (e.g. Ashraful Islam et al., 2016; Hoque et al., 2019) or from those that use qualitative techniques to derive more precision-focussed mapping products to delineate the level of exposure or risk at the household, neighbourhood or catchment level (e.g. Canevari-Luzardo et al., 2017; Cubelos et al., 2019; Huang & London, 2016) to multiple hazards. While the combined physical output of participatory mapping sessions may be less amenable to the preparation of detailed spatial plans or adaptation measures for a particular location, they do allow for the visualisation of areas that are socially, culturally and agriculturally important, as well as areas that are impacted by different environmental hazards. The complex linkages between land, river, sea and people, and the ways in which people modify their use of the land- and seascapes in response to the impact of natural hazards, demonstrate the importance of a landscape approach in planning for multiple, potentially competing land uses (Sayer et al., 2013).

The discussion that follows reflects on the findings of the research, and particularly the third research objective concerning the extent to which local knowledge aids in preparing for and responding to multiple climate-related hazards. We also consider how participatory mapping could be used to demonstrate the importance of traditional lands and seas during environmental impact assessment processes, and highlight how the Fijian government and NGOs are already using local knowledge and participatory processes to inform planning and policy.

Landscapes, Livelihoods and Cumulative Impacts of Multiple Hazards

The temporal and spatial extent and impact of hazards (floods, cyclones, droughts and bank erosion) was variable within and between communities. The clustered nature of dwellings within each of the three villages meant that the impact of cyclonic winds was fairly consistent within the boundaries of each village, with research participants explicitly stating that Cyclone Winston affected everyone equally in Nawaqarua and Votua. Beyond the dwellings, there was spatial variability in terms of the areas where crops such as cassava (Navala) and natural resources such as mangroves (Nawaqarua) were damaged. In terms of flooding, some dwellings on slightly higher ground in Votua were less impacted than those closest to the river; however, all agricultural lands were equally affected with total crop loss. Drought differs from acute shocks such as floods and cyclones as drought is a slow-onset hazard that affects all members of the community. Having a diverse set of resources from which to draw is likely important in terms of distributing risk associated with different hazards.

As the livelihoods and hazard impacts demonstrate (Figs. 4.2 and 4.3), multiple hazards directly impact the same location. For instance, Nawaqarua and Votua villages are directly affected by floods, cyclones and riverbank erosion. These hazards have different modes of impact, so that the coping and adaptation strategies to reduce risk are different. In a cyclone, participants indicated that single-storey dwellings felt safer, whereas during a flood, double-storey dwellings were preferred. Reconstruction or repair following a flood or cyclone may be more strongly directed to dwelling types built to better endure the most recent hazard, and may not be designed to withstand another set of hazards. One couple's solution was to shelter with family members in a nearby village during Cyclone Winston, where recently built houses are equipped with cyclone straps, and to shelter in Votua during floods on the second storey of their dwelling. With adequate warning, preparation and transport, this kind of multi-location strategy could be adapted for broader use in locations where communities have access to lands that vary in their exposure to different hazards.

Local Knowledge in Preparing for and Responding to Hazards

Some of the elders who participated in mapping sessions shared elements of local knowledge of the advent of particular hazards, particularly in relation to cyclones and floods. The means of predicting severe cyclones were similar to other reported knowledge from the Pacific and further afield to Timor-Leste, the Philippines and Indonesia (Hiwasaki et al., 2014; Janif et al., 2016). For the floodplain communities of Votua and Nawaqarua, regular flooding occurs more frequently than the direct impact of cyclones, and there are well established patterns that indicate a flood is likely following several days of torrential rain (these are often associated with the passage of tropical storms and depressions, and are widely publicised in the media). Women in particular played a leading role in preparing households, goods, children and the elderly in advance of floods (Bennett et al., 2020, Chapter 5, this volume). The same holds true for cyclones; in Navala one group of women described the gendered division of tasks prior to the cyclone using a cooking metaphor, as 'women are like the pots, and men are like the lids'. When questioned, the explanation of this metaphor was that cooking (like hazard preparation) is more effective if both pots and lids are used (in other words, both women and men), but it can still be done without lids if necessary.

Despite elders holding the knowledge of the local indicators of impending hydro-meteorological hazards, and specific warnings provided via media and/or local leaders, some community members did not heed warnings and were not fully prepared for the arrival of cyclonic winds in particular. This may be an indication of the relative novelty of cyclones in the communities visited (as highlighted by several participants who said that they were not prepared for a cyclone to come from the west), or it could be related to a gradual loss of traditional oral narratives shared between elders and youth, as young people move away from rural areas to seek income, as highlighted by Janif et al. (2016). In addition, the pace of environmental change may be more rapid than the evolution of local knowledge associated with new or infrequent hazards. There is also likely to be more detailed knowledge and observation around long-term climatic trends and more recent patterns held by community members which were not explicitly discussed during participatory mapping sessions. Rapid climate change means that adaptation strategies will need to be diverse, incorporating both scientific and local knowledge (de Andrade & Szlafsztein, 2015).

Community members held detailed knowledge about areas of riverbank erosion and accumulation, with considerable agreement among sessions and participants on the locations of areas that are currently being eroded. The Ba River presents modelling complexities due to the very flat topography and hydro-dynamic uncertainties in how water moves through tributaries in different situations (Dutch Risk Reduction Team, 2019); incorporation of local knowledge in hydraulic and hydrological modelling could assist with increasing accuracy (Laborde, Imberger, & Toussaint, 2012). Participants in Votua and Nawaqarua attributed bank erosion and river widening to increased wave action from boat wakes and flooding. Recent dredging funded by the state is intended to reduce flood risk, and participants in Nawaqarua tended to agree that dredging has reduced the impact of floods (at least, at the time of field research; subsequent to this study the communities were again flooded in April 2018). A recent report commissioned by the Fijian government recommended continuation of dredging as well as construction of dykes and revegetation of the riparian zone, in order to protect the town of Ba from the worst effects of flooding (Dutch Risk Reduction Team, 2019). The report did not include consideration of how other communities are impacted by flood mitigation measures (such as reduced fish catch following dredging, as discussed by some participants), highlighting the need for broad consultation on floodplain management.

During the mapping sessions, there was often curiosity expressed as to why the research team were interested in which areas were used for fishing, crabbing, farming and other activities, when much of the research concerned the impact of acute hazards. At the time of this research (2016), participatory mapping was used as a tool to understand the temporal dynamics and spatial dimensions of local livelihoods rather than as a means of developing a very detailed spatial representation of local knowledge and resource use. When the research team returned to present the results of the study to the coastal communities in 2019 (including a version of Fig. 4.2), iron sand dredging had started off the coast of the Ba River, and there was great concern as to what the impact of dredging activities might have on the livelihoods of coastal communities. In this context, having a map drawn directly from local people's knowledge and clearly indicating the importance of mangroves and nearshore waters *prior* to the commencement of dredging activities could form documentary evidence of the importance of these regions. Importantly, the hybrid format (a digitised map on a precise base layer using imprecise representations of knowledge and resource boundaries) can be mutually understood and potentially considered by both local communities and external entities (such as government agencies or corporate entities). Production of detailed local resource and hazard maps can be a very lengthy process (Corbett, 2009; Gaillard et al., 2015); the method described here is relatively rapid and could be deployed in similar contexts to document the importance of lands, seas and coastal habitats that do not fall neatly within parcels of titled land.

In Fiji, there are a number of examples where consideration is given to the inclusion of local knowledge in resource management decisions. Among the most widely known is the network of around 150 Fiji Locally Managed Marine Areas (FLMMA), where communities, NGOs, government departments and academic institutions work together to promote sustainable use of *qoliqoli* (Thaman et al., 2013). Extensive work has been done in Votua village to establish the basis for community-based natural resource management along these lines (Veitayaki, Tawake, & Aalbersberg, 2003), and Votua village has a registered LMMA (Atlas of Marine Protection, 2020). The Fijian Ministry of *iTaukei* Affairs embarked on a 'Cultural Mapping Program' commencing in 2005, with the goal of collecting, recording and documenting traditional knowledge and expressions of culture (in other words, intangible cultural heritage) from each of the more than 1,000 *iTaukei* villages in all 14 Fijian provinces (Sevudredre, 2009; Turagaiviu, 2018). Ba Province was the last to be mapped, with mapping activities commencing in 2018. Fiji is also in the process of implementing measures to operationalise the Nagoya Protocol to the Convention Biological Diversity on Access to Genetic Resources and the Fair and Equitable Sharing of Benefits Arising from their Utilization (ABS) (SPREP, 2017); Fiji acceded to the protocol in 2012. These initiatives highlight that participatory approaches to mapping and understanding cultural landscapes have been recognised by government and non-government agencies in Fiji.

CONCLUSIONS

Communities within the Ba River catchment of Fiji are experiencing increased physical exposure to hazards due to a range of processes, including deforestation throughout the catchment, and shifting weather patterns that alter the frequency and intensity of tropical storm systems. In response, communities have employed a variety of adaptation techniques, many of which are tied to strong social networks (Neef et al., 2018; Yila et al., 2013). The persistence of communities to maintain their cultural integrity and socio-economic activities following repeated exposure to floods, cyclones and drought is testament to their resilience and ingenuity (echoing the findings of McNamara & Prasad, 2014), and ability to draw on a wide range of resources throughout the land- and seascape. These landscapes and seascapes may not all be equally impacted during hazard events and recover at different times. It remains to be seen whether there is a threshold of repeated hazard intensity or frequency beyond which communities will encounter severe difficulties with recovery.

The use of participatory approaches to understand local livelihoods and experiences of climate change is imperative for the development of inclusive, sustainable adaptation planning and management strategies. For example, mitigation measures designed to reduce the impact of floods in larger population centres may have unintended impacts in nearby communities if floodwaters are simply diverted elsewhere; likewise, a mining operation that might appear to have only a small spatial footprint may also affect a broader web of social-ecological relationships. Documentation of how communities use land, rivers, estuaries, coastal habitats and nearshore marine areas can provide a powerful visualisation of local experiences in regions that may otherwise be 'hidden' from view due to remoteness or small size. In rapidly changing environments such as those in the lower Ba River catchment, repeating participatory mapping and allied approaches at regular intervals can help document the dynamic nature of resource availability and hazard impacts. Such approaches can form part of social impact assessment as well as frame future planning for climate adaptation.

NOTES

1. Throughout this chapter, the term 'local knowledge' is used as a generic term that incorporates the rich experiential, often tacit, implicit and 'informal' knowledge held by farmers, fishers, community members and Indigenous peoples about their environment, as contrasted with 'formal' expert and scientific knowledge.
2. Prior to Cyclone Winston, around three-quarters of all houses in Navala were *bures*. One year after the cyclone, there was an increase in the number of non-traditional houses, with many of these being 'temporary' housing and a smaller number of permanent modern houses (Miyaji et al., 2017). In a survey of 72 residents of Navala following the passage of Cyclone Winston, 70% of respondents considered *bures* to be safer than modern houses in cyclonic winds, as debris from thatched roofs does not pose the same danger as flying metal sheeting from modern roofs (Miyaji et al., 2017). As the construction of a *bure* is labour-intensive, it is challenging to build large numbers of these houses in any given year.

ACKNOWLEDGEMENTS

We extend our thanks to the Ba Provincial Council, and the leaders and residents of the villages of Nawaqarua, Votua and Navala for permitting and participating in the research, and especially thank Viti and Celestino for hosting authors, G.I. and R.V. The authors would like to thank Dr Peter Jones, Prof. Andreas Neef, Dr Eberhard Weber, Kahukura Bennett, Talica Nauvi, Robert Varea, Dr Eleanor Bruce, Dr Floris van Ogtrop, Dr John Duncan and Mark Williams for their involvement in the research. This research was made possible through funding and support provided by the Asia-Pacific Network for Global Change Research (CAF2016-RR05-CMY-Neef, 'Climate Change Adaptation in Post-Disaster Recovery Processes: Flood-Affected Communities in Cambodia and Fiji', led by Prof, Andreas Neef at the University of Auckland) and the University of Western Australia (Research Collaboration Award RA/1/1200/755, 'Risk, resilience and recovery: A participatory approach to integrating local and scientific knowledge for disaster preparedness of communities in flood-prone catchments in Fiji').

REFERENCES

Arksey, H. (1996). *Collecting data through joint interviews*. Social Research Update (Vol. 15). Guilford: University of Surrey. Retrieved from http://sru.soc.surrey.ac.uk/SRU15.html

Armour, G. (2010). Communities communicating with formal and informal systems: Being more resilient in times of need. *Bulletin of the American Society for Information Science and Technology, 36*, 34–38. doi:10.1002/bult.2010.1720360510

Asare-Kyei, D., Kloos, J., & Renaud, F. G. (2015). Multi-scale participatory indicator development approaches for climate change risk assessment in West Africa. *International Journal of Disaster Risk Reduction, 11*, 13–34. doi:10.1016/j.ijdrr.2014.11.001

Ashraful Islam, M., Mitra, D., Dewan, A., & Akhter, S. H. (2016). Coastal multi-hazard vulnerability assessment along the Ganges deltaic coast of Bangladesh – A geospatial approach. *Ocean & Coastal Management, 127*, 1–15. doi:10.1016/j.ocecoaman.2016.03.012

Atlas of Marine Protection. (2020). Fiji. Marine Conservation Institute. Retrieved from http://www.mpatlas.org/region/country/FJI/

Bennett, K., Neef, A. & Varea, R. (2020). Embodying resilience: Narrating gendered experiences of disasters in Fiji. In A. Neef & N. Pauli (Eds.), *Climate-induced disasters in the Asia-Pacific region: Response, recovery, adaptation* (pp. 87–112). Bingley: Emerald Publishing.

Brandt, K., Graham, L., Hawthorne, T., Jeanty, J., Burkholder, B., Munisteri, C., & Visaggi, C. (2019). Integrating sketch mapping and hot spot analysis to enhance capacity for community-level flood and disaster risk management. *The Geographical Journal, 186*(2), 198–212. doi:10.1111/geoj.12330

Canevari-Luzardo, L., Bastide, J., Choutet, I., & Liverman, D. (2017). Using partial participatory GIS in vulnerability and disaster risk reduction in Grenada. *Climate and Development, 9*(2), 95–109. doi:10.1080/17565529.2015.1067593

CARE Australia. (2018). *Republic of Fiji, Tropical Cyclone Josie and Tropical Cyclone keni rapid gender, protection and inclusion analysis.* Canberra: CARE Australia. Retrieved from https://reliefweb.int/report/fiji/republic-fiji-tropical-cyclone-josie-and-tropical-cyclone-keni-rapid-gender-protection

CDKN. (2014). *The IPCC's fifth assessment report: What's in it for small island development states?* London: Climate and Development Knowledge Network. Retrieved from https://cdkn.org/wp-content/uploads/2014/08/IPCC-AR5-Whats-in-it-for-SIDS_WEB.pdf

Ceccato, L., Giannini, V., & Giupponi, C. (2011). Participatory assessment of adaptation strategies to flood risk in the Upper Brahmaputra and Danube river basins. *Environmental Science and Policy, 14*(8), 1163–1174. doi:10.1016/j.envsci.2011.05.016

Chambers, C. (2019). Mba ironsands shipment to depart next week. *Fiji Sun.* Retrieved from https://www.pressreader.com/fiji/fiji-sun/20190824/282303911793234

Chaudhury, F. (2012). Fiji flood road damage exacerbated by land use changes. *Pacific Islands Report.* Retrieved from http://www.pireport.org/articles/2012/02/03/fiji-flood-road-damage-exacerbated-land-use-changes

CIA. (2017). World Factbook: Fiji. Retrieved from https://www.cia.gov/library/publications/the-world-factbook/geos/print_fj.html

Corbett, J. (2009). Good practices in participatory mapping: A review prepared for the International Fund for Agricultural Development (IFAD). Retrieved from https://www.ifad.org/documents/38714170/39144386/PM_web.pdf/7c1eda69-8205-4c31-8912-3c25d6f90055

Cubelos, C., Shyam Kularathna, A. H. T., Valenzuela, V. P. B., Iliopoulos, N., Quiroz, M., Yavar, R., ... Esteban, M. (2019). Understanding community-level flooding awareness in remote coastal towns in northern Chile through community mapping. *Geosciences, 9*(7), 279. doi:10.3390/geosciences9070279

Dadhich, A. P., & Nadaoka, K. (2012). Analysis of terrestrial discharge from agricultural watersheds and its impact on nearshore and offshore reefs in Fiji. *Journal of Coastal Research, 28*(5), 1225–1235. doi:10.2112/jcoastres-d-11-00149.1

Dadhich, A. P., & Nadaoka, K. (2014). Modeling hydrological response to land use change in watersheds of Viti Levu Island, Fiji. *Journal of Environmental Research and Development, 8*(3), 492–503.

de Andrade, M., & Szlafsztein, C. (2015). Community participation in flood mapping in the Amazon through interdisciplinary methods. *Natural Hazards, 78*(3), 1491–1500. doi:10.1007/s11069-015-1782-y

Dube, E., & Munsaka, E. (2018). The contribution of indigenous knowledge to disaster risk reduction activities in Zimbabwe: A big call to practitioners. *Jàmbá – Journal of Disaster Risk Studies, 10*(1), a493. doi:10.4102/jamba.v10i1.493

Dutch Risk Reduction Team. (2019). DRR mission report Fiji: Scoping mission for flood alleviation measures for Ba & Rakiraki towns (and associated water catchments). Retrieved from https://www.drrteam-dsswater.nl/wp-content/uploads/2019/11/116224-19-016.139-repf02-DRR-Fiji-main-report-revision_08-10-2019.pdf

ESRI. (2014). *ArcGIS 10.3.* Redlands: Environmental Systems Research Institute.

Fa'avae, D., Jones, A., & Manu'atu, L. (2016). *Talanoa'i 'a e talanoa* – Talking about talanoa: Some dilemmas of a novice researcher. *AlterNative: An International Journal of Indigenous Peoples, 12*(2), 138–150. doi:10.20507/AlterNative.2016.12.2.3

Feresi, J., Kenny, G. J., de Wet, N., Limalevu, L., Bhusan, J., & Ratukalou, I. (2000). *Climate change vulnerability and adaptation assessment for Fiji: Technical report.* Hamilton: The International Global Change Institute, University of Waikato.

Gaillard, J., Hore, K., & Cadag, J. (2015). Participatory mapping for disaster risk reduction: A review. *The Globe, 76*, 31–38.

Gallina, V., Torresan, S., Critto, A., Sperotto, A., Glade, T., & Marcomini, A. (2016). A review of multi-risk methodologies for natural hazards: Consequences and challenges for a climate change impact assessment. *Journal of Environmental Management, 168*, 123–132. doi:10.1016/j.jenvman.2015.11.011

Giardino, A., Nederhoff, K., & Vousdoukas, M. (2018). Coastal hazard risk assessment for small islands: Assessing the impact of climate change and disaster reduction measures on Ebeye (Marshall Islands). *Regional Environmental Change, 18*(8), 2237–2248. doi:10.1007/s10113-018-1353-3

Google LLC. (2019). Google Earth Pro (Version 7.3.2.5776).

Gravelle, G., & Mimura, N. (2008). Vulnerability assessment of sea-level rise in Viti Levu, Fiji Islands. *Sustainability Science, 3*(2), 171–180. doi:10.1007/s11625-008-0052-2

Hagenlocher, M., Renaud, F. G., Haas, S., & Sebesvari, Z. (2018). Vulnerability and risk of deltaic social-ecological systems exposed to multiple hazards. *Science of the Total Environment, 631–632*, 71–80. doi:10.1016/j.scitotenv.2018.03.013

Hay, J. E. (2006). *Republic of the Fiji Islands: Preparing the renewable power sector development project.* Mandaluyong City, Philippines: Asian Developmenet Bank. Retrieved from http://prdrse4all.spc.int/system/files/climate_proofing_power_sector_develop_projects.pdf

Hiwasaki, L., Luna, E., Syamsidik, & Shaw, R. (2014). Process for integrating local and indigenous knowledge with science for hydro-meteorological disaster risk reduction and climate change adaptation in coastal and small island communities. *International Journal of Disaster Risk Reduction, 10*(A), 15–27. doi:10.1016/j.ijdrr.2014.07.007

Hoque, M. A.-A., Ahmed, N., Pradhan, B., & Roy, S. (2019). Assessment of coastal vulnerability to multi-hazardous events using geospatial techniques along the eastern coast of Bangladesh. *Ocean & Coastal Management, 181*, 104898. doi:0.1016/j.ocecoaman.2019.104898

Huang, G., & London, J. K. (2016). Mapping in and out of "messes": An adaptive, participatory, and transdisciplinary approach to assessing cumulative environmental justice impacts. *Landscape and Urban Planning, 154*, 57–67. doi:10.1016/j.landurbplan.2016.02.014

iTaukei Institute of Language and Culture and Ministry of Itaukei Affairs. (2016). *Navala Pdna report.* Suva: Government of Fiji.

Janif, S., Nunn, P., Geraghty, P., Aalbersberg, W., Thomas, F., & Camailakeba, M. (2016). Value of traditional oral narratives in building climate-change resilience: Insights from rural communities in Fiji. *Ecology and Society, 21*(2), 7. doi:10.5751/ES-08100-210207

Jin, F. F., Boucharel, J., & Lin, I. I. (2014). Eastern Pacific tropical cyclones intensified by El Niño delivery of subsurface ocean heat. *Nature, 516*(7529), 82–85. doi:10.1038/nature13958

Kelman, I. (2017). How can island communities deal with environmental hazards and hazard drivers, including climate change? *Environmental Conservation, 44*(3), 244–253. doi:10.1017/S0376892917000042

Kienberger, S. (2014). Participatory mapping of flood hazard risk in Munamicua, District of Búzi, Mozambique. *Journal of Maps, 10*(2), 269–275. doi:10.1080/17445647.2014.891265

Kuleshov, Y., McGree, S., Jones, D., Charles, A., Cottrill, A., Prakash, B., … Seuseu, S. K. (2014). Extreme weather and climate events and their impacts on island countries in the Western Pacific: Cyclones, floods and droughts. *Atmospheric and Climate Sciences, 4*(5), 16. doi:10.4236/acs.2014.45071

Laborde, S., Imberger, J., & Toussaint, S. (2012). Contributions of local knowledge to the physical limnology of Lake Como, Italy. *Proceedings of the National Academy of Sciences of the United States of America, 109*(17), 6441–6445. doi:10.1073/pnas.1113740109

Lebel, L. (2013). Local knowledge and adaptation to climate change in natural resource-based societies of the Asia-Pacific. *Mitigation and Adaptation Strategies for Global Change, 18*(7), 1057–1076. doi:10.1007/s11027-012-9407-1

McGree, S., Herold, N., Alexander, L., Schreider, S., Kuleshov, Y., Ene, E., … Tahani, L. (2019). Recent changes in mean and extreme temperature and precipitation in the western Pacific Islands. *Journal of Climate, 32*(16), 4919–4941. doi:10.1175/jcli-d-18-0748.1

McGree, S., Yeo, S., & Devi, S. (2010). *Flooding in the Fiji Islands between 1840 and 2009.* Sydney: Risk Frontiers, Macquarie University. doi:10.13140/RG.2.2.24364.67202

McLeod, E., Bruton-Adams, M., Förster, J., Franco, C., Gaines, G., Gorong, B., … Terk, E. (2019). Lessons from the Pacific Islands – Adapting to climate change by supporting social and ecological resilience. *Frontiers in Marine Science, 6*, 289. doi:10.3389/fmars.2019.00289

McNamara, K., & Prasad, S. (2014). Coping with extreme weather: Communities in Fiji and Vanuatu share their experiences and knowledge. *Climatic Change, 123*(2), 121–132. doi:10.1007/s10584-013-1047-2

Meo-Sewabu, L. (2014). Cultural discernment as an ethics framework: An Indigenous Fijian approach. *Asia Pacific Viewpoint, 55*(3), 345–354. doi:10.1111/apv.12059

Mercer, J., Dominey-Howes, D., Kelman, I., & Lloyd, K. (2007). The potential for combining indigenous and western knowledge in reducing vulnerability to environmental hazards in small island developing states. *Environmental Hazards, 7*(4), 245–256. doi:10.1016/j.envhaz.2006.11.001

Miyaji, M., Fujieda, A., Waqalevu, S. V., & Kobayashi, H. (2017). Challenges for self-recovery from cyclone disasters in a traditional Fijian village: The case of Navala village after Tropical Cyclone Winston. *WIT Transactions on the Built Environment, 173*, 161–172. doi:10.2495/DMAN170161

Morgan, D. (1997). *Focus groups as qualitative research.* London: Sage.

Nakalevu, T. (2006). *CV&A: A guide to community vulnerability and adaptation assessment and action.* Apia: Secretariat of the Pacific Regional Environment Programme. Retrieved from https://www.sprep.org/att/publication/000437_CVAGuideE.pdf

Neef, A., Benge, L., Boruff, B., Pauli, N., Weber, E., & Varea, R. (2018). Climate adaptation strategies in Fiji: The role of social norms and cultural values. *World Development, 107*, 125–137. doi:10.1016/j.worlddev.2018.02.029

Noy, I. (2015). *Natural disasters and climate change in the Pacific Island countries: New non-monetary measurements of impacts.* School of Economics and Finance Working Paper 08/2015, Victoria University of Wellington, Wellington, New Zealand. Retrieved from http://hdl.handle.net/10063/4200

Noy, I., & Edmonds, C. (2016). *The economic and fiscal burdens of disasters in the Pacific.* School of Economics and Finance Working Paper 25/2016. Victoria University of Wellington, Wellington, New Zealand. Retrieved from https://www.wgtn.ac.nz/sef/research/pdf/2016-papers/SEF-Working-Paper-25-2016.pdf

Nunn, P. D. (2007). *Climate, environment and society in the Pacific during the last millennium.* Amsterdam: Elsevier.

Payne, G., & Payne, J. (2004). *Key concepts in social research.* London: Sage.

PICCAP. (2005). *Climate change the Fiji Islands response. Fiji's first national communication under the framework convention on climate change.* Suva: Pacific Islands Climate Change Assistance Programme (PICCAP) Fiji Islands and Department of Environment Fiji. Retrieved from https://unfccc.int/resource/docs/natc/fjinc1.pdf

Piguet, E., & Laczko, F. (Eds.). (2014). *People on the move in a changing climate: The regional impact of environmental change on migration.* Dordrecht: Springer.

Preston, B., Yuen, E., & Westaway, R. (2011). Putting vulnerability to climate change on the map: A review of approaches, benefits, and risks. *Sustainability Science, 6*(2), 177–202. doi:10.1007/s11625-011-0129-1

Qamese, S. (2015). *Catchment scale modeling of the impact of climate change on hydrology and water quality.* Doctoral dissertation, University of the South Pacific, Suva, Fiji.

Radio New Zealand. (2018, May 1). Cyclones Josie and Keni cost Fiji $US3 million. Retrieved from https://www.rnz.co.nz/international/pacific-news/356391/cyclones-josie-and-keni-cost-fiji-us3-million

Rampengan, M. M. F., Law, L., Gaillard, J. C., Boedhihartono, A. K., & Sayer, J. (2016). Engaging communities in managing multiple hazards: Reflections from small islands in North Sulawesi, Indonesia. *Singapore Journal of Tropical Geography, 37*(2), 249–267. doi:10.1111/sjtg.12148

Rawalai, L. (2019, September). 'Activities worsen climate impacts': Research team disseminates findings with local communities. *The Fiji Times.* Retrieved from https://www.pressreader.com/fiji/the-fiji-times/20190928/282355451472271

Reichel, C., & Frömming, U. U. (2014). Participatory mapping of local disaster risk reduction knowledge: An example from Switzerland. *International Journal of Disaster Risk Science, 5*(1), 41–54. doi:10.1007/s13753-014-0013-6

Rhee, J., & Yang, H. (2018). Drought prediction for areas with sparse monitoring networks: A case study for Fiji. *Water, 10*(6), 788. doi:10.3390/w10060788

Sayer, J., Sunderland, T., Ghazoul, J., Pfund, J.-L., Sheil, D., Meijaard, E., … Buck, L. E. (2013). Ten principles for a landscape approach to reconciling agriculture, conservation, and other competing land uses. *Proceedings of the National Academy of Sciences, 110*(21), 8349–8356. doi:10.1073/pnas.1210595110

Sevudredre, S. (2009). Cultural mapping program: Fiji's ICH inventory-making and the establishment of the traditional knowledge and expression of culture (TKEC) information system.

In S.-Y. Park (Ed), *Information & networking for the safeguarding of intangible cultural heritage* (pp. 103–115). Daejeon: UNESCO Intangible Cultural Heritage Centre for Asia and the Pacific (ICHCAP). Retrieved from https://www.unesco-ichcap.org/eng/ek/sub8/pdf_file/01/ E03-3_Cultural_Mapping_Program.pdf

Simpson, J. (2016). *Assessing indicators of socio-ecological resilience in flood-prone coastal areas using remote sensing*. Bachelor of Science (Advanced) (Honours) dissertation, The University of Sydney, Sydney, Australia.

SPREP. (2017). About the GEF ABS project. Secretariat of the Pacific Regional Environment Programme. Retrieved from https://www.sprep.org/abs

Srinivasan, P. (2020, January). Fiji's black sand mining project draws international scrutiny. *ABC Radio Australia, Pacific Beat*. Retrieved from https://www.abc.net.au/radio-australia/programs/ pacificbeat/fijis-black-sand-mining-project-draws-international-scrutiny/11865334

Sullivan-Wiley, K. A., & Short Gianotti, A. G. (2017). Risk perception in a multi-hazard environment. *World Development, 97*, 138–152. doi:10.1016/j.worlddev.2017.04.002

Takor Group. (2016). *Mappt*. Perth: Takor Group. Retrieved from http://www.mappt.com.au/

Tauzer, E., Borbor-Cordova, M. J., Mendoza, J., De La Cuadra, T., Cunalata, J., & Stewart-Ibarra, A. M. (2019). A participatory community case study of periurban coastal flood vulnerability in southern Ecuador. *PloS One, 14*(10), e0224171–e0224171. doi:10.1371/journal.pone.0224171

Terry, J. P., & Raj, R. (2002). *The 1997–98 El Niño and drought in the Fiji Islands*. Paper presented at the Second International Colloquium on Hydrology and Water Management in the Humid Tropics, Panama, Republic of Panama, 22–26 March 1999.

Thaman, R., Lyver, P., Mpande, R., Perez, E., Cariño, J., & Takeuchi, K. (Eds.). (2013). *The contribution of indigenous and local knowledge systems to IPBES: Building synergies with science*. IPBES Expert Meeting Report, UNESCO and United Nations University. Paris: UNESCO. Retrieved from https://unesdoc.unesco.org/ark:/48223/pf0000225242

Tilloy, A., Malamuda, B. D., Winter, H., & Joly-Laugel, A. (2019). A review of quantification methodologies for multi-hazard interrelationships. *Earth-Science Reviews, 196*, 102881. doi:10.1016/ j.earscirev.2019.102881

Turagaiviu, E. (2018, May 29). *iTaukei* affairs ministry completes cultural mapping exercise. *Fijian Broadcasting Corporation*. Retrieved from https://www.fbcnews.com.fj/news/itaukei-affairs-ministry-completes-cultural-mapping-exercise/

UNICEF. (2009). Fiji flood 2009: Early assessments. Retrieved from http://www.pacificdisaster.net/ pdnadmin/data/original/FJI_IM_2009_Flood_assessment.pdf

UNISDR. (2015). *Making development sustainable: The future of disaster risk management*. Global Assessment Report on Disaster Risk Reduction. United Nations Office for Disaster Risk Reduction (UNISDR), Geneva, Switzerland. Retrieved from https://www.preventionweb.net/ english/hyogo/gar/2015/en/gar-pdf/GAR2015_EN.pdf

UNOCHA. (2016). *Fiji: Severe Tropical Cyclone Winston*. Situation Report No. 8. Suva, Fiji: United Nations Office for the Coordination of Humanitarian Affairs (OCHA) Regional Office for the Pacific. Retrieved from http://reliefweb.int/sites/reliefweb.int/files/resources/ocha_tc_winston_ situation_report_8.pdf

Veitayaki, J., Tawake, A., & Aalbersberg, B. (2003). Empowering local communities: Case study of Votua, Ba, Fiji. *Ocean Yearbook, 17*(1), 449–463. doi:10.1163/221160003X00177

Walshe, R., & Nunn, P. (2012). Integration of indigenous knowledge and disaster risk reduction: A case study from Baie Martelli, Pentecost Island, Vanuatu. *International Journal of Disaster Risk Science, 3*(4), 185–194. doi:10.1007/s13753-012-0019-x

Williams, M., Pauli, N., & Boruff, B. (2020) Participatory GIS and community based adaptation to climate change and environmental hazards: A Cambodian case study. In A. Neef & N. Pauli (Eds.), *Climate-induced disasters in the Asia-Pacific region: Response, recovery, adaptation* (pp. 113–134). Bingley: Emerald Publishing.

Yen, B. T., Son, N. H., Tung, L. T., Amjath-Babu, T. S., & Sebastian, L. (2019). Development of a participatory approach for mapping climate risks and adaptive interventions (CS-MAP) in Vietnam's Mekong River Delta. *Climate Risk Management, 24*, 59–70. doi:10.1016/j.crm.2019.04.004

Yila, O., Weber, E., & Neef, A. (2013). The role of social capital in post-flood response and recovery among downstream communities of the Ba River, Western Viti Levu, Fiji Islands. In A. Neef & R. Shaw (Eds.), *Risks and conflicts: Local responses to natural disasters* (pp. 79–107). Bingley: Emerald Group Publishing Limited.

CHAPTER 5

EMBODYING RESILIENCE: NARRATING GENDERED EXPERIENCES OF DISASTERS IN FIJI

Kahukura Bennett, Andreas Neef and Renata Varea

ABSTRACT

This chapter explores the local narration of gendered experience of disasters in two iTaukei (Indigenous Fijian) communities, Votua and Navala, both located in the Ba River catchment, Fiji. The methodology consisted of semi-formal interviews, talanoa, mapping sessions and journal entries from community members in Votua and Navala. Local narratives of post-disaster response and recovery in the aftermath of 2016 Tropical Cyclone Winston showed that women were not perceived as embodying a heightened vulnerability to disasters in comparison to men in either Votua or Navala. Rather perceptions of vulnerability were based on the experiences of those who physically struggled, such as people with disabilities, the elderly and those who had lost their homes. While gender roles and responsibilities underlay perceptions and gender relations, the roles and responsibilities were predominantly perceived as changing over time, either to a more shared sense of responsibilities or a shift from male responsibilities to female. This shift may lay the foundations for future changes in vulnerability and experiences towards disasters.

Keywords: Disaster resilience; post-disaster response; disaster recovery; vulnerability; gender; Fiji; South Pacific

Climate-Induced Disasters in the Asia-Pacific Region: Response, Recovery, Adaptation
Community, Environment and Disaster Risk Management, Volume 22, 87–112
Copyright © 2021 by Emerald Publishing Limited
All rights of reproduction in any form reserved
ISSN: 2040-7262/doi:10.1108/S2040-726220200000022004

INTRODUCTION: NARRATING DISASTERS

In February 2016, Tropical Cyclone (TC) Winston, a category 5 storm and the largest recorded storm to hit the southern hemisphere, struck Fiji (Mohd, 2016). The primary narrative following Cyclone Winston was one of devastation, fear and widespread homelessness (Holmes, 2016; Leask, 2016). According to FAO (2016), approximately 40% of the Fijian population was affected by Cyclone Winston, with 100% of crops destroyed in the hardest hit regions. Technology is said to have played a significant role in reducing the devastation of TC Winston through early warning systems that allowed community members to reach safer ground (Kohona, 2016). The Pacific Islands, including Indigenous Fijians, have a long history of adaptation and resilience to extreme weather events that have been weaved into the fabric of culture (McCubbin, Smit, & Pearce, 2015). However, in recent decades there has been a widespread unravelling of traditional knowledge and livelihoods that have dramatically impacted people's way of life, food systems and settlement patterns (McCubbin et al., 2015).

Many studies exist that project and quantify the effects of climate change on communities throughout the Pacific. Yet there are fewer studies that target an understanding of local-level interpretation of climate change, adaptation processes, perceived vulnerabilities and experiences (Betzold, 2015). As a result, there is an urgent need for adapted and sustainable livelihoods to be developed in the Pacific Islands, which incorporate environmental and cultural contexts (Nunn, 2013). The aim of this study is to trace a narrative of disaster experience in Votua and Navala, both located in the Ba River catchment, Fiji, within the wider context of Fijian history, social relations, politics and culture. Both communities experience a life disrupted by weather extremes, yet these hazards occur upon a pre-existing fabric of day-to-day living.

The leading objective of this study is to understand the localised knowledge and gendered experiences of *iTaukei* (Indigenous) Fijians within the frame of a changing climate as well as to explore the embodiment of resilience through the narrative of lived experience. The aim is underscored by a desire to understand individual experience and the importance of culture, tradition, politics and history in determining vulnerability. To this end, gender relations were examined as well as family dynamics and key livelihood activities. In order to address this, the following questions guided this study:

• Are there gendered divisions in livelihood activities at a household level?
• Do gendered divisions in livelihood activities affect vulnerability to disasters?
• Is there a perceived gendered vulnerability to disasters?

The study approaches these questions through the utilisation of both traditional qualitative modes of data collection as well as principles of a *talanoa* methodology. The incorporation of *talanoa* into this research sought to elicit individual stories and experiences in relation to a particular event, in this case Cyclone Winston, through less structured means of data collection. This hybrid approach was deemed contextually appropriate for Fiji.

Within the disaster risk reduction community, there is the common desire to move populations from a state of vulnerability to one of resilience. However, as this chapter will explore, notions of vulnerability and resilience are predetermined on assumptions which often undermine the value and are blind to the needs of certain members of society. The following section will explore the feminisation of vulnerability and delve deeper into the literature of postcolonial feminism within a Pacific context.

EN*GENDER*ING DISASTERS, DISASTERING GENDERS: POSTCOLONIAL FEMINISM

Within international development discourse, rural women tend to be regarded as one of the most vulnerable demographic groups to climate change and disasters due to an array of locally and globally constructed dynamics (Aipira, Kidd, & Morioka, 2017; Andersen, Verner, & Manfred, 2016; Nawaz, 2013). The feminisation of vulnerability and disaster stems from the notion of inequality between men and women as well as systems of labour division where women are more likely to take part in climate-sensitive activities such as water collection and agriculture, while simultaneously having different, often inferior, access to land, resources, labour markets and mobility (Aipira et al., 2017; Andersen et al., 2016; Bradshaw, 2014). While much research identifies that women on average work much longer hours than men in developing rural settings, due to their duties both within and outside the home, women have significantly less decision-making power, occupying a space of voicelessness, domestically, locally and internationally (Manata & Papazu, 2009). However, despite these inequalities, women are also perceived to embody a secondary identity, being the cornerstone of climate change adaptation, processing traditional forms of knowledge that can see households and communities through disasters as well as holding the mental map to clean water and having a deeper understanding of the best crops to grow during times of disaster (Aipira et al., 2017; Morioka, 2012). These contrasting perceived identities require further consideration and exploration in the development of disaster risk reduction policies and projects to be sustainable, utilising a gendered lens in order to incorporate myriad experiences and unique knowledge (Aipira et al., 2017; MacGregor, 2010b). Yet, simultaneously, these perceived identities are themselves layered and formed within the unequal power relations between local communities and external organisations (including government officials, development practitioners and researchers). This silencing of individual stories and embodied realities by broader power structures undermines the ability of those at the forefront of climate-related disasters to adapt, as it shifts the decisions and resources into external hands with external actors, and internally powerful actors, controlling people's identities and the consequent distribution of capabilities to adapt (cf. Foucault, 1982).

Although the concepts of vulnerability and resilience are seemingly synonymous with climate change adaptation, Mikulewicz (2019) critiques the use of resilience within development programmes, arguing that when applied, resilience continues to dehumanise disasters and ignores local contexts, with even the parameters for what constitutes a state of resilience coming from external agencies (MacKinnon & Derickson, 2013). This critique is echoed by other scholars who perceive resilience to sit within a systems approach and inadvertently privileging and reinforcing dominant systems of oppression (MacKinnon & Derickson, 2013) rather than challenging and transforming the structures which increase the vulnerability of certain community members (Mikulewicz, 2018). These structures of oppression and privilege are not only interwoven into the fabric of local communities but within global power structures most evidently seen the privileging of certain forms of knowledge (MacKinnon & Derickson, 2013). As Nightingale (2015) further explores, the promotion of resilience brings to question adaption not of how (to adapt) but of who (adapts), leaving the need to democratise resilience and consequently adaptation and resituate it within communities and interventions (cf. Mikulewicz, 2018). Consequently, it can be argued that the contending identity of 'women' as naturally resilient can result in the adaptation measures not grounded in local contexts or implementing strategies which focus on those less 'naturally' resilient, missing the opportunity to further social justice (Mikulewicz, 2019).

In contrast to the concept of vulnerability, susceptibility to harm is nestled in issues of social justice connecting the fields of disaster risk reduction and adaptation to local power structures (Adger, 2006), but nevertheless is plagued by structures beyond community. As reiterated throughout this chapter, who is regarded as vulnerable is often not defined by those at the forefront of disasters but by external actors, be they researchers, bureaucrats or humanitarians. It is at this junction that we seek alternative literature which places the 'vulnerable' at the centre of their own experiences.

Since the late 1990s, women have increasingly been identified as agents of change (Sen, 1999), the missing key to unlocking a more sustainable and socially just world. Women's empowerment, according to the United Nations Population Fund (cited in Manata & Papazu, 2009, p. 11), includes components such as a 'women's sense of self-worth; their right to have and to determine choices; their right to have access to opportunities and resources; their right to have the power to control', and gaining the capability to access and acquire strategic life choices (Kabeer, 1999). This notion of women as agents of change aligns with a study undertaken in South Africa, which found female agriculturalists were more concerned about the imminent implications and risks of global climate change than their male counterparts due to their sense of domestic responsibility and family survival (Thomas, Twyman, Osbahr, & Hewitson, 2011). However, attaining such ideals of empowerment can be regarded as foreign templates and can dismiss Pacific avenues of change (Nabalarua, 2005). Furthermore, the process of women's empowerment has not been without criticism, primarily concerning the process of feminising responsibility and reinforcing stereotypes (Bradshaw, 2014), particularly when based upon incompatible models.

The significant push for the concept of 'women in development' in the 1970s stemmed from a foundation of perceived gender blindness within development discourse (Hyndman, 2008), and hoped to bring to light and address the forgotten experiences of women globally (Boris, 2014). However, this concept began to shift away from a focus exclusively upon women, to one of gender relations and to the incorporation of other undercutting and intersecting issues such as class, ethnicity and geographic location (Hyndman & de Alwis, 2003). This conceptual alteration of understanding gender relations is significant as it explores the field of power and opens a space for analysing the root of female vulnerability within patriarchal systems, and the need to target men, as well as women, in order to achieve equality (Farré, 2013). An understanding of the array of issues that underscore inequality and differences in experiences between women and men, and among women, develops a more nuanced context and provides the potential for more targeted approaches to development, particularly in light of climate change and disasters.

Taking the concept of gender blindness as well as gendered power relations within development and applying it to climate change discourse, MacGregor (2010b) argues that the 'scientising' of climate change instantaneously categorises it in the traditional realm of masculine hegemony, while female reproductive rights continue to be challenged, with the imminent threat and perceived relationship between population growth and sustainability. Although the field of science is changing, engaging more women, contemporary decisions regarding climate change are still predominantly within the realm of men. A study undertaken by Kruse (2014) explored the representation of women within UN climate change negotiations and found that nations that demonstrate a higher level of development and political gender equality have a higher representation of female delegates. Although this study focusses predominantly on rural women within two Fijian communities, it is important to note the absence and oppression of the female voice at every level of climate change and disaster discourse. As recently as 2009, people were still calling for the effective incorporation of gender into disaster risk reduction at the international level (Bradshaw, 2014).

Meanwhile, the binary of women's experiences and men's experiences continues to take place within the dichotomy of Western perceptions of gender, where in fact in many societies, including in the Pacific, gender is extended beyond scientific classification (Gaillard et al., 2016). Neglect to incorporate third genders/ gender minorities within climate change and disaster literature can lead to inadequate policy development and exclusion from programmes aimed at disaster risk reduction (Gaillard et al., 2017). Although there is little available literature regarding the experiences of Fiji's third gender *vaka sa lewa lewa*, a study undertaken by Gaillard et al. (2017) explored the role *fa'afafine* in Samoa played following the 2009 Tsunami and Cyclone Evan in 2012. This study found that the ability for *fa'afafine* to undertake both traditional male and female roles meant that they were at the front line of disaster response and recovery, while also experiencing discrimination, particularly in public shelters where they neither identified as male or female, and facilities were not accessible.

The nature of enforcing vulnerability based on gender leads to the homogenisation of experiences, where the identity of 'woman' is synonymous with 'vulnerable', and *vaka sa lewa lewa* are excluded or grouped into the experiences of men or women. It also does not account for the multitude of experiences and fragmented identities which an individual embodies as an actor within a socio-cultural context (Tschakert, 2012). It is therefore the extraction of experiences and of the individual voice that is required to contextualise climate change research and develop meaningful disaster risk reduction policies (Bradshaw, 2014).

Within the Pacific context, there is vast heterogeneity at the national level to the extent to which gender has been incorporated into climate change strategies, and – in general – is still in its relatively early stages (Aipira et al., 2017). Aipira et al. (2017) highlight that the effectiveness of the incorporation of gender into climate change policies, or conversely climate change incorporated into gender policies, is heavily context-dependent. Studies that focus on contextualising experience within the Pacific are sorely lacking, and as a result, there is the tendency to generalise the experiences of these island states, despite their large differences historically, culturally, physically, topographically and demographically.

Beyond policy and at the individual level, how 'women' experience disasters is vastly different and not simply set upon biological determinants (a view that has often resulted in the homogenisation of experiences), but upon social norms which vary between contexts (Mohanty, 1984). Furthermore, disasters have been shown to be a destabilising force within communities and households with the power to change intrahousehold relations (Hyndman, 2008). In its most expressive form, this destabilisation leads to an escalation in violence towards women, a significant dimension of female vulnerability (Griffen, 2006). Furthermore, in relation to diversifying household livelihoods as a means of improving resilience, Farré (2013) explores the complex literature around livelihood diversification and domestic violence. While livelihood diversification has been positively attributed to the reduction of household violence due to female empowerment and power through economy, in some societies where patriarchy is deeply engrained within social systems and worldviews, violence is used as a means of re-establishing power and control. The patriarchal nature of *iTaukei* (Indigenous Fijian) culture would lend some weight to further delving into understanding such complexities within differing *iTaukei* communities in contemporary Fiji (Charan, Kaur, & Singh, 2016). These potential changes are instrumental in addressing inequality and vulnerability within a rapidly changing climate and reassessing how we as practitioners and researchers challenge structures of power that we operate within and listen to individuals (Charan et al., 2016; Mikulewicz, 2019).

A HYBRID RESEARCH METHODOLOGY

The overarching approach to this research is ethnographic, an attempt to understand the reality (Meo-Sewabu, 2014) of those living in Votua and Navala (for more details of the geographic locations of Votua and Navala, refer to Irvine, Pauli, Varea, & Boruff, 2020 – Chapter 4, this volume), using the Pacific principles of *talanoa* as well as interviews and supplemented by mapping sessions, participant journal entries as the primary tools for data collection and analysis.

Talanoa

Talanoa is an encompassing methodological approach to conducting research in the Pacific Island region. It is regarded by Meo-Sewabu (2014) as a methodological tool to collect and analyse data within an oral tradition. The formal aspects of *talanoa* include protocols, such as a *yaqona* ceremony, that occur when entering onto the land, which were conducted during the cultural ceremonies held on first arrival to the villages (Meo-Sewabu, 2014). The remaining '*talanoa* sessions' took a far more informal approach. *Talanoa* sessions in particular were regarded as encounters which took place in an informal manner, where participants were aware of the research project but no formal request to be interviewed was made. *Talanoa* sessions primarily occurred in a group, usually while undertaking another activity such as cooking, walking to a fishing spot or gardening and usually with participants with whom the researcher had conversed on more than one occasion. Following these criteria, two *talanoa* sessions were conducted in each community. Both these sessions significantly aided in contextualising this research, as did *talanoa* conversations in Nawaqarua, a satellite village of Votua. Consequently, these conversations provided an initial basis for which to move forward and contextualise the more formal interviews.

Interviews

Interviews can take several forms ranging from open conversations to intensely structured questionnaires (Stewart-Withers, Banks, McGregor, & Meo-Sewabu, 2014). This research utilised two predominant forms: semi-structured interviews and formal interviews. Again, the disaggregation between semi-structured and formal depended upon the relationship between the researcher and the interviewee. Still wanting to maintain *talanoa* principles, subjectivity played a strong role in determining whether the interview was semi-structured or formal, which was developed as the interview evolved.

Participatory Mapping Sessions

Participatory mapping sessions were led by undergraduate researcher Gracie Irvine from University College London and the University of Western Australia, and usually involved four to seven community members, disaggregated according to their gender, the first author and two translators. The mapping sessions provided a spatial overview of a large scale of livelihood activities as well as stimulating conversation regarding the effects of natural hazards upon the community and demonstrating the heterogeneous experiences of different community members towards natural disasters (for more details on the sessions, see Irvine et al., 2020 – Chapter 4, this volume).

Journals

Journals were distributed and collected from 38 households in Navala, with a set of questions enquiring about people's experiences during Cyclone Winston. The distribution of journals attempted to gain a good coverage of the community ensuring that both those living in traditional thatched homes, also known as bures, modern homes and tents were all selected as well as families living on the periphery and those more central. A further 50 journal transcriptions from Votua were incorporated which had been collected during previous research visits. This technique involved the researches and translators traversing the village and selecting households based on the aforementioned traits. The *turaga-ni-koro* (elected village leader) announced to the households when the journals were to be returned to the research team.

The primary data were derived from 16 interviews conducted in Votua and 12 in Navala as well as four focus groups. These data were supplemented by five mapping sessions held in Votua and six in Navala as well as the 38 journals distributed and collected throughout Navala. All participants resided predominantly in either Votua or Navala, with some participants having a second home in Etatoko – a community resettled after the 2012 flood (cf. Neef et al., 2018) – or being away due to their employment contracts. Each form of data collection provided a differing viewpoint of individual or community-wide experience of living through and dealing with disasters.

A thematic analysis was conducted in this study through first codifying leading themes around livelihoods, gendered experiences, vulnerability, resilience, social networks and the changes experienced by an individual following a disaster event. As narratives and events occur along a temporal scale, the analysis is presented from a pre-, during and post-disaster perspective (Ellsberg, Pena, Herrera, Liljestrand, & Winkvist, 2000).

NARRATING GENDER AND RESILIENCE: AN ANALYSIS OF GENDERED ROLES IN FIJI'S DISASTER LANDSCAPES

The prevalence of gender inequalities within Pacific cultures has been used to explain the increased vulnerability of women and girls in the face of disasters (Aipira et al., 2017). Conceptualising narrative into gender roles can provide a basis for perceived power and decision-making relations within a household and at the community level. This section constructs the narratives of gender within this study, in particular exploring the gendered division of responsibility within the household, the perceptions of vulnerability to disasters within Votua and Navala, and finally, whether there are different ways and responsibilities in which men and women prepare and recover from disasters.

Conceptualising a narration of gender and resilience within this study is to not only provide the dominant narrative that emerged from interviews, journals and mapping sessions, but primarily to tease out the other voices and notions that contradict or run parallel to dominant community narratives, to share the various stories of experience that exist within Votua and Navala. Strict cultural and patriarchal systems embed inequalities into the 'structural layers' of communities and households, dominating the lives of many women within the Pacific (Cutter, 2017; Underhill-Sem, Cox, Lacey, & Szamiers, 2014). In both Votua and Navala, these power structures that determined roles and responsibilities were expressed as being intrinsic features of men and women, while acknowledging social changes that were occurring in these roles. While gender was often not an outwardly expressed determinant of vulnerability for participants, the notion of women's increased workload and significant responsibilities within the household and towards other community members was a recurring theme.

Responsibilities and Livelihoods within the Household

The majority of households that were interviewed consisted of a wide range of family members, including a central husband and wife unit, children, grandparents, aunties and uncles. Female-headed households were not uncommon, primarily consisting of widowed elderly women. There were several households which included additional family members and neighbours compared with ordinary circumstances, as a result of the impact of Cyclone Winston in February 2016 and the floods which followed in Votua. Many homes were destroyed during the cyclone and – as a consequence – household membership increased, or families moved into smaller temporary housing situations, such as their kitchens, waiting for their homes to be rebuilt either through their own resources, family and community assistance or waiting for government subsidies. This sub-section seeks to directly understand perceptions of household responsibility, gender divisions and livelihoods separate from a disaster setting.

A Woman's Place as Provider

Gender has predetermined the responsibilities and roles of household members globally. In particular, there is the prevalent notion that women take care of the domestic realm including caring for the home and the members in it, while men hold the responsibility as the head of families, being the primary wage earner. This notion is shared by some of the individuals interviewed.

> Women stay home. Men farm. Women are only helpers, but everything is the man's responsibility. (Male community leader, interview, Navala)

This perception reflects not only the value that is placed on different activities conducted by different members of the household, but an engrained conception of the worth of these contributions based upon gender, as repeated throughout the interview with this community leader. This statement additionally embodies the often-expressed notion of the reliance of women on men and emphasises male control of resources (Plate 5.1). In essence, this simple statement of 'women are only helpers' encapsulates a key cultural source of realised inequalities based on gender and the physical embodiment of unequal power relations in the form of violence, reliance and neglect (Eastin, 2018; Tschakert, 2012). This idea was echoed by a number of individuals who believed men to be the head of the household.

This notion of a gender divide in responsibilities is apparent in many of the systems that operate within Fiji. Many women feared for the sustainability of their livelihood once their husbands passed away, as evidenced by the following quote:

> Our only income is from my husband's pension. Every six months, we have to update a form to say that my husband is still alive. I cannot get the pension as I have never worked formally. When my husband dies, I do not know whether I can continue to receive his pension. (Elderly woman, interview, Votua)

Pensions in Fiji are based upon formal work experience, a domain from which women have historically been absent, due to the notion of male-headed households and men being the primary breadwinner. Women interviewed who had lost their husbands were receiving social welfare in the form of a FJD50 food voucher

(a) Women preparing dinner for visitors   (b) Men preparing the *kava* ceremony

Plate 5.1.   Embodied Gender Roles in Navala. *Source*: A. Neef.

and FJD30 cash per month. This was supplemented through family support and continued farming and travelling to the market to sell produce.

Women's roles within the household and communities were thought to be expanding by many participants. However, this trend was not triggered by increased opportunities to take part in roles that have often been relegated to men nor an increase in power, but a result of necessity.

> Men are more relaxed than women, especially those (women) that catch prawns. Women mostly do more because they know they have to prepare whereas men just rely on women. If the mother leaves, the father does not look after the children, instead they are looked after by other female family members such as their grandmother or aunty. (Elderly woman, interview, Votua)

This necessity could stem from women's leading role within the domestic sphere and as providers for the family, in a society with deeply embedded gender roles. Where men turn to 'grogging/*kava*[1] drinking', women must take on additional roles in order to complete their responsibility as carer for the members of the household. While women's roles as caregivers and providers emerged through this shift towards social drinking of *kava*, it is perceived as a necessity to expand women's responsibilities as their domestic domain.

> Men's and women's roles are changing. Women are now going fishing and farming, while men stay at home reading, cleaning and grogging. Because men drink a lot of grog, it affects the roles that men and women play, with men getting lazier. (Young woman, interview, Votua)

> In Votua, women earn more than men. The mentality is that men go fishing for cigarettes or *kava*. (Retired fisherman, interview, Votua)

> Roles are changing as men do less work, they just sleep, and women take on more jobs. Men stay up late drinking *kava*. (Female farmer, interview, Navala)

Yet the diversity of women's roles may not be a new phenomenon, nor one directly resulting from increased *kava* consumption, which has been identified by many community members. One interviewee describes the roles of members within her household as follows:

> My mother goes to the market to buy and sell vegetables, as well as looking after the house and cooking. I go fishing for eels, while my father usually goes to the farm. (Female student, interview, Navala)

This demonstrates a broader range of responsibilities held by some women, while in other households and other experiences, men are expressed as undertaking the broader range of income-generating responsibility.

> I go to the farm twice a week, collect firewood, clean around the house. My family's main source of income comes from the *kava* field. My son and I go to the *kava* field together, and the money we get is used to pay for school fees. (Male farmer, interview, Navala)

However, some households' primary form of income is through a joint effort by both husband and wife.

> Both my husband and I go fishing together for a number of days, before we both go to the market in Nailaga to sell our catch. Our family's main source of income comes from our fishing. (Fisherwoman, interview, Votua)

At the opposing end of the scale is the experience of a 35-year-old woman in Votua, whose husband places strict restrictions upon her to remain at home and complete domestic tasks, such as caring for the house and their children. However, in order to provide for her children's needs, she goes fishing to gain an independent income. Such narratives exemplify the need to push aside our assumptions and listen to the stories of the individual for while some women express their liberation from past oppressions, others continue to navigate their way within a continued oppressive reality.

Diversified Livelihoods and Changing Gender Roles

Fishing and agriculture continue to be significant livelihood activities for people in Votua, despite the majority of households having at least one member employed within the formal sector. Agricultural activities, in particular harvesting *kava*, are the primary source of income for many households in Navala, in particular households that have a male head. Widowed women would stop going to the *kava* fields following their husband's death, perhaps due to the distance (for approximate distances to *kava* plantations refer to Irvine et al., 2020 – Chapter 4, this volume) and effort for one person and/or their age.

Domestic duties, selling produce at markets and tourism were the leading forms of income for women in Navala, although it is unknown how this income is distributed at the household level. Though tourism was the domain and responsibility of women, there were different levels of access to the tourism industry. While there was a cooking roster which allocated cooking responsibilities to each household when tourists arrived and the entry fee into Navala was set aside for community use, the opportunity to be guides for tourists or to sell souvenirs was not available to everyone. As a female farmer in Navala expressed:

> Tourism only seems to really benefit those who are in the main centre of Navala. As I am in the corner of the village, no tourists come here.

While during one of the focus groups youth discussed their desire to continue farming, some youth had left Navala to work for the police force or army. Key activities for youth are similar to those of adults, including being involved in tourism and cutting sugarcane for three months of the year. The roles of women are also changing as they begin joining sectors that are dominated by men including clearing up and building homes as well as cutting sugarcane, despite earning only FJD10 per day as opposed to men who earn FJD12.

Many interviewees aligned with the notion that there are gendered responsibilities; however, both men and women were able to complete the tasks. A female school teacher in Votua stated:

> Although women usually have more home-orientated roles, as long as there is agreement it works. Only a few women go fishing, most stay at home, look after children, do washing and cooking ... [My husband] helps a lot with the cooking, washing, planting and cleaning as well as some farming. He also goes fishing and diving for crabs.

Some men have also noticed a shift within their own households as well as the broader community (Plate 5.2):

> Before we used to carry out roles separately. My wife did the housework while I was working, but now we share the work. (Male assistant pastor, interview, Votua)

There were different views of gender roles between Votua and Navala, with many interviewees from Navala aligning more with what would be considered 'traditional' gender roles, perhaps reflecting the different forms of access individuals and households had to formal employment. Votua had more exposure in general to formal employment and urban settings, while Navala is a community that is effectively promoted through tourism as a remnant of traditional Fijian life.

For women entering the formal sector, however, they are faced with structural inequalities in which jobs are perceived appropriate for women, such as teaching, while others experience a lower pay than men. While both women and men are faced with structural constraints and roles, the potential for men to earn more in a similar role lends weight for women to continue to fulfil domestic duties and perpetuates the physical manifestation of gender inequality (in the form of

(a) Husband and wife going fishing together   (b) Both men and women catch highly priced crabs

Plate 5.2.   Converging Gender Roles in Votua. *Source*: A. Neef.

access to resources and control over finances) despite changing perceptions of roles. Consequently, changing gender roles must be addressed at all levels in order to reduce the gendered dimensions of inequality.

Perceptions of Vulnerability to Disasters

There Is No Vulnerability Differentiated by Gender

Vulnerability encompasses predetermined characteristics of an individual or group, which within a certain social, physical and cultural setting leads them to be more affected by disasters. Throughout all the interviews conducted, there was no individual that perceived gender to be a determining factor of vulnerability in either Votua or Navala. This was primarily attributed to the strong social networks that underlie the communities as expressed in the following quote:

> No groups are more vulnerable before, during or after a disaster. Everyone makes sure everyone else is ok and then the government comes. (Female farmer, interview, Votua)

Social networks and government assistance were significant contributors to reducing perceived vulnerabilities in Votua and Navala. Even while acknowledging the different roles that men and women play within the community, a fisherwoman and farmer in Votua stated:

> While men and women have different roles, they are affected by disasters equally.

Women and men were perceived in both Votua and Navala as experiencing similar if not equal levels of vulnerability towards disasters. This conception, particularly within the patriarchal nature of Indigenous Fijian culture, could be explained through the notion of lived experiences, or in this circumstance, lived vulnerabilities. As FAO's (2016) report outlines,

> Fijian women – a majority of whom rely on agriculture as their sole source of income – are particularly vulnerable to food insecurity, and must be a key focus of response efforts. (p. 1)

Consequently, as the disaster response by the Fijian government in the form of food rations occurred extremely quickly following Cyclone Winston, the area in which women are regarded as most vulnerable was subsidised and addressed. A further example, as provided by an elderly female interviewee in Navala, demonstrates the varying degrees by which vulnerability is measured and the consequent notion of resilience by stating,

> It doesn't matter if you have sugar, as long as you have cassava with salt, as long as you live.

Resilience in the face of hardship is a common theme throughout many of the social aspects of disasters and climate change, and often stems from a strong belief in a higher being (cf. Cox et al., 2020). A further explanation for conceptualising the vulnerable, or lack thereof, is the ability to predict, anticipate and prepare for disasters. A female interviewee in Navala highlighted the consistent expectation of increased extreme weather events between December and April, and maintained a consistent supply of food containers and water during this period. However, her and her family's ability to stockpile food and water may be a result of both her and her husband being a part of the formal sector and having a secure cash flow. She further mentioned in the interview the increased cost of living in Fiji and stated the need for both the husband and wife to have a regular income.

Vulnerability Is Perceived through Experience
Despite there being no perceived gendered vulnerability in the face of disasters, there were still particular groups of people who were identified as vulnerable. These primarily included the elderly, those with disabilities and those who had lost their home. Many interviewees who identified a particular group as vulnerable experienced first-hand that kind of vulnerability. One female interviewee in Votua noted that people with disabilities are most affected, citing the particular disaster experience of her brother-in-law:

> My husband's older brother couldn't walk, so I had to stay back at the house during and after the flood. The school, which was our evacuation centre, was too far and hard to reach with his disability. It was also overcrowded there. People with disabilities are the most affected by disasters.

A further example was provided by a female farmer in Navala who stated:

> Men and women are affected in the same [way] in disasters, there are no superheroes. The most vulnerable are the old people. Like this 85-year old woman who lives with me, her house was destroyed and she had to be carried to the evacuation centre.

This opinion was further supported by a mixed focus group in Navala which considered the families with elderly members as the most vulnerable during disasters as they cannot reach the school, which acted as an evacuation centre during and following TC Winston. Focus group participants highlighted that it was the elderly who remained in their houses during extreme weather events.

As can be seen from these reflections, the notion of vulnerability by some is based upon the personal experiences of interviewees primarily concerning the ability to access safety and services. This is also demonstrated at a regional level in Vanessa Griffen's (2006) reflection on the Association for Women's Rights in Development Forum where she suggested that the predominant Pacific women's issues which were discussed throughout the Forum were those that were experienced personally by attendees. Further, vulnerability was linked significantly to physical loss, in particular to housing destruction. Physical loss is more evident, and for many, the damage incurred by TC Winston was very apparent within both Votua and Navala.

The Unprepared Are Vulnerable
Within Votua and Navala, as demonstrated earlier, the narrative of vulnerability is readily interwoven within the fabric of social networks and assistance, and is related to physical access, such as an evacuation centre, a physical loss of home or being ill-prepared. As mentioned earlier, there are many individuals, and – by extension – many households, who cannot physically reach the evacuation centres. In Votua, the evacuation centre/school is located in the far corner of the village, while in Navala, it is located at the top of the hill. Evacuation centres were

said to be overcrowded, with some community members preferring to stay in their homes or in some cases taking a bus to another village.

A question arose of the role that evacuation centre location plays in developing vulnerability. One *talanoa* conversation described everyone as being

equally affected by disasters, but those who go to the evacuation centre are safer.

The notion of not being prepared was echoed by many as a key indicator of vulnerability.

Doesn't matter who is male or female, just who is better prepared for the disasters. (Retired woman, interview, Votua)

If we were to follow the path of established gendered responsibilities as perpetuated by some interviewees or with the notion that women are taking on both their own gendered responsibilities and men's, then the space of preparedness is inevitably gendered. However, some community members connected a lack of preparation to the failure of early warning radio systems,

I would like to share one thing only regarding the cyclone that passed and that is that the radio broadcasts did not tell us where and what time the cyclone was to hit which is why we were not well prepared. (Female villager, journal entry, Votua)

If radio broadcasting stations were to take more responsibility in disseminating disaster information, this may not necessarily result in increased preparedness by community members. Some respondents who heard the radio broadcasts chose not to heed warnings due to perceptions of cyclone weather not aligning with the sunny day they were observing.

Preparing for Disasters

As explored in the previous section, a lack of preparation is perceived to increase the vulnerability of individuals and households towards disasters. There are two leading but parallel narratives regarding disaster preparation within Votua and Navala: one developing around taking preparatory measures and the other around taking last-minute or no measures for Cyclone Winston.

Only two interviewees in Votua perceived a gendered differentiation in how disasters were prepared for. Both developed a narrative of male complacency contrasted with maternal care and female domestic responsibilities as a leading driver behind the elevated role women play in disaster preparations.

There is a difference between men and women. Men, they just relax, but women prepare for everything. They prepare utensils and food to take with them. This is because women look after the household, while men say 'just leave everything'. (Elderly fisherwoman, interview, Votua)

Women are more affected (in preparing for) disasters as they worry about the children. It is more stress for women as men just drink *kava* and forget about it. We men think about how to build houses, not how to feed children. (Retired fisherman, interview, Votua)

These individual notions of gendered responses to disaster preparation were further reified during two mapping sessions: one with men from Votua and the other by men in Navala. The men's mapping session in Navala reiterated the role women play in the collection of food for disasters while the men's mapping session in Votua stated that:

> Men were not as prepared for Cyclone Winston compared to women. Women prepare all the food and cooking utensils because women naturally focus on households and men focus more on being out in the field.

What can be uniquely drawn out from the mapping session in Votua is the perceived 'natural' element to the roles men and women play within the household, suggesting innate gendered responsibilities. One individual story that was shared in a journal from Votua, however, contradicts the notion of men's ill preparation for disasters, while highlighting how some preparatory techniques can take place within what would be regarded as the men's domain.

> A few days before the hurricane struck, warnings were broadcasted over the radio and television and I even saw signs appear within my surroundings, such as trees which were dying and falling fruits, indicators that were used by our ancestors. When I started seeing these signs, I began my preparations. I went to the farm to gather vegetables and root crops. I stacked up of groceries from the supermarket as well as gallons of water, a first aid kit and some clothes. (Young fisherman, journal entry, Votua)

Preparation of the farm for a cyclone was only expressed by one female interviewee in Votua who described her husband as cutting the cassava branches so that they would not be uprooted after he heard the radio warning. She and her husband also moved belongings such as cooking equipment and food to a relative's house which was located at higher ground.

Similarly, throughout the Votuan journals, although not dictating the gendered differences in preparation, men often wrote of their and their families' preparation techniques prior to Cyclone Winston.

There were further contending perceptions of disaster preparation at the community level. One respondent noted:

> Since we have faced numerous floods and cyclones, we know exactly what to expect and how to prepare. (Male trade assistant, journal entry, Votua)

Others wrote about the fear and confusion of how to prepare and cope with a disaster.

> I was undecided and confused, I didn't know what to keep safe, my home, my furniture, everything in my kitchen, my family. I wanted to save everything but I didn't know where to start. (Elderly woman, journal entry, Votua)

Post-Disaster Recovery

As mentioned earlier, Cyclone Winston is regarded as one of the most devastating storms to have reached Fiji. As one respondent shared their story:

> When the cyclone was behind us, we were in an absolute state of poverty. Our food and our clothes were damaged, our houses torn apart and roads blocked and devastated. (Elderly woman, journal entry, Navala)

In Navala, up to 100% of the farms were said to be destroyed, according to the male focus group, with only some below-ground crops being salvaged, such as cassava and kava roots, for selling in the market. Participants also discussed the harvesting of wild chillies and lemons to sell at the market, in order to purchase staple foods such as rice until further assistance arrived. For many, their livelihoods were destroyed; they had lost access to water, food and shelter. The road to recovery was arduous and many households, particularly in Navala, were still recovering at the time of the fieldwork, with some families living in tents, sharing homes with family members or still waiting for their farmland to recover. The destruction of plantations significantly impacted many households as this is a primary source of food and money.

Disasters pose a significant threat to food security as was discussed during one *talanoa* conversation:

We have to plant more food so we do not have a food shortage. If there is no cyclone, there is no food shortage, when a cyclone comes though we have a shortage.

The women discussed their consumption levels falling following Cyclone Winston and continuing to November 2016:

For now, we are only eating rice, flour and roti. The cassava hasn't grown back yet, but we manage to buy cabbage from the market. We had to replant our cassava a few months ago, as a large tree fell and destroyed all the plants. We didn't have enough stems to replant, so we asked our neighbours for help.

The recovery process following disaster events evidently leaves communities in a state of reliance upon social networks as well as restricting the variety of food consumed. This is a significant divergence in the conceptualisation of vulnerability between community members and external stakeholders.

This relationship draws attention to the alignment of strategies to reduce gender inequality in disaster risk reduction measures. It also requires an adequate and meaningful alignment of different forms of knowledge and knowledge development which inadvertently brings to light the power relations through identifying who determines the vulnerable, whose cultural values are placed in higher esteem and which networks of utilisation are promoted. This is not to say that internal autonomous movements for women's rights are not present in the Pacific, as they very much are, nor that the gender disparities can be justified, but rather the realisation of the importance of critical thought.

Recovery from disasters was gendered primarily through the spaces which men and women occupied in the recovery process:

After Cyclone Winston everybody cleaned up together – men repaired the house, whilst women clean up inside and outside the house. (Mixed youth focus group, Navala)

Disparities between men and women within everyday social, cultural, economic and politic spheres weaken 'resilience and recovery' for women following disasters, in particular due to their heightened responsibilities for the welfare of family and home (Moreno-Walton & Koenig, 2016). This notion of responsibility was echoed in both Votua and Navala.

It is mainly men that do everything after a cyclone. They do all the cleaning. The women only cook and help to clean the drains. (Female farmer, interview, Navala)

One respondent outlined her difficulties following Cyclone Winston:

For me, as a single mother, it was very hard to look after my family because it was difficult to find food to store and in addition there was no electricity. My children found it a challenge to do their school work due to the lack of electricity. (Single mother, journal entry, Votua)

Another female interviewee in Votua described how she and her children left for the Fijian capital Suva following a large flooding event, while her husband remained home to clean and clear their house. The movement of women and children to safer locations following a disaster would increase the husband's exposure to post-disaster health risks, suggesting the potential for men to have an increased level of vulnerability following disasters.

Both in Votua and Navala, there is an undercurrent of the breakdown of traditional gender roles through both increased opportunities for women to involve themselves in the formal sector as well as the prolific effects of anecdotally expressed *kava* culture. Utilising a gendered lens into reduction of vulnerability within Votua and Navala could benefit through targeting the perceived gendered issues within both these communities such as *kava* consumption. Excluding an explicit focus on women has inextricably led to an increase in workload for women in both communities and at a national level providing social welfare schemes that do not inherently disable women's 'security' at an older age.

DISCUSSION: EMBODYING RESILIENCE

This study aimed to develop and present an understanding of the gender and knowledge landscapes in two disaster-prone villages in Fiji: Votua and Navala. The purpose was to understand the extant forms of knowledge utilised in preparing, adapting and recovering from climate change-induced disasters as well as the specific gendered experiences. As Gero et al. (2015) highlight, successful climate change projects begin with a holistic approach and adequate incorporation of local communities, rather than translocating solutions implemented in vastly different regions (cf. Nunn, 2009). Consequently, the employment of a narrative approach was conceived due to the communal and individual experience that narratives provide. It draws upon stories of experience, of worldviews and understandings. Narrative furthermore supplies an alternative conception to that developed through a scientific lens (Lejano, Tavares-Reager, & Berkes, 2013) elevating the space for other forms of understanding.

Gender, Livelihoods and Disasters

Gendered perspectives and experiences in Pacific disaster discourse are a relatively new area of inquiry and action (Lane & McNaught, 2009). A significant conception that was recognised throughout this research, and drawn from other sources, is the complexity of experience. This calls for stepping away from conceiving the world through a lens of binaries, instead conceiving experience as a complex interaction of intersecting social constructions (Carr & Thompson, 2014; Kaijser & Kronsell, 2014; Tschakert, 2012). This study aligns with the conception that women play a leading role in agriculture and, however, remain predominantly invisible due to the prevalence of predetermined roles and responsibilities. It is often argued that to make bounds in gender equality, the diversity of roles women encompass needs to be recognised (Carr & Thompson, 2014; Underhill-Sem et al., 2014). This was principal in how women perceived their 'occupation' within journal entries when compared to interviews. Throughout the majority of journal entries completed by women, their primary occupation was 'domestic duties'. Perhaps this reflects the range of duties that women do in fact undertake, such as farmer, fisher, produce seller, carer, cook, cleaner, souvenir seller, tour guide, and so on. However, all these positions are hidden, particularly during data collection which elicits short answer responses. This is further complicated when 'domestic duties' are not expanded upon and – as demonstrated through interviews – 'domestic duties' can encompass a multitude of roles that differ between women from different households and, in some cases, differ between women within the same household and is then disaggregated via age. However, similar to broader studies, in female-headed households, women take on the role of farm management (Arun, 2012) and other activities often vacated by men (Vepa, 2005). This was seen in both Votua and Navala with women undertaking a greater role in farming and fishing management as men turned to *kava* drinking.

A field of concern within contemporary climate change literature is that of food security and livelihood security among subsistence level households and communities. Food security and sustainability within Pacific Island states has greatly deteriorated due to a multitude of external influences. Global weather patterns and climatic extremes placed further pressure and destruction upon farming and fishing communities. In addition to this, social, economic and political dynamics such as colonisation, the introduction of new religious institutions, capitalism and globalisation have altered, added and negated many worldviews, coping mechanisms and national-level developments for decades (Campbell, 2015). These varying and colliding impacts are not felt uniformly throughout communities but rely upon roles, responsibilities and identity (Carr & Thompson, 2014). This view of reduced food security is partially consistent with that seen in Votua and Navala, in particular the absence of food preservation and a reliance on imported food, a remnant of a colonial past and contemporary effects of globalisation. However, the perception of food insecurity held by villagers was not in accordance with this perception. Climate was greatly affecting crop yields, overfishing was depleting fish stocks and natural hazards such as floods and TCs devastated agriculture. However, the presence of social networks, diversified livelihoods in Votua, as well as assistance through the church, government and NGO sectors ensured a decrease in food insecurity, in particular for women.

Women are regarded as especially susceptible to food insecurity in Fiji due to their reliance upon agriculture as a leading, and often only, form of income (FAO, 2016). However, it was identified that in both Votua and Navala, elder women were almost always the household member who went to market to sell produce, often over an entire day or two per week. While selling produce at markets was the leading income-generating activity for the many, several women interviewed also partook in other complimentary income-generating activities, while others no longer took part in subsistence activities. While teaching and working in restaurants were significant sources of income for some women, others opened their own shops or canteens, selling such commodities as hygiene products as well as canned and packaged goods within the village. In Navala particularly, tourism offered a key income for many women either as tour guides, selling souvenirs or cooking for tourists. The tourism industry in Navala was perceived as solely within the domain of female roles. Although, as previously stated, only those located in the centre of Navala truly benefitted from this industry.

While rural women have generally been regarded collectively as vulnerable towards disasters (Alston, 2013), some outcomes from this study have highlighted the need to disaggregate data further. There are many cross-cutting issues which increase or decrease an individual's or a household's exposure to increased risk in the face of a changing climate. While common narratives emerged through interviews, mapping sessions and journals, there were community members who held a different perspective or had a different experience. These diverse experiences in livelihoods and capacities to adapt demonstrate the intersection of realities within one individual, influenced by socio-cultural expectations and necessity. Individual experience is diverse, changing spatially and temporally. The movement of individuals and households between rural and urban centres as well as to other neighbouring villages further disrupts the conception of generalised statements of vulnerability and resilience based along gender lines.

The gendered landscape of Votua and Navala as analysed through community member's experiences and views is diverse. Of particular note is that both men and women did not view gender as a deciding factor of vulnerability and while women were often expressed as having increasingly more responsibilities within the household, this did not seem to equate to an increase in power. Globally, gender relations stem from institutional and systematic norms (Jaggar, 2009). A study undertaken in Bangladesh emphasised that although women experience and bear the brunt of greatest vulnerability towards natural disasters, they do so furtively (Rahman, 2013). Social norms that impose restrictions on behaviour and access to assets are at the core of gendered vulnerability (Perez et al., 2015; Sugden et al., 2014). These conceptions could be used to explain in part the lack of perceived gender vulnerability to disasters in Votua and Navala. However, it also brings to light the spaces that are still to be explored in relation to contextualised experiences, particularly directly following disasters, in the space of potential gender-based violence that is heightened during this time.

Conceptualising vulnerability as arising from interacting social factors provides an insight into spaces behind unperceived vulnerability by understanding the engrained nature of gender roles. In Votua and Navala, gender roles were seen to be either changing, with men and women's roles combining or with women taking on more responsibilities, or as immutable. Within these set roles, women have less ownership over agricultural land, as plantations are relegated to male responsibilities as well as less access to formal employment. Furthermore, the conception that men are the 'breadwinners' of the household was prevalent. This notion was expressed explicitly by one respondent whose husband believed a woman's place was at home and restricted his wife's movements. As discussed in Nussbaum (2003, p. 34), gender injustice has led to female adaptation as 'second-class'. Consequently, if women's roles and voices were to be acknowledged and incorporated into social systems, then they can partake in a furthering successful climate change adaptation locally, in line with empowering their own forms of knowledge and power (Charan et al., 2016).

The conception that women and men have varying responsibilities and roles in the Pacific is not new (Charan et al., 2016). However, reflecting upon the perceived notion of these roles and responsibilities is not something that is often discussed. As aforementioned, the absence of reflecting upon gendered responsibilities and the effects this may have at an individual level may be a leading reason for the lack of perceived gendered vulnerability. The pivotal role that women play in determining household and national sustainable development and well-being is an area of study which has been extensively explored. Yet, while women engage in various other roles, the transition of increased power and decision-making is still in the hands of men, and the role of household leaders remains reserved for the husband. This notion aligns with other studies which have noted that, within a Fijian context, women are expected to care for domestic and community tasks (Enarson & Fordham, 2001).

Although the perception of gendered vulnerability was absent from respondent narratives, gender responsibilities and unequal access to resources were not. Consequently, gendered vulnerability may still be prevalent without explicit expression. However, as discussed in MacGregor (2010a), a shift is required in presenting and assuming female victimhood and vulnerability to further understanding the relationships between genders. Through conceiving gender relations in regard to local contexts, this shift, as well as one towards contextualised social justice, can begin to alter this perception.

The Value of Social Networks

The significant role that social networks play in reducing household vulnerability, when viewed through an *iTaukei* worldview, is paramount in understanding resilience within these communities (Neef et al., 2018; Yila, Weber, & Neef, 2013). The foundations of co-operation and support are inherent within village life and Fijian tradition (Bricker & Kerstetter, 2006). Social networks are often perceived through a Western lens as predominantly reliance upon others. However, as expressed by Campbell (2015), this perception fails to see the reciprocal nature of such exchanges, particularly with regard to remittances. Furthermore, other researchers have highlighted the potential threat of reduced social reliance as a result of urban movement resulting in a loss of connection with 'place' in addition to the deterioration of traditional structures through external influences (Baird & Gray, 2014; Mimura, 1999). These networks are still well maintained and drawn upon, as was evident in the interviews and journal entries. According to Aldrich (2012), it is social networks that best explain the efficiency of community recovery following disasters.

Furthermore, if we were to extrapolate this perception of social networks to a broader scale, such as the relationship between households, communities and the government, we can see the reciprocity in tasks, and developing a conception of interdependency. For example, within Fiji utilising social networks in order to support food security and housing aspects of recovery within kinship groups, as well as through church support allows the government to focus on infrastructural recovery. Yet, as seen through some experiences in Navala, social networks and assistance are not guaranteed, although all respondents had received some form of assistance from their immediate family.

Consequently, rather than conceptualising social networks through a lens of reliance, we can view it through a lens of reciprocity and division of tasks in the context of *iTaukei* communities. According to Baird and Gray (2014), much research has focussed on the role social networks have in conveying information and within the realm of governance as opposed to the physical exchange of goods. They draw attention to the relationship between natural resource exchange and the implications this has on natural resource management. This chapter focussed purely upon the activation of social networks within a disaster setting as opposed to the broader utilisation of exchange systems within everyday life. However, some respondents alluded to the 'Pacific way' of exchange systems, as an engrained aspect of Pacific culture, 'emphasising trust and reciprocity and the establishment of strong ties' (Ingold, 2017, p. 416).

Consequently, this study aligns with other studies that purport social networks as increasing resilience towards climate change (Chamlee-Wright & Storr, 2011; Ingold, 2017; Murphy, 2007). As social networks and religious institutions were demonstrated to be the first steps in coping and recovery following a disaster, working together in order to rebuild housing destruction, provide materials as well as coordinate recovery efforts (Chamlee-Wright & Storr, 2011). These responses were exemplified in both Votua and Navala with community-led village analyses of destruction, identifying community members most in need and ensuring resources were allocated to where they were required to go, as well as the provision of food, clothing and housing for those whose homes were destroyed.

CONCLUSION

The embodiment of resilience is a conception that comprises historical influences, not only forming from the onset of colonisation but of generations of adaptation and knowledge formation, with a need to capture such diverse and varied narratives and collating them into a framework which can be collaborated within the contemporary project and policy frameworks. Evidently while these conceptions are still dominated by Western rhetoric which seeks to categorise and form binaries, the space to incorporate alternative knowledge is limited. As stated by Underhill-Sem et al. (2014), the greatest difficulty with transforming practices is the combining of other concepts.

Furthermore, adaptations cannot only incorporate technical aspects while negating cultural contexts, nor only technical responses (Mimura, 1999), particularly within environments where strong social networks are already established. This not only fails to leverage off existing resilient practices but also continues the cycle of deteriorating traditional knowledge, some aspects which have already disappeared within Votua and Navala. There is also the conception by some respondents that traditional knowledge is no longer adequate within this rapidly changing climate.

Gender-specific knowledge and coping strategies were only partially developed here, primarily due to the perception by respondents that women and men experience disasters similarly. Although it was argued that deeply rooted gender roles within traditional structures may have rendered a gendered dimension to vulnerability invisible within both communities, it was evident that changes within these roles were occurring. Janif et al. (2016, p. 7) perhaps articulate the importance of social dimensions and traditional knowledge in maintaining resilient individuals and communities, stating:

> among the components of resilience are traditional environmental knowledge, community unity, respected decision-making processes, abundant communication and discussion opportunities, and community self-belief in their ability to manage their own futures.

The knowledge systems that are drawn upon by respondents in Votua and Navala provide a collective community narrative of hope, resilience and faith.

Women face multiple pulling forces from recent movements of gender equality, entrenched traditional gender roles and their own agency, leading to complex embodiments of diversity (Underhill-Sem et al., 2014). Throughout the Pacific, women are thought to continuously be navigating the power relations formed by political, economic and cultural aspects (Underhill-Sem et al., 2014). This conception, however, did not emerge as a uniform narrative from Votua and Navala. While some women and men acknowledged the evident dissidence in power between genders, in particular in the weight of increased livelihood responsibility becoming the onus of women, others believed that gender roles were becoming less fixed or alternatively that gendered roles were not necessarily negative conceptions. This does not negate the place for gendered disparities and power relations in Votua and Navala but highlights the heterogeneity within communities not only in experiences but also conceptions.

NOTE

1. *Kava* (*Piper methysticum*) is a popular Pacific plant from the pepper family whose roots are used to produce a drink with mildly sedative effects. It plays an important part in cultural protocols and social life in many parts of the Pacific.

ACKNOWLEDGEMENTS

We thank the leaders and residents of the villages of Votua and Navala for their hospitality and for generously sharing their perspectives and knowledge. We are grateful to the research assistants Talica Nauvi and Robert Varea for supporting the fieldwork. This research was made possible through funding and support provided by the Asia-Pacific Network for Global Change Research (CAF2016-RR05-CMY-Neef, 'Climate Change Adaptation in Post-Disaster Recovery Processes: Flood-Affected Communities in Cambodia and Fiji').

REFERENCES

Adger, W. (2006). Vulnerability. *Global Environmental Change, 16*(3), 268–281.

Aipira, C., Kidd, A., & Morioka, K. (2017). Climate change adaptation in Pacific countries: Fostering resilience through gender equality. In W. L. Filho (Ed.), *Climate change adaptation in Pacific countries: Fostering resilience and improving the quality of life* (pp. 225–240). Cham: Springer International Publishing.

Aldrich, D. P. (2012). Social, not physical, infrastructure: The critical role of civil society after the 1923 Tokyo earthquake. *Disasters, 36*(3), 398–419.

Alston, M. (2013). Women and adaptation. *WIREs Climate Change, 4*, 351–358.

Andersen, L E., Verner, D., & Manfred, W. (2016). Gender and climate change in Latin America: An analysis of vulnerability, adaptation and resilience based on household surveys. *Journal of International Development, 29*(7), 857–876

Arun, S. (2012). 'We are farmers too': Agrarian change and gendered livelihoods in Kerala, South India. *Journal of Gender Studies, 21*(3), 271–284.

Baird, T. D., & Gray, C. L. (2014). Livelihood diversification and shifting social networks of exchange: A social network transition? *World Development, 60*, 14–30.

Betzold, C. (2015). Adapting to climate change in small island developing states. *Climate Change, 133*, 481–489.

Boris, E. (2014). Mothers, household managers, and productive workers: The International Labor Organization and Women in Development. *Global Social Policy, 14*(2), 189–208.

Bradshaw, S. (2014). Engendering development and disasters. *Disasters, 39*(1), 54–75.

Bricker, K. S., & Kerstetter, D. (2006). Exploring sense of place in the rural highlands of Fiji. In G. Jennings & N. Nickerson (Eds.), *Quality tourism experiences* (pp. 99–109). Burlington: Elsevier Butterworth-Heinemann.

Campbell, J. R. (2015). Development, global change and traditional food security in Pacific Island countries. *Regional Environmental Change, 15*(7), 1313–1324.

Carr, E. R., & Thompson, M. C. (2014). Gender and climate change adaptation in agrarian settings: Current thinking, new directions, and research frontiers. *Geography Compass, 8*(3), 182–197.

Chamlee-Wright, E., & Storr, V. H. (2011). Social capital as collective narratives and post-disaster community recovery. *The Sociological Review, 59*(2), 266–282.

Charan, D., Kaur, M., & Singh, P. (2016). Indigenous Fijian women's role in disaster risk management and climate change adaptation. *Pacific Asia Inquiry, 7*(1), 107–122.

Cox, J., Varea, R., Finau, G., Tarai, J., Kant, R., Titifanue, J., & Neef, A. (in press). Disaster preparedness and the abeyance of agency: Christian responses to Tropical Cyclone Winston in Fiji. *Anthropological Forum, 30*(1–2), 125–140.

Cutter, S. L. (2017). The forgotten casualties redux: Women, children and disaster risk. *Global Environmental Change, 42*, 117–121.

Eastin, J. (2018). Climate change and gender equality in developing states. *World Development, 107*, 289–305.

Ellsberg, M., Pena, R., Herrera, A., Liljestrand, J., & Winkvist, A. (2000). Candies in hell: Women's experiences of violence in Nicaragua. *Social Science & Medicine, 51*(11), 1595–1610.

Enarson, E., & Fordham, M. (2001). From women's needs to women's rights in disasters. *Environmental Hazards, 3*(3–4), 133–136.

FAO. (2016). *Fiji: Tropical Cyclone Winston: Situation report – 16 March 2016*. Rome: FAO. Retrieved from http://www.fao.org/resilience/resources/resources-detail/en/c/396283/

Farré, L. (2013). The role of men in the economic and social development of women: Implications for gender equality. *The World Bank Research Observer, 28*(1), 22–51.

Foucault, M. (1982). The subject and power. *Critical Inquiry, 8*(4), 777–795.

Gaillard, J. C., Cadag, J. R., Gampell, A., Hore, K., Le Dé, L., & McSherry, A. (2016). Participatory numbers for integrating knowledge and actions in development. *Development in Practice, 26*(8), 998–1012.

Gaillard, J. C., Sanz, K., Balgos, B., Dalisay, S., Gorman-Murray, A., Smith, F., & Toelupe, V. (2017). Beyond men and women: A critical perspective on gender and disaster. *Disasters, 41*(3), 429–447.

Gero, A., Fletcher, S., Rumsey, M., Thiessen, J., Kuruppu, N., Buchan, J., Daly, J., & Willetts, J. (2015). Disasters and climate change in the Pacific: Adaptive capacity of humanitarian response organisations. *Climate and Development, 7*(1), 35–46.

Griffen, V. (2006). Local and global women's rights in the Pacific. *Development, 49*(1), 108–112.

Holmes, O. (2016). Cyclone Winston: Tens of thousands homeless in Fiji a week after storm. *The Guardian.* Retrieved from https://www.theguardian.com/world/2016/feb/29/cyclone-winston-forces-thousands-fijians-out-of-homes

Hyndman, J. (2008). Feminism, conflict and disasters in post-tsunami Sri Lanka. *Gender, Technology and Development, 12*(1), 101–121.

Hyndman, J., & de Alwis, M. (2003). Beyond gender: Towards a feminist analysis of humanitarianism and development in Sri Lanka. *Women's Studies Quarterly, 31*(3–4), 212–226.

Ingold, K. (2017). How to create and preserve social capital in climate adaptation policies: A network approach. *Ecological Economics, 131*, 414–424.

Irvine, G., Pauli, N., Varea, R., & Boruff, B. (2020). A participatory approach to understanding the impact of multiple natural hazards in communities along the Ba River, Fiji. In A. Neef & N. Pauli (Eds.), *Climate-induced disasters in the Asia-Pacific region: Response, recovery, adaptation* (pp. 51–86). Bingley: Emerald Publishing.

Jaggar, A. M. (2009). Transnational cycles of gendered vulnerability: A prologue to a theory of global gender justice. *Philosophical Topics, 37*(2), 33–52.

Janif, S. Z., Nunn, P. D., Geraghty, P., Aalbersberg, W., Thomas, F. R., & Camailakeba, M. (2016). Value of traditional oral narratives in building climate-change resilience: Insights from rural communities in Fiji. *Ecology and Society, 21*(2), 7.

Kabeer, N. (1999). Resources, agency, achievements: Reflections on the measurement of women's empowerment. *Development and Change, 30*(3), 435–464.

Kaijser, A., & Kronsell, A. (2014). Climate change through the lens of intersectionality. *Environmental Politics, 23*(3), 417–433.

Kohona, P. (2016). Climate change – Are we really confronting this challenge? *Environmental Policy and Law, 46*(2), 109–111.

Kruse, J. (2014). Women's representation in the UN climate change negotiations: A quantitative analysis of state delegations, 1995–2011. *International Environmental Agreements: Politics, Law and Economics, 14*, 349–370.

Lane, R., & McNaught, R. (2009). Building gendered approaches to adaptation in the Pacific. *Gender and Development, 17*(1), 67–80.

Leask, A. (2016). Cyclone Winston's fury evident throughout Fiji. *New Zealand Herald.* Retrieved from http://www.nzherald.co.nz/world/news/article.cfm?c_id=2&objectid=11593860

Lejano, R. P., Tavares-Reager, J., & Berkes, F. (2013). Climate and narrative: Environmental knowledge in everyday life. *Environmental Science and Policy, 31*, 61–70.

MacGregor, S. (2010a). 'Gender and climate change': From impacts to discourse. *Journal of the Indian Ocean Region, 6*(2), 223–238.

MacGregor, S. (2010b). A stranger silence still: The need for feminist social research on climate change. *The Sociological Review, 57*(2), 12–140.

MacKinnon, D., & Derickson, K. (2013). From resilience to resourcefulness: A critique of resilience policy and activism. *Progress in Human Geography, 37*(2), 253–270.

Manata, S., & Papazu, I. (2009). Gendering climate change. A perspective on the overlooked gender dimension of climate change in the developing world. *Approaches to Development.* Retrieved from http://ps.au.dk/fileadmin/Statskundskab/Dokumenter/subsites/Uland/GenderingClimateChange.pdf

McCubbin, S., Smit, B., & Pearce, T. (2015). Where does climate fit? Vulnerability to climate change in the context of multiple stressors in Funafuti, Tuvalu. *Global Environmental Change, 30*, 43–55.

Meo-Sewabu, L. (2014). Cultural discernment as an ethics framework: An Indigenous Fijian approach. *Asia Pacific Viewpoint, 55*(3), 345–354.

Mikulewicz, M. (2018). Politicizing vulnerability and adaptation: On the need to democratize local responses to climate impacts in developing countries. *Climate and Development, 10*(1), 18–34.

Mikulewicz, M. (2019). Thwarting adaptation's potential? A critique of resilience and climate-resilient development. *Geoforum, 104*, 267–282.

Mimura, N. (1999). Vulnerability of island countries in the South Pacific to sea level rise and climate change. *Climate Research*, *12*, 137–143.

Mohanty, C. T. (1984). Under western eyes: feminist scholarship and colonial discourse. *Boundary 2*, *12*(3), 333–358.

Mohd, S. (2016). I have no words to tell you. *Bulletin of the American Meteorological Society*, *97*(6), 901.

Moreno-Walton, L., & Koenig, K. (2016). Disaster resilience: Addressing gender disparities. *World Medical & Health Policy*, *8*(1), 46–57.

Morioka, K. (2012). *A climate for change: Understanding women's vulnerability and adaptive capacity to climate change from ActionAid's rights-based approach – Case studies from Papua New Guinea and Solomon Islands*. Sydney: ActionAid.

Murphy, B. L. (2007). Locating social capital in resilient community-level emergency management. *Natural Hazards*, *41*(2), 297–315.

Nabalarua, E. (2005). Making a difference where it counts: A case of activism, advocacy and action-research with two women's groups in Fiji. *Fijian Studies*, *3*(2), 295–310.

Nawaz, F. (2013). Power, empowerment and participatory development: Conceptual linkages. *Open Journal of Social Science Research*, *1*(2), 26–30.

Neef, A., Benge, L., Boruff, N., Pauli, N., Weber, E., & Varea, R. (2018). Climate change adaptation strategies in Fiji: The role of social norms and cultural values. *World Development*, *107*, 125–137.

Nightingale, Andrea J. (2012). The embodiment of nature: fishing, emotion, and the politics of environmental values. In E. Brady & P. Phemister (Eds.), *Human-environment relations* (pp. 135–47). Dordrecht: Springer Netherlands.

Nunn, P. D. (2009). Responding to the challenges of climate change in the Pacific islands: Management and technological imperatives. *Climate Research*, *40*, 211–231.

Nunn, P. D. (2013). The end of the Pacific? Effects of sea level rise on Pacific Island livelihoods. *Singapore Journal of Tropical Geography*, *34*(2), 143–171.

Nussbaum, M. (2003). Capabilities as fundamental entitlements: Sen and social justice. *Feminist Economics*, *9*(2–3), 33–59.

Perez, C., Jones, E. M., Kristjanson, P., Cramer, L., Thornton, P. K., Forch, W., & Barahona, C. (2015). How resilient are farming households and communities to a changing climate in Africa? A gender-based perspective. *Global Environmental Change*, *34*, 95–107.

Rahman, S. (2013). Climate change, disaster and gender vulnerability: A study on two divisions of Bangladesh. *American Journal of Human Ecology*, *2*(2), 72–82.

Sen, A. (1999). *Development as freedom*. New York: Anchor Books.

Stewart-Withers, R., Banks, G., McGregor, A., & Meo-Sewabu, L. (2014). *Qualitative research in development fieldwork: A practical guide* (2nd ed.). London: SAGE Publications.

Sugden, F., Maskey, N., Clement, F., Ramesh, V., Philip, A., & Rai, A. (2014). Agrarian stress and climate change in the Eastern Gangetic Plains: Gendered vulnerability in a stratified social formation. *Global Environmental Change*, *29*, 258–269.

Thomas, D. S. G., Twyman, C., Osbahr, H., & Hewitson, B. (2011). Adaptation to climate change and variability: Farmer responses to intra-seasonal precipitation trends in South Africa. *African Climate and Climate Change*, *43*, 155–178.

Tschakert, P. (2012). From impacts to embodied experiences: Tracing political ecology in climate change research. *Geografisk Tidssdrift-Danish Journal of Geography*, *112*(2), 144–158.

Underhill-Sem, Y., Cox, E., Lacey, A., & Szamiers, M. (2014). Changing market culture in the Pacific: Assembling a conceptual framework from diverse knowledge and experiences. *Asia Pacific Viewpoint*, *55*(3), 306–318.

Vepa, S. (2005). Feminisation of agriculture and marginalisation of their economic stake. *Economic and Political Weekly*, *40*(25), 2563–2568.

Yila, O., Weber, E., & Neef, A. (2013). The role of social capital in post-flood response and recovery among downstream communities of the Ba River, Western Viti Levu, Fiji Islands. In A. Neef & R. Shaw (Eds.), *Risks and conflicts: Local responses to natural disasters* (pp. 79–107). Bingley: Emerald.

CHAPTER 6

PARTICIPATORY GIS AND COMMUNITY-BASED ADAPTATION TO CLIMATE CHANGE AND ENVIRONMENTAL HAZARDS: A CAMBODIAN CASE STUDY

Mark Williams, Natasha Pauli and Bryan Boruff

ABSTRACT

Climate change, deforestation and hydropower dams are contributing to environmental change in the Lower Mekong River region, the combined effects of which are felt by many rural Cambodians. How people perceive and manage the effects of environmental change will influence future adaptation strategies. The objective of this research was to investigate whether the use of a low-cost, explicitly spatial method (participatory mapping) can help identify locally relevant opportunities and challenges to climate change adaptation in small, flood-prone communities. Four villages along the banks of the Mekong River in Kratie Province, Cambodia, were the subject of this research. To identify perceived environmental hazards and adaptive responses, eight workshops were conducted using focus-group interviews and participatory mapping. The communities' responses highlight the evolving nature of environmental hazards, as droughts increase in perceived importance while the patterns of wet season flooding were also perceived to be changing. The attribution of the drivers of these hazards was strongly skewed towards local factors such as deforestation and less towards regional or global drivers affecting the hydrology of the Mekong and climate patterns. Combining participatory mapping with focus-group interviews allowed a greater depth of understanding of the vulnerabilities

Climate-Induced Disasters in the Asia-Pacific Region: Response, Recovery, Adaptation
Community, Environment and Disaster Risk Management, Volume 22, 113–134
Copyright © 2021 by Emerald Publishing Limited
All rights of reproduction in any form reserved
ISSN: 2040-7262/doi:10.1108/S2040-726220200000022005

and opportunities available to communities than reliance on a single qualitative method. The study highlights the potential for a bottom-up transfer of information to strengthen existing climate change policies and tailor adaptation plans to local conditions.

Keywords: Participatory mapping; climate change adaptation; natural hazards; Cambodia; Mekong River; local knowledge

INTRODUCTION

Climate change is altering rainfall and temperature patterns throughout Southeast Asia (Ge et al., 2019; Kingston, Thompson, & Kite, 2011; Tangang et al., 2018; Västilä, Kummu, Sangmanee, & Chinvanno, 2010), with projected increases in rainfall intensity and frequency combined with expected increased occurrences of flooding and drought (Hoang et al., 2016; Räsänen, Koponen, Lauri, & Kummu, 2012; Yamamauchi, 2014). These impacts affect populations and economies of big cities, small towns and rural communities (Bonatti et al., 2016). Alongside climate change, alterations in land-use patterns are contributing to environmental change and may increase the exposure of communities to natural hazards in vulnerable areas. Understanding how humans are vulnerable and adapt to environmental hazards in the context of climate change is an urgent task for researchers (Few & Tran, 2010; Halsnæs, Larsen, & Kaspersen, 2018; Sovacool, Linnér, & Klein, 2017). If people can adjust and respond to the changing environment, it reduces vulnerability to hazards and provides examples for adaptation that can be applied in related circumstances the world over.

Cambodia has previously been characterised as particularly vulnerable to climate change based on a series of broad indicators (Yusuf & Francisco, 2009), and a recent assessment by CRED and UNISDR (2015) found that the proportion of the Cambodian population affected by weather-related hazards was one of the highest in the world. In recognition of the challenges faced by the country, multilateral funding for climate change adaptation in Cambodia was the highest of all countries in the Southeast Asia region in 2016 (Dedicatoria & Diomampo, 2019). Future climatic changes are projected to affect Cambodia by increasing annual precipitation by 10% (Kingston et al., 2011), at the same time altering the timing of rainfall patterns and increasing exposure to seasonal drought, and longer dry spells during the wet season (Yamamauchi, 2014). The Mekong River is expected to experience more frequent and intense high-flow events, with increased flood risk (Hoang et al., 2016). Cambodia suffered through a severe drought in 2015–2016 associated with an El Niño event (Besant, 2016). The drought, officially recognised by the Mekong River Commission and the Cambodian Ministry of Water Resources and Management, resulted in an alteration of the River's annual flood regime in 2015 starving its inhabitants of the resource on which they have built their livelihoods and delayed monsoon rains in 2016.

Moreover, 90% of the country's poor live in rural areas (Sok & Yu, 2015) and depend on agriculture for their food and income activities. Rice is the predominant crop within the Cambodian agricultural sector with the Lower Mekong Basin accounting for 84% of the nation's production (Mekong River Commission, 2019). Research based on 24 years of data from field trials found that rice yield declined by 10% for every 1°C increase in minimum temperatures during the dry season (Peng et al., 2004). With a 3–4°C increase in land surface temperatures projected from 1986–2005 to 2081–2100 (IPCC, 2014b), the nation could see a 40% decrease in rice production by the end of the century. The agricultural sector and water supply (quality and quantity) are two of the top priority areas for climate change adaptation within Cambodia (Dedicatoria & Diomampo, 2019).

Tonle Sap and the Lower Mekong Basin are the two broad regions within Cambodia projected to be on the receiving end of the most extreme climate-related events – Tonle Sap and the Lower Mekong Basin (Doch, Diepart, & Heng, 2015), both experience seasonal flood-pulse events around which agricultural and livelihood activities are centred. The north-eastern province of Kratie, within the Lower Mekong Basin, is expected to face an increase in the frequency of larger flooding events (Eastham et al., 2008) with one recent model predicting an increase in the overall annual flooded extent for Kratie Province from 1,000 km² (Arias et al., 2012) to ~3,800 km² (Eastham et al., 2008). Kratie Province is also affected by the advent of reservoirs used to generate hydroelectricity along the Mekong and its tributaries; the dams needed for hydropower generation have been associated with reduced water levels downstream (Lu, Li, Kummu, Padawangi, & Wang, 2014). The development of dams is considered the catalyst for the greatest relative change to the flow of water for the area (Grumbine & Xu, 2011; Keskinen et al., 2010). There are up to 165 proposed dams along the Mekong (Räsänen et al., 2012); as a consequence, the yearly flood regimes could be further modified (Johnston & Kummu, 2012; Kummu & Sarkkula, 2008; Piman, Lennaerts, & Southalack, 2013; Pokhrel et al., 2018). Deforestation, expansion of cultivated land and irrigation are further drivers of environmental, social and economic change in Kratie Province (Arias et al., 2012). The research presented in this chapter explored the perceptions, resilience and adaptive capacity of several communities along the banks of the Mekong River in Kratie Province in Cambodia, alongside the perceived causes, actual impacts and local responses to a range of environmental hazards.

Vulnerability and Adaptive Capacity

The research presented here is framed by the concepts of vulnerability, adaptive capacity and resilience as they have been described in literature around natural hazards and disasters. The extent to which hazards become disasters is, in part, a function of vulnerability. The concept of vulnerability has become particularly important within natural hazard and disaster research (Birkholz, Muro, Jeffrey, & Smith, 2014; King & MacGregor, 2000), and is used as an analytical lens that incorporates how social context shapes risk and by extension, natural disasters such as flood events. Vulnerability is often described as a result of a system's exposure and sensitivity to stress and its capacity to absorb, or cope with, the effects of these stressors (McLeod et al., 2015). Three components are often described as key to understanding vulnerability: exposure to a hazard, susceptibility to harm and adaptive capacity (López-Marrero & Tschakert, 2011; Smit & Wandel, 2006). Adaptive capacity is often influenced by social capital, linked by social learning and knowledge exchange which are essential to the capacity of social–ecological systems to adapt and shape change (Folke, 2006). Adaptation to climate change is often thought of as strategies that take gradual effect over the long term to guard against the risks associated with new climate futures, while coping strategies are generally perceived as short-term measures taken for survival or persistence through a particular event. Coping strategies can provide a mechanism for transitioning to long-term adaptation (Neef et al., 2018); in this research, we discuss short-term coping and long-term adaptation strategies together to highlight how such transitions can occur.

The Intergovernmental Panel on Climate Change (IPCC, 2014a) has identified that people who are socially, economically, culturally, politically, institutionally or otherwise marginalised are especially vulnerable to climate change. Furthermore, people in these marginalised groups are also vulnerable to some externally led adaptation and mitigation responses. Through evaluating climate vulnerability, people or places that are most susceptible to harm can be identified and actions that will reduce their susceptibility can be formulated (Polsky, Neff, & Yarnal, 2007). A key aim of climate change adaption then is the reduction of vulnerability and subsequent enhancement of resilience (Gero, Méheux, & Dominey-Howes, 2011). Previous research into vulnerability and adaptation has found that understanding vulnerabilities and coping strategies of both people and the responsible institutions is vital for designing disaster preparedness and adaptation strategies (Burrel, Davar, & Hughes, 2007). Furthermore, recent hazard research has found that shared learning experiences help develop the capacity to accept different perspectives on risk and employ alternative innovatory responses to threats (Birkholz et al., 2014).

Methods to Assess Community-based Adaptation

In the last several decades, community-based approaches (CBA), such as participatory rural appraisal, rapid rural appraisal and participatory learning and action, have become increasingly popular in research on climate change adaptation (Schipper, Ayers, Reid, Huq, & Rahman, 2014). This is arguably due to the benefits of recognising and valuing local culture, conditions and development issues (Gero et al., 2011). In the analysis of CBA, the conditions that interact to shape exposures, sensitivities and adaptive capacities are community-specific and therefore create needs and opportunities for adaptation (Smit & Wandel, 2006).

To understand and reduce the risk of hazards, it is seen as increasingly important to include local knowledge for identifying community risks (Mercer, 2010). These diverse sources of knowledge aid the management of complex and uncertain situations (Folke, Hahn, Olsson, & Norberg, 2005). While scientific knowledge has been shown to be valuable with infrequent or unprecedented incidents, local knowledge is vital in comprehending historical hazards (Mercer, Dominey-Howes, Kelman, & Lloyd, 2007). As they are most affected, local communities are on the frontline of response when a disaster strikes (Butler et al., 2015;

Delica-Willison & Willison, 2004). When communities are involved in the entire research process, incorporating local and scientific knowledge, the application of management strategies is ultimately more effective (Fazey et al., 2010). Additionally, building strong two-way relationships between differing points of view will lead to more informed management (Raymond et al., 2010).

The analysis of spatial information is key to the design of adaptation projects because the impacts of climate change and hazards on communities vary across space (Seneviratne et al., 2012). The use of geographic information systems (GIS) in hazard analysis is long-standing (Liu, Gebremeskel, De Smedt, Hoffmann, & Pfister, 2003; Townsend & Walsh, 1998; Van Der Knijff, Younis, & De Roo, 2010), as is its use in the policy realm (Esnard, 1998; Radil & Jiao, 2016). It has been argued that the methodologies of traditional, technically focussed GIS help decision makers in a top-down approach, and ignore complex forms of local land ontologies, thereby de-legitimising local knowledge (Cullen, 2015; Dunn, 2007). Participatory mapping (PGIS) is a response to these concerns and arose in the mid-1990s as the use of GIS for community engagement increased (Rinner, Keßler, & Andrulis, 2008). The approach uses a range of tools including mental mapping, ground mapping, participatory sketch mapping, transect mapping and participatory three-dimensional modelling with more recent developments including the use of Global Positioning Systems, aerial photos and remotely sensed images and GIS (Corbett, 2009).

Participatory mapping allows for the visualisation of local spatial knowledge, which is rarely available on official maps; the information is spatially specific, implying that it concerns local priorities, values and perceptions. The process itself is driven by local interests and priorities; it is socially inclusive, representative of the interests and values of the community as well as of individuals; feelings of 'ownership' and the legitimacy of actions. Communities and groups can be empowered by involvement in PGIS processes, thereby improving self-confidence and technical and political capacities. By making use of formalised systematic mapping and analysis of local spatial knowledge, which are relevant to hazards, vulnerability and risk, PGIS provides the added value of digital data for use in a GIS environment (Brown & Kyttä, 2014). Integrating local spatial knowledge into a PGIS can be used to forecast flood hazards, understand vulnerability and coping strategies, and therefore estimate risk much more effectively (McCall, 2003; van Aalst, Cannon, & Burton, 2008).

Successful adaptation to altered hydrological regimes associated with climate change requires local involvement and capacity, acknowledgement of local spatial differences, high-level support and reliable data. Local and Indigenous knowledge has historically often been overlooked in the formulation of climate change policies and plan, including within the IPCC assessment reports (Ford et al., 2016). There is growing recognition of the importance of understanding local indicators of climate change for effective adaptation planning (Makondo & Thomas, 2018) and the potential of including community-based observation networks to contribute to co-produced knowledge of environmental change (Alessa et al., 2016). A recent review (Nkoana, Verbruggen, & Hugé, 2018) identified best practices in involving rural communities in climate change adaptation efforts, highlighting the need for effective participatory processes that allow for two-way communication of climate risk. In rural, data-poor communities, there is often little available information, or adaptation plans are generalised and not locally relevant. This increases the difficulties for communities on the frontline of climate change, such as those small villages along the Mekong that are often first affected. There is very little research combining climate change and hazard perceptions, CBA and participatory mapping to explore these issues.

Research Aim and Objectives

The objective of this research was to investigate whether the use of a low-cost, explicitly spatial method (participatory mapping in a focus-group setting) can help identify locally relevant opportunities and challenges to climate change adaptation in small, flood-prone communities, which are also exposed to other environmental hazards. It is hoped that the results of this research may help inform locally relevant strategies and measures for adaptation planning. The specific objectives for the research were to:

(1) explore local understanding of spatial and temporal changes in environmental conditions, including climate-related hazards;
(2) highlight and map local vulnerabilities to environmental change and hazards; and
(3) elucidate coping mechanisms and adaptation strategies associated with environmental change.

METHODS

Study Area

The research encompassed four villages to the south of the town of Kratie in Kratie Province, approximately 300 km from Phnom Penh in the northeast of Cambodia (Fig. 6.1). The population of Kratie Province in the 2008 census was approximately 38,000 with the majority living along the Mekong River (NCCC, 2013). Kratie Province ranked 17th out of 19 provinces in vulnerability to climate change, with flood and drought named by residents as the most severe climate-related hazards (Khim & Phearanich, 2012). The villages involved in this study (Thma Reab, Ou Lung, Dei Doh Kraom and Kbal Kaoh) were selected as representative of villages in the region that are physically vulnerable to flooding, ranging from small communities largely dependent on income from smallholder agriculture to larger communities with more diversified economies including small businesses. The study area includes villages that are located in close proximity to the mainstream of the river, including an inhabited island (Koh Tasuy) within the Mekong River itself.

Much of the rural population has a subsistence economy based largely on agricultural activities including rice and maize production, wild fisheries and livestock rearing (Mekong River Commission, 2010). The farmers of the study area

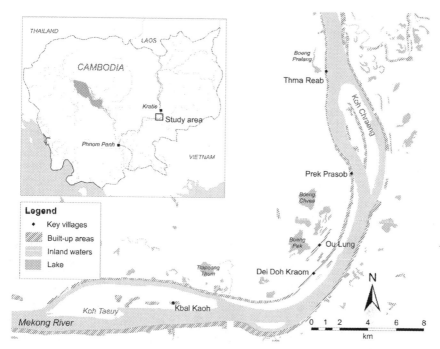

Fig. 6.1. Map of the Study Area Showing Village Locations and Built-up Areas. Prek Prasob is the largest settlement in the district and location of the district government. Numerous other villages are located within the regions marked as built-up areas. *Source*: Authors' own.

generally grow one or two rice crops per year, following the patterns of rainfall and flooding specific to each wet season. The first rice crop is sown at higher elevations less susceptible to flooding at the beginning of the wet season and is rainfed; severe flood events can result in loss or damage to this crop. The second rice crop and maize are planted at lower elevations as floodwaters recede, and may need to be irrigated, particularly if floodwaters are not extensive or recede quickly so that the soil does not hold sufficient moisture. On the island of Koh Tasuy, the tobacco that was formerly grown as a cash crop has been replaced largely by maize (rice is not grown on the island). Numerous other crops are grown in the study area, including various tree crops (cashew, mango and rubber are among the more extensive in the area), sesame and a wide range of vegetables. Fish are a major source of protein caught throughout the year and may be consumed fresh, preserved for later consumption or sold at market.

Research Design

Participatory workshops focussed on environmental hazards, coping mechanisms and adaptation strategies were conducted in the four villages in June 2016. Two group participatory mapping sessions occurred in each village, following

Table 6.1.   Number of Participants and Gender Composition of the
Workshops Held as Part of This Research.

Village	Number of Women (%)	Number of Men (%)	Total Participants
Thma Reab	6 (40)	9 (60)	15
Ou Lung	11 (65)	6 (35)	17
Dei Doh Kraom	12 (67)	6 (33)	18
Kbal Kaoh	7 (41)	10 (59)	17

the approaches detailed by Corbett (2009), NOAA (2009) and Forrester, Cook, Bracken, Cinderby, and Donaldson (2015). Sessions were held in Khmer, facilitated by research assistants, with groups ranging from six to ten community members at a time (comprising groups of women, men and mixed genders). Each workshop ran for 60–90 minutes. Workshop participants were organised by the village or commune leader. The total number of participants across the entire study was 67 (see Table 6.1 for participant breakdown). Each of the workshops was conducted underneath a participant's house (Plate 6.1). This area is commonly used as a resting place and provides an open area that is accessible to others within the social norms of the community.

A semi-structured focus-group technique was conducted to allow workshop participants to direct the conversation, raise issues relevant to them, and for researchers to add follow-up questions (Bernard, 2006; Gero et al., 2011). Heeding Hinkel's (2011) call to design vulnerability assessment methods from the specific case considered, the questions for this study were developed and adjusted based

Plate 6.1.   Depiction of Participatory Mapping Workshop. This photograph was drawn from a mixed-gender workshop in the village of Kbal Kaoh. Translator and facilitator Sengponleur Yuk wears a chequered shirt. Children were also present as onlookers at many workshops, which were held in open areas underneath houses where families and villagers often socialise and eat during the day.

Table 6.2. Question Themes and Example Prompts Used During the Workshops.

Theme	Example Prompts
Introductory and livelihoods	• Where is your village on this image? • Where are [other] important areas on this image? • Where are the agricultural areas, and what is grown there? • Which areas are used for fishing, and how is the catch used?
Environmental change	• Have there been any changes to the environment over the last few years? • What do you think are causing changes to the environment?
Hazards	• Can you describe the flooding in the area around your community? • Which areas are most affected by floods? • Has the extent of flooding changed over time compared with now? • Are there areas that are prone to disease or illness? • How does drought affect your community? • Which areas are affected by droughts? • What are the impacts of floods and droughts?
Vulnerability	• Which households are most affected by floods? • Which households are most affected by droughts? • Which groups of people in the community are most affected by [hazards]?
Coping mechanisms (during hazard events)	• Who/where do villagers stay [with] during the floods? • Where are crops grown during flooding? • Are fish caught during the floods, and where are they caught? • What work or labour is done during the floods? • Does anyone in the village have access to insurance? • Where are valuables moved during floods? • How and where is food stored during floods and drought times?
Adaptation strategies (over longer timescales)	• How has agriculture changed to deal with changes in flooding conditions? • How has agriculture changed to deal with drought and changes in rainfall? • If heat continues to increase and precipitation continues to decline, have you thought about what you will do in the future?

Note: Many of the questions incorporate a spatial element and were discussed with reference to a 1:25,000 satellite image, with participants encouraged to draw responses on the image.

on observations gathered during pilot interviews by members of the research team earlier in 2016, around themes of perceptions, vulnerability and adaptation (see Table 6.2 for question themes). Due to the nature of the focus-group technique, not every workshop had the same order of questions or the same wording of questions so as to enable the direction of each workshop to flow naturally. The timescale (i.e. how far into the past or future the participants delved) was left open, to enable more freedom with regard to social memory (Folke, 2006).

Printed satellite images at 1:25,000 scale (current at the time of study) were used as a tool to discuss and map important areas, livelihoods, flooding extent, flooding patterns, impacts of natural hazards and adaptation strategies. Topographic maps were also prepared at the same scale; however, the workshop participants expressed a clear preference for the satellite images. Following López-Marrero and Tschakert (2011), a transparent plastic sheet was placed over the top of the printed map, on which participants were invited to draw responses to questions. The participants were asked to map out the important locations around their community (e.g. infrastructure, safe places, agricultural areas), areas impacted by hazards (floods, droughts) and how hazards develop over time (e.g. how floodwaters move through the landscape). At the conclusion of each session, notes were compiled and discussions held among the research team to ensure consistency and note any omissions. Participants' map markings were later digitised with the aid of mapping control points (Corbett, 2009).

Data Analysis

The notes taken on workshop participants' responses were grouped by themes and coded with reference to patterns of responses and recurrent concepts and words. Results were organised into tables and represented in map form. The participatory maps from the workshops were scanned and georeferenced; the features drawn on the maps were digitised into vector layers using ArcGIS 10.3 (ESRI, 2014). Once the participatory maps were digitised and the responses coded, the data were critically analysed in relation to the objectives of the study and with consideration given to spatial aspects. Comparative analysis was also undertaken where applicable, including examining the responses between women and men, and between different communities.

RESULTS AND DISCUSSION

This section synthesises results and insights for each of the three major objectives, in turn, concluding some comments on limitations of the study and recommendations for application and further research.

Perceptions of Environmental Changes and Climate-related Hazards

At the outset, it is important to note the unusual weather conditions experienced prior to and during the research. Because the villages in the study regularly experience flooding, which is expected to increase in severity under future scenarios of climatic change in the region (Hoang et al., 2016), the research was initially conceived primarily as a means to understand local communities' resilience and adaptation strategies in the face of flooding. However, the timing of the research coincided with a severe drought that affected much of Cambodia (including the study region), with delayed onset of monsoon rains and diminished seasonal flooding in both 2015 and 2016. As a result, discussions around environmental changes expanded to encompass multiple climate-related hazards, and villagers were more immediately concerned with drought than with flooding. 'Drought' is understood to mean increased daytime temperatures and greatly reduced rainfall during the dry season, often coupled with early cessation of the wet monsoon, and/or delayed onset of the following wet season rains. These conditions lead to water deficit and severe stress on crops grown wholly or partially during the drier months.

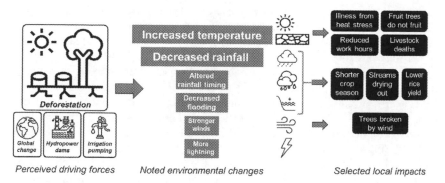

Perceived driving forces   *Noted environmental changes*   *Selected local impacts*

Fig. 6.2. Representation of Workshop Participants' Perceived Environmental Changes, Causes and Impacts. Responses derived from workshop participants' answers to questions on the theme of environmental change. The sizes of the icons for perceived driving forces, and the size of the grey bars for noted environmental changes, are proportional to the frequency with which these elements were mentioned across the eight workshops. Impacts are not scaled (based on the frequency of mention) due to the diversity of impacts mentioned. Note that several impacts are cumulative, resulting from multiple environmental changes.

When asked to nominate any environmental changes that have occurred, participants in almost all workshops mentioned increased temperature and decreased rainfall. Fig. 6.2 provides a graphical representation of perceived changes, causes and selected impacts associated with these environmental changes. Other changes noted by workshop participants included altered timing of rainfall (such as delayed onset of monsoon rains or early cessation), a reduction in the extent of flooded lands and the duration of flooding, stronger and gustier winds, more frequent storms and lightning, and reduced predictability in the direction of prevailing winds and storms. One commune leader also noted that rainfall is now patchier, whereas once large areas received similar rainfall during regular monsoon rains, there is now much more localised variability during individual rainfall events.

When discussing the causes of these environmental changes, the perceived driver universally mentioned was deforestation. Deforestation means not only the loss of natural forests from upland areas but also their replacement with plantations of trees (in the region, the most common tree crops planted are mango, cashew and rubber). Forests were thought to hold water, and their loss consequently reduced the availability of water further down the catchment. Global change and natural fluctuations were also identified as potential drivers by participants in approximately one quarter of the workshops, along with the construction of hydropower dams and pumping for irrigated agriculture at a similar frequency (Fig. 6.2). One participant mentioned that he had heard on the radio that the cause for all the floods was deforestation, raising the potential for this perception to have been more widely disseminated within the community through radio broadcasts. A similar commonly held belief that forested upland regions can prevent or reduce floods has been noted by Tran, Marincioni, and Shaw (2010) in Vietnam; in that case, the view was perpetuated by the Vietnamese government and mass media but was at odds with the much greater likelihood that floods were largely due to variance in rainfall (Tran et al., 2010).

Specific impacts associated with higher temperatures and exacerbated by drought conditions included: people becoming ill from heat stress (a particular concern for children); deaths of chickens and pigs from heat-related distress and illness; reduced fruit borne by trees (mango grown as cash crops were highlighted); a reduction in the time spent in agricultural fields due to high temperatures (during the heat of the day, many farmers and some labourers retreat to shaded areas); and reduced fish stocks (see Fig. 6.2). Changes in rainfall patterns, volume and flooding regimes impacted agricultural productivity, with decreased time available to grow crops (villagers cited only being able to grow one rice crop per wet season rather than two as had once been regularly possible), reduced crop yield and decreased soil fertility. Participants in Dei Doh Kraom mapped areas that were once used for rice cultivation and had been changed to cultivation of sesame and corn, which have lower water requirements. Stronger winds associated with more intense storms led to damage to valuable trees grown as cash crops and to supplement household diets.

Broadly speaking, workshop participants were more concerned with the impacts of drought than they were with floods. Women participants from Thma Reab noted that during times of flood, people can move away, and the floods replenish agricultural land; with drought, by contrast, it is not possible to move away, and everyone is affected in a negative way. Participants from workshops in Dei Doh Kraom, the largest village in the study area with the most diverse economy, were equally concerned with both droughts and severe floods. The time periods over which these changes were noted varied among participants, with estimates ranging from the previous 10–11 years to the previous 5–8 years.

Local Vulnerabilities to Environmental Hazards

Participants in workshops identified a number of physical and socio-economic vulnerabilities to climate-related hazards, some of which were also mapped (an example is shown in Fig. 6.3). The participatory map and the results detailed in the following text together highlight that many people within the communities are exposed to multiple environmental hazards, some of which overlap in space and time.

With regard to flooding, for the most part, dwellings are constructed on the highest elevation land available along the river; however, in some years, even the land around dwellings is inundated. Typhoid and mosquito-borne illnesses including dengue and malaria are associated with floods (Fig. 6.3 depicts perceptions of areas most prone to mosquitoes); diarrhoea was highlighted as a particular concern among the young. Temples are situated on land of higher elevation and are used as refuges by community members during times of very high flood. When the land around the village is inundated, boats are used for transport by those with access.

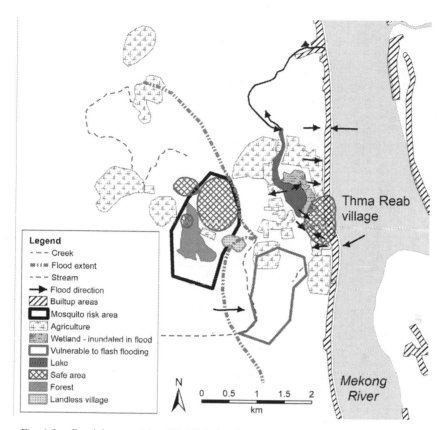

Fig. 6.3. Participatory Map Highlighting Exposure to Multiple Environmental Hazards. The map presents a digitised version of participatory maps from two workshops in the village of Thma Reab. During the flooding season, much of the land near the village (including agricultural land) is inundated, with the maximum flooded extent indicated. Floodwaters generally enter over the course of days to weeks via streams, lakes and wetlands within the backswamp of the Mekong, and only directly enter overland across the natural levee banks in times of very high flood. Flash flooding occurs after very heavy rain as a result of overland flow from upland areas. Safe areas are well known within the community and are generally elevated. Some of the known safe areas are within an area that is thought to be prone to mosquito-borne disease, the threat of which is greatest during the wet season. The area marked as 'forest' is used by many as a place to maintain livestock (cattle, buffalo) during floods and is within the mosquito-prone area. One settlement away from the main village is vulnerable to drought, as they have limited access to water, and is also at risk of inundation during severe floods. Note that not all agricultural fields were drawn on these maps; most of the land shown on this map is cultivated for crops such as rice, corn and sesame, or is planted with cashew, teak, rubber, mango or green pepper.

Roads have been damaged in the past by floods and may be repaired by the private ferry operator (if not severe – without vehicles the demand for the ferry service across the Mekong drops), government (if severe), or in the case of Kbal Kaoh, by the islanders themselves. Culverts, levees, bridges and wells may also be damaged during flood events. Much of the island of Koh Tasuy is inundated every year from August to October, including the villages. Because of the predictability of this flooding, residents are ready their boats by July and prepare to catch fish directly from their houses during the floods.

The variable price of crops at the market (in relation to climate shocks) was raised by participants in each workshop and across all the communities. Participants in Dei Doh Kraom and Kbal Kaoh highlighted the risks of over-supply in good years reducing prices for growers. The volatility of the market and crop failure in poor years (flood and drought) was associated with microfinance borrowing, documented in Thma Reab, Dei Doh Kraom and Kbal Kaoh. Perhaps half of the residents of one village use microfinance for seed or livestock purchases, and in some villages, microfinance lenders come to the village directly to offer money to borrow.

Coping Mechanisms and Adaptation Strategies in the Face of Climate Hazards

There were a number of coping mechanisms and adaptation strategies used in the four study villages in relation to the major hazards of drought and floods and changes to rainfall distribution, highlighting a variety of methods and alternative sources of livelihoods and sustenance used to establish resilience to short-term and slow-onset climate shocks and stressors (Table 6.3 and Plate 6.2). Fishing was universally mentioned as a means of providing nutrition and some income during periods of flood when little other fresh food is available (fish are also preserved throughout the year). Storage of food and water within homes and movement of people (particularly the young and elderly) and livestock (chiefly buffalo and cows) to safe, dry areas are well-established seasonal rhythms within the communities.

Coping and adaptation strategies vary among and within villages. For example, on the mainland villages, not all families have access to pumps to draw water from the Mekong, whereas on the island of Koh Tasuy (village of Kbal Kaoh), almost all families have access to pumps. Kbal Kaoh residents tended to place less emphasis on moving away during flood or moving crops; this is likely due to their insular nature with greater restrictions on movement especially during times of high flood. Residents on the island had even constructed a communal area of higher ground for livestock through earthworks and planting bamboo to reduce erosion. The majority of households in Kbal Kaoh have boats, and work starts in July to prepare for the coming floods (Plate 6.2).

Adaptation strategies were discussed in greater depth during workshops with predominantly women participants, although it was often mentioned that people beyond just women use these strategies. Women spoke more often than men about pumping water and also using boats in times of flood. These tasks often fall more strongly to women within the study area – men with livestock will leave

Table 6.3. Coping Mechanisms and Adaptation Strategies Mentioned in Workshops in the Four Villages of the Research.

Strategy	Hazard	Time Frame	Thma Reab Workshops ♀	Thma Reab Workshops ♂	Om Lung Workshops ♀	Om Lung Workshops ♂	Dei Doh Kraom Workshops ♀	Dei Doh Kraom Workshops ♂	Kbal Kaoh Workshops ♀♂	Kbal Kaoh Workshops ♀♂	Kbal Kaoh Workshops ♀♂
Fishing (for consumption and sale)	(flood)	Seasonal									
Store food and water	(flood)	Seasonal									
Move to safe areas (temple, school or upland)	(flood)	Seasonal									
Use boats for transport	(flood)	Seasonal									
Plant crops at higher elevation	(flood)	Seasonal									
Stay with friends or family	(flood)	Seasonal									
Microfinance borrowing	(flood/drought)	Seasonal to medium term									
Wage work outside village	(flood/drought)	Seasonal to long term									
Pump water (domestic and agricultural use)	(drought)	Seasonal to long term									
Dig ponds as water reservoirs over dry season	(drought)	Long term									
Change/new crops (to better suit conditions)	(flood/drought)	Long term									

Note: ♀ (women) and ♂ (men) refer to the dominant gender at each workshop. Workshops in Kbal Kaoh were mixed gender. The icons refer to flood (house on stilts) and drought (cracked fields). Grey shading indicates that this strategy was mentioned by participants in each respective workshop. Note that the lack of shading does not imply that nobody in these villages uses these strategies, just that it was not mentioned during workshops.

Plate 6.2. Adaptation Mechanisms Implemented by Communities. The photos highlight different adaptation measures implemented by communities in the study area. (A) The former tobacco drying shed is surrounded by maize on Kbal Kaoh, juxtaposing the older and newer dominant crops grown by villagers (both are grown for cash). (B) A water pump aside the Mekong provides water to a crop in Kbal Kaoh. (C) A safe, forested area near the village of Thma Reab, used as a refuge during times of flood. (D) Residents of this household on Koh Tasuy have prepared their boat in June in preparation for seasonal flooding.

for higher ground while women use boats to transport fodder to livestock, food to menfolk and fish catches to market. Women also discussed changes in crops; for example, in the most socio-economically disadvantaged village of Ou Lung, women noted that one benefit of drier conditions is that lotus root is growing better in the lakes with shallower water depth; the roots are collected by women and sold to a middleman as a new crop.

The photos highlight different adaptation measures implemented by communities in the study area. (A) The former tobacco drying shed is surrounded by maize on Kbal Kaoh, juxtaposing the older and newer dominant crops grown by villagers (both are grown for cash). (B) A water pump aside the Mekong provides water to a crop in Kbal Kaoh. (C) A safe, forested area near the village of Thma Reab, used as a refuge during times of flood. (D) Residents of this household on Koh Tasuy have prepared their boat in June in preparation for seasonal flooding.

There was broad recognition that changing environmental conditions may mean changes to traditional or current agricultural practices, but many respondents expressed uncertainty as to what to do as they follow practices traditional to the area, and know that agriculture involves taking risks. In Thma Reab, agricultural extension agents have introduced rainfed rice varieties with shorter growing seasons. An NGO provided seeds of alternative crops that were thought to be more suitable for changed climatic conditions; however, these trials were not sustained, and the seed supply was exhausted. When asked if the increase in temperature and decrease in rainfall were to continue into the future, there was marked uncertainty as to what people would do in response, with most initial responses along the lines of 'I don't know' or 'do nothing'. Some workshop participants mentioned digging small reservoirs and using these as a source of water for irrigation, thereby extending the short-term strategy of pumping water into a longer term strategy of irrigation infrastructure, digging wells, farming only around the lake where there is water (which may not be enough land for all), and moving further away for permanent wage work. In this latter case, a short-term strategy used in times of flood may change to a longer term strategy to adapt to repeated drought and decreased rainfall.

Some Comments on Limitations of the Research

While this study produced important findings in the application of PGIS for research in climate change adaptation and environmental hazards, there are some important limitations. The participants included in the study were selected by the village or commune chief, due to the logistical constraints on organising workshops within short time periods; the research team is therefore dependent on the local leader to organise a group of participants who are representative of the community. The data collected in the field were heavily reliant on translation, often in real-time situations, which can introduce a source of bias through the interpretation process, whereby nuanced discussions and dissent may not be completely captured (Scott, Miller, & Lloyd, 2006). Having a visual cue such as the maps aided in the translation process and in cross-cultural understanding. Allied research conducted in the same four villages (Henningsen, Pauli, & Chhom, 2020, Chapter 7, Volume 22) has echoed similar sentiments and findings to those noted here, which suggests that the overall picture that has emerged is robust and representative of local conditions.

CONCLUDING REMARKS

This study demonstrates how combining a community-based focus group with participatory mapping can provide valuable insights into the local knowledge of communities facing climate change and other environmental hazards. The participatory approach also provides an avenue to reinforce the ongoing transfer of ecological knowledge within the communities and between generations. For example, most workshops had young children around, who were listening to the stories and watching elders map and discuss impacts, adaptations and past and current agricultural practices. The perceived changes in increased temperature and decreased rainfall were keenly felt by participants across all workshops, likely exacerbated by the drought conditions prevailing during the fieldwork.

Communities had complex adaptive strategies to deal with regular floods (large, damaging floods occur perhaps once every 5 years, but the seasonal flood-pulse of the Mekong occurs annually) and had started to adopt changes that may help adjust to the impact of reduced rainfall and increased temperature. The adaptive strategies that are used by communities were wide-ranging and represented all five facets of adaptation practice categorised by Agrawal and Perrin (2008) across mobility, storage, diversification, communal pooling and market exchange. The diverse range of strategies used in the Cambodian villages studied was also reflected in villages in Fiji subject to similar changes in climatic conditions (Neef et al., 2018). Uncertainty of what the future holds is of major concern, and the causes of environmental change were largely attributed to processes over which local people hold very little influence. The resilience and entrepreneurship of individuals and communities was demonstrated with many examples, and this is perhaps nowhere more evident than on the island of Koh Tasuy, where isolation from outside sources of assistance has driven residents to undertaken their own earthworks, establish household-level water and energy supply, and remain in place during times of flood. From a policy perspective, aiding local communities to establish reliable and equitable sources of clean water for domestic consumption and agricultural irrigation would aid in reducing vulnerability to numerous climate-related hazards.

ACKNOWLEDGEMENTS

The authors wish to thank the communities of Thma Reab, Ou Lung, Dei Doh Kraom and Kbal Kaoh for participating in this research and hosting the first author. The research would not have been possible without three research assistants and translators from the Royal University of Phnom Penh: Ms Hak Sochanny, Mr Yuk Sengponleur and Mr Sa Kimleng, together with the support of Mr Touch Siphat and the Cambodian Ministry of Rural Development. The research was made possible through funding and support provided by the Asia-Pacific Network for Global Change Research (CAF2015-RR10-NMY-Neef, 'Climate Change Adaptation in Post-Disaster Recovery Processes: Flood-Affected Communities in Cambodia and Fiji') and the University of Western Australia (Research Collaboration Award RA/1/1200/755, 'Risk, resilience and recovery: A participatory approach to integrating local and scientific knowledge for disaster preparedness of communities in flood-prone catchments in Fiji'). Icons used in Fig. 6.2 and Table 6.3 made by surang [deforestation, hydropower], smashicons [global change], turkkub [pumping, drought, lightning], iconixar [reduced flooding], Freepik [wind, decreased rainfall, flooding] and Those Icons [rainfall]; available via www.flaticon.com.

REFERENCES

Agrawal, A., & Perrin, N. (2008). *Climate adaptation, local institutions, and rural livelihoods.* Working Paper No. W081-6. International Forestry Resources and Institutions Program, University of Michigan. Retrieved from http://www.umich.edu/~ifri/Publications/W0816%20Arun%20 Agrawal%20and%20Nicolas%20Perrin.pdf

Alessa, L., Kliskey, A., Gamble, J., Fidel, M., Beaujean, G., & Gosz, J. (2016). The role of Indigenous science and local knowledge in integrated observing systems: Moving toward adaptive capacity indices and early warning systems. *Sustainability Science, 11*(1), 91–102. doi:10.1007/s11625-015-0295-7

Arias, M. E., Cochrane, T. A., Piman, T., Kummu, M., Caruso, B. S., & Killeen, T. J. (2012). Quantifying changes in flooding and habitats in the Tonle Sap Lake (Cambodia) caused by water infrastructure development and climate change in the Mekong Basin. *Journal of Environmental Management, 112*, 53–66. doi:10.1016/j.jenvman.2012.07.003

Bernard, H. R. (2006). *Research methods in anthropology: Qualitative and quantitative approaches.* Lanham, MD: AltaMira Press.

Besant, D. (2016, March). Cambodia faces severe and prolonged drought. *Southeast Asia Globe.* Retrieved from https://southeastasiaglobe.com/cambodia-drought-water-scarcity-mekong-river/

Birkholz, S., Muro, M., Jeffrey, P., & Smith, H. M. (2014). Rethinking the relationship between flood risk perception and flood management. *Science of the Total Environment, 478*, 12–20. doi:10.1016/j.scitotenv.2014.01.061

Bonatti, M., Sieber, S., Schlindwein, S. L., Lana, M. A., de Vasconcelos, A. C. F., Gentile, E., … Malheiros, T. F. (2016). Climate vulnerability and contrasting climate perceptions as an element for the development of community adaptation strategies: Case studies in Southern Brazil. *Land Use Policy, 58*, 114–122. doi:10.1016/j.landusepol.2016.06.033

Brown, G., & Kyttä, M. (2014). Key issues and research priorities for public participation GIS (PPGIS): A synthesis based on empirical research. *Applied Geography, 46*, 122–136. doi:10.1016/j.apgeog.2013.11.004

Burrel, B. C., Davar, K., & Hughes, R. (2007). A review of flood management considering the impacts of climate change. *Water International, 32*(3), 342–359. doi:10.1080/02508060708692215

Butler, J. R. A., Wise, R. M., Skewes, T. D., Bohensky, E. L., Peterson, N., Suadnya, W., … Rochester, W. (2015). Integrating top-down and bottom-up adaptation planning to build adaptive capacity: A structured learning approach. *Coastal Management, 43*(4), 346–364. doi:10.1080/08920753.2015.1046802

Corbett, J. (2009). *Good practices in participatory mapping: A review prepared for the International Fund for Agricultural Development (IFAD).* Rome: International Fund for Agricultural Development (IFAD). Retrieved from https://www.ifad.org/documents/38714170/39144386/PM_web.pdf/7c1eda69-8205-4c31-8912-3c25d6f90055

CRED & UNISDR. (2015). *The human cost of weather related disasters 1995–2015.* Brussels: Centre for Research on the Epidemiology of Disasters (CRED) and The United Nations Office for Disaster Risk Reduction (UNISDR).

Cullen, A. (2015). Making sense of claims across institutional divides: Critical PGIS and mapping customary land in Timor-Leste. *Australian Geographer, 46*(4), 473–490. doi:10.1080/00049182.2015.1080344

Dedicatoria, R. M. M., & Diomampo, C. B. (2019). Status of climate change adaptation in Southeast Asia region. In M. Alam, J. Lee, & P. Sawhney (Eds.), *Status of climate change adaptation in Asia and the Pacific* (pp. 153–182). Cham: Springer.

Delica-Willison, Z., & Willison, R. (2004). Vulnerability reduction: A task for the vulnerable people themselves. In G. Bankoff, G. Frerks, & D. Hilhorst (Eds.), *Mapping vulnerability: Disasters, development and people* (pp. 145–158). London: Earthscan.

Doch, S., Diepart, J.-C., & Heng, C. (2015). A multi-scale flood vulnerability assessment of agricultural production in the context of environmental change: The case of the Sangkae River watershed, Battambang province. In J.-C. Diepart (Ed.), *Learning for resilience: Insights from Cambodia's rural communities* (pp. 19–49). Phnom Penh: The Learning Institute.

Dunn, C. E. (2007). Participatory GIS – A people's GIS? *Progress in Human Geography, 31*(5), 616–637. doi:10.1177/0309132507081493

Eastham, J., Mpelasoka, F., Mainuddin, M., Ticehurst, C., Dyce, P., Hodgson, G., … Kirby, M. (2008). *Mekong River Basin water resources assessment: Impacts of climate change.* Canberra: CSIRO Water for a Healthy Country National Research Flagship. Retrieved from http://hdl.handle.net/102.100.100/120292?index=1

Esnard, A.-M. (1998). Cities, GIS, and ethics. *Journal of Urban Technology, 5*(3), 33–45. doi:10.1080/10630739883822

ESRI. (2014). *ArcGIS 10.3.* Redlands: Environmental Systems Research Institute (ESRI).

Fazey, I., Kesby, M., Evely, A., Latham, I., Wagatora, D., Hagasua, J.-E., … Christie, M. (2010). A three-tiered approach to participatory vulnerability assessment in the Solomon Islands. *Global Environmental Change, 20*(4), 713–728. doi: 10.1016/j.gloenvcha.2010.04.011

Few, R., & Tran, P. G. (2010). Climatic hazards, health risk and response in Vietnam: Case studies on social dimensions of vulnerability. *Global Environmental Change*, *20*(3), 529–538. doi:10.1016/j.gloenvcha.2010.02.004

Folke, C. (2006). Resilience: The emergence of a perspective for social-ecological systems analyses. *Global Environmental Change*, *16*(3), 253–267. doi:10.1016/j.gloenvcha.2006.04.002

Folke, C., Hahn, T., Olsson, P., & Norberg, J. (2005). Adaptive governance of social-ecological systems. *Annual Review of Environment and Resources*, *30*, 441–473. doi:10.1146/annurev.energy.30.050504.144511

Ford, J. D., Cameron, L., Rubis, J., Maillet, M., Nakashima, D., Willox, A. C., & Pearce, T. (2016). Including indigenous knowledge and experience in IPCC assessment reports. *Nature Climate Change*, *6*(4), 349–353. doi:10.1038/nclimate2954

Forrester, J., Cook, B., Bracken, L., Cinderby, S., & Donaldson, A. (2015). Combining participatory mapping with Q-methodology to map stakeholder perceptions of complex environmental problems. *Applied Geography*, *56*, 199–208. doi:10.1016/j.apgeog.2014.11.019

Ge, F., Zhu, S., Peng, T., Zhao, Y., Sielmann, F., Fraedrich, K., ... Ji, L. (2019). Risks of precipitation extremes over Southeast Asia: Does 1.5 °C or 2 °C global warming make a difference? *Environmental Research Letters*, *14*(4), 044015. doi:10.1088/1748-9326/aaff7e

Gero, A., Méheux, K., & Dominey-Howes, D. (2011). Integrating community based disaster risk reduction and climate change adaptation: Examples from the Pacific. *Natural Hazards and Earth System Sciences*, *11*(1), 101–113. doi:10.5194/nhess-11-101-2011

Grumbine, R. E., & Xu, J. (2011). Mekong hydropower development. *Science*, *332*(6026), 178–179. doi:10.1126/science.1200990

Halsnæs, K., Larsen, M. A. D., & Kaspersen, P. S. (2018). Climate change risks for severe storms in developing countries in the context of poverty and inequality in Cambodia. *Natural Hazards*, *94*(1), 261–278. doi: 10.1007/s11069-018-3387-8

Henningsen, S., Pauli, N., & Chhom, C. (2020). Seasonal livelihoods and adaptation strategies for an uncertain environmental future: Results from participatory research in Kratie, Cambodia. In A. Neef & N. Pauli (Eds.), *Climate-induced disasters in the Asia-Pacific region: Response, recovery, adaptation* (pp. 135–165). Bingley: Emerald Publishing.

Hinkel, J. (2011). "Indicators of vulnerability and adaptive capacity": Towards a clarification of the science–policy interface. *Global Environmental Change*, *21*(1), 198–208. doi:10.1016/j.gloenvcha.2010.08.002

Hoang, L. P., Lauri, H., Kummu, M., Koponen, J., van Vliet, M. T. H., Supit, I., ... Ludwig, F. (2016). Mekong River flow and hydrological extremes under climate change. *Hydrology and Earth System Science*, *20*, 3027–3041. doi:10.5194/hess-20-3027-2016

IPCC. (2014a). *Climate change 2014: Impacts, adaptation, and vulnerability. Part A: Global and sectoral aspects. Contribution of working group II to the fifth assessment report of the Intergovernmental Panel on Climate Change*. Geneva: Intergovernmental Panel on Climate Change.

IPCC. (2014b). *Climate change 2014: Synthesis report. Contribution of working groups I, II and III to the fifth assessment report of the Intergovernmental Panel on Climate Change*. Geneva: Intergovernmental Panel on Climate Change.

Johnston, R. M., & Kummu, M. (2012). Water resource models in the Mekong Basin: A review. *Water Resources Management*, *26*, 429–455. doi:10.1007/s11269-011-9925-8

Keskinen, M., Chinvanno, S., Kummu, M., Nuorteva, P., Snidvongs, A., Varis, O., & Västilä, K. (2010). Climate change and water resources in the Lower Mekong River Basin: Putting adaptation into the context. *Journal of Water and Climate Change*, *1*(2), 103–117. doi:10.2166/wcc.2010.009

Khim, L., & Phearanich, H. (2012). Climate resilience in rural Cambodia: Adaptation mainstreaming, water resource management and agricultural practice. *Asian Journal of Environment and Disaster Management*, *4*(4), 447–468. doi:10.3850/S1793924012100067

King, D., & MacGregor, C. (2000). Using social indicators to measure community vulnerability to natural hazards. *Australian Journal of Emergency Management*, *15*(3), 52–57.

Kingston, D. G., Thompson, J. R., & Kite, G. (2011). Uncertainty in climate change projections of discharge for the Mekong River Basin. *Hydrology and Earth System Sciences*, *15*(5), 1459–1471. doi:10.5194/hess-15-1459-2011

Kummu, M., & Sarkkula, J. (2008). Impact of the Mekong River flow alteration on the Tonle Sap flood pulse. *Ambio*, *37*(3), 185–192. Retrieved from www.jstor.org/stable/25547881

Liu, Y. B., Gebremeskel, S., De Smedt, F., Hoffmann, L., & Pfister, L. (2003). A diffusive transport approach for flow routing in GIS-based flood modeling. *Journal of Hydrology*, *283*(1), 91–106. doi:10.1016/S0022-1694(03)00242-7

López-Marrero, T., & Tschakert, P. (2011). From theory to practice: Building more resilient communities in flood-prone areas. *Environment and Urbanization*, *23*(1), 229–249. doi:10.1177/0956247810396055

Lu, X. X., Li, S., Kummu, M., Padawangi, R., & Wang, J. J. (2014). Observed changes in the water flow at Chiang Saen in the Lower Mekong: Impacts of Chinese dams? *Quaternary International*, *336*, 145–157. doi:10.1016/j.quaint.2014.02.006

Makondo, C. C., & Thomas, D. S. G. (2018). Climate change adaptation: Linking indigenous knowledge with western science for effective adaptation. *Environmental Science & Policy*, *88*, 83–91. https://doi.org/10.1016/j.envsci.2018.06.014

McCall, M. K. (2003). Seeking good governance in participatory-GIS: A review of processes and governance dimensions in applying GIS to participatory spatial planning. *Habitat International*, *27*(4), 549–573. doi:10.1016/S0197-3975(03)00005-5

McLeod, E., Margles weis, S. W., Wongbusarakum, S., Gombos, M., Dazé, A., Otzelberger, A., ... Wiggins, M. (2015). Community-based climate vulnerability and adaptation tools: A review of tools and their applications. *Coastal Management*, *43*(4), 439–458. doi:10.1080/08920753.2015.1046809

Mekong River Commission. (2010). *State of the basin report 2010*. Vientiane, Lao PDR: Mekong River Commission.

Mekong River Commission. (2019). *State of the basin report 2018*. Vientiane, Lao PDR: Mekong River Commission.

Mercer, J. (2010). Disaster risk reduction or climate change adaptation: Are we reinventing the wheel? *Journal of International Development*, *22*(2), 247–264. doi:10.1002/jid.1677

Mercer, J., Dominey-Howes, D., Kelman, I., & Lloyd, K. (2007). The potential for combining indigenous and western knowledge in reducing vulnerability to environmental hazards in small island developing states. *Environmental Hazards*, *7*(4), 245–256. doi:10.1016/j.envhaz.2006.11.001

NCCC. (2013). *Cambodia Climate Change Strategic Plan 2014-2023*. National Climate Change Committee. Phnom Penh: Royal Government of Cambodia.

Neef, A., Benge, L., Boruff, B., Pauli, N., Weber, E., & Varea, R. (2018). Climate adaptation strategies in Fiji: The role of social norms and cultural values. *World Development*, *107*, 125–137. doi:10/1016/j.worlddev.2018.02.029

Nkoana, M. E., Verbruggen, A., & Hugé, J. (2018). Climate change adaptation tools at the community level: An integrated literature review. *Sustainability*, *10*(3), 1–21. doi:10.3390/su10030796

NOAA. (2009). *Stakeholder engagement strategies for participatory mapping*. Charleston: National Oceanic and Atmospheric Administration.

Peng, S., Huang, J., Sheehy, J. E., Laza, R. C., Visperas, R. M., Zhong, X., ... Cassman, K. G. (2004). Rice yields decline with higher night temperature from global warming. *Proceedings of the National Academy of Sciences of the United States of America*, *101*(27), 9971–9975. doi:10.1073/pnas.0403720101

Piman, T., Lennaerts, T., & Southalack, P. (2013). Assessment of hydrological changes in the Lower Mekong Basin from basin-wide development scenarios. *Hydrological Processes*, *27*, 2115–2125. doi:10.1002/hyp.9764

Pokhrel, Y., Burbano, M., Roush, J., Kang, H., Sridhar, V., & Hyndman, W. D. (2018). A review of the integrated effects of changing climate, land use, and dams on Mekong River hydrology. *Water*, *10*(3), 266. doi:10.3390/w10030266

Polsky, C., Neff, R., & Yarnal, B. (2007). Building comparable global change vulnerability assessments: The vulnerability scoping diagram. *Global Environmental Change*, *17*(3), 472–485. doi:10.1016/j.gloenvcha.2007.01.005

Radil, S. M., & Jiao, J. (2016). Public participatory GIS and the geography of inclusion. *The Professional Geographer*, *68*(2), 202–210. doi:10.1080/00330124.2015.1054750

Räsänen, T. A., Koponen, J., Lauri, H., & Kummu, M. (2012). Downstream hydrological impacts of hydropower development in the Upper Mekong Basin. *Water Resources Management*, *26*(12), 3495–3513. doi:10.1007/s11269-012-0087-0

Raymond, C. M., Fazey, I., Reed, M. S., Stringer, L. C., Robinson, G. M., & Evely, A. C. (2010). Integrating local and scientific knowledge for environmental management. *Journal of Environmental Management*, *91*(8), 1766–1777. doi:10.1016/j.jenvman.2010.03.023

Rinner, C., Keßler, C., & Andrulis, S. (2008). The use of Web 2.0 concepts to support deliberation in spatial decision-making. *Computers, Environment and Urban Systems, 32*(5), 386–395. doi:10.1016/j.compenvurbsys.2008.08.004

Schipper, E. F., Ayers, J., Reid, H., Huq, S., & Rahman, A. (Eds.). (2014). *Community-based adaptation to climate change*. London: Routledge.

Scott, S., Miller, F., & Lloyd, K. (2006). Doing fieldwork in development geography: Research culture and research spaces in Vietnam. *Geographical Research, 44*(1), 28–40. doi:10.1111/j.1745-5871.2006.00358.x

Seneviratne, S., Nicholls, N., Easterling, D., Goodess, C., Kanae, S., Kossin, J., ... Zhang, X. (2012). Changes in climate extremes and their impacts on the natural physical environment. In C. B. Field, V. Barros, T. F. Stocker, D. Qin, D. J. Dokken, K. L. Ebi, ... P. M. Midgley (Eds.), *Managing the risks of extreme events and disasters to advance climate change adaptation. A special report of working groups I and II of the Intergovernmental Panel on Climate Change (IPCC)* (pp. 109–230). Cambridge: Cambridge University Press.

Smit, B., & Wandel, J. (2006). Adaptation, adaptive capacity and vulnerability. *Global Environmental Change, 16*(3), 282–292. doi:10.1016/j.gloenvcha.2006.03.008

Sok, S., & Yu, X. (2015). Adaptation, resilience and sustainable livelihoods in the communities of the Lower Mekong Basin, Cambodia. *International Journal of Water Resources Development, 31*(4), 575–588. doi:10.1080/07900627.2015.1012659

Sovacool, B. K., Linnér, B.-O., & Klein, R. J. T. (2017). Climate change adaptation and the Least Developed Countries Fund (LDCF): Qualitative insights from policy implementation in the Asia-Pacific. *Climatic Change, 140*(2), 209–226. doi:10.1007/s10584-016-1839-2

Tangang, F., Supari, S., Chung, J., Cruz, F., Salimun, E., Ngai, S., ... Hein-Griggs, D. (2018). Future changes in annual precipitation extremes over Southeast Asia under global warming of 2°C. *APN Science Bulletin, 8*(1). Advance online publication. doi:10.30852/sb.2018.436

Townsend, P. A., & Walsh, S. J. (1998). Modeling floodplain inundation using an integrated GIS with radar and optical remote sensing. *Geomorphology, 21*(3), 295–312. doi:10.1016/S0169-555X(97)00069-X

Tran, P., Marincioni, F., & Shaw, R. (2010). Catastrophic flood and forest cover change in the Huong river basin, central Viet Nam: A gap between common perceptions and facts. *Journal of Environmental Management, 91*(11), 2186–2200. doi:10.1016/j.jenvman.2010.05.020

van Aalst, M. K., Cannon, T., & Burton, I. (2008). Community level adaptation to climate change: The potential role of participatory community risk assessment. *Global Environmental Change, 18*(1), 165–179. doi:10.1016/j.gloenvcha.2007.06.002

Van Der Knijff, J. M., Younis, J., & De Roo, A. P. J. (2010). LISFLOOD: A GIS-based distributed model for river basin scale water balance and flood simulation. *International Journal of Geographical Information Science, 24*(2), 189–212. doi:10.1080/13658810802549154

Västilä, K., Kummu, M., Sangmanee, C., & Chinvanno, S. (2010). Modelling climate change impacts on the flood pulse in the Lower Mekong floodplains. *Journal of Water and Climate Change, 1*(1), 67–86. doi:10.2166/wcc.2010.008

Yamamauchi, K. (2014). Climate change impacts on agriculture and irrigation in the Lower Mekong Basin. *Paddy and Water Environment, 12*(S2), 227–240. doi:10.1007/s10333-013-0388-9

Yusuf, A. A., & Francisco, H. (2009). *Climate change vulnerability mapping for Southeast Asia* (EEPSEA Special and Technical Paper tp200901s1). Philippines: Economy and Environment Program for Southeast Asia. Retrieved from https://ideas.repec.org/p/eep/tpaper/tp200901s1.html

CHAPTER 7

SEASONAL LIVELIHOODS AND ADAPTATION STRATEGIES FOR AN UNCERTAIN ENVIRONMENTAL FUTURE: RESULTS FROM PARTICIPATORY RESEARCH IN KRATIE PROVINCE, CAMBODIA

Savuti Henningsen, Natasha Pauli and Chanchhaya Chhom

ABSTRACT

The effects of environmental change are becoming more noticeable in the Lower Mekong Basin, where there is growing pressure on the agriculture-based livelihoods of communities living along the mainstream of the Mekong River. This chapter presents an investigation of temporal seasonal variability in four communities of Kratie Province, Cambodia, including identification of locally developed strategies to adapt to temporal changes in weather patterns. A mixed-methods approach was adopted, combining historical hydrometeorological data with participatory seasonal calendars and daily routine diaries. Seasonal calendars were compiled from nine workshops across four villages in Kratie Province, and daily diaries were collected from seven individuals across three villages. The results indicate that patterns in rainfall, flooding and drought have become more variable due to the impacts of environmental change; a phenomenon that will likely continue into the future. Without effective, locally appropriate adaptation measures, changing weather patterns will likely continue to have adverse impacts on communities in the region due to their reliance on reliable seasonal rainfall and

Climate-Induced Disasters in the Asia-Pacific Region: Response, Recovery, Adaptation
Community, Environment and Disaster Risk Management, Volume 22, 135–165
Copyright © 2021 by Emerald Publishing Limited
ISSN: 2040-7262/doi:10.1108/S2040-726220200000022006

flooding events for crop cultivation. Households and communities in the study region have already developed a number of approaches to mitigate the adverse impacts of environmental change. This research also reiterated the importance of incorporating both local knowledge and scientific data to gain the most accurate understanding of the impacts of environmental change in a given region.

Keywords: Mekong River; Cambodia; seasonal variability; local knowledge; gender; climate change adaptation

INTRODUCTION

Over the last decade, the impacts of environmental change[1] on livelihoods in developing countries have become more pronounced (Piya, Maharjan, & Joshi, 2019). In particular, the Lower Mekong Basin (LMB) region is expected to be significantly impacted by environmental change, with climate change models projecting increases in seasonality, severe flooding and drought events (Doch, Diepart, & Heng, 2015; Hoang et al., 2016; Kingston, Thompson, & Kite, 2011). While the aggregated effects of climate change have often been emphasised (such as an increase in annual average temperature, or decline in average annual rainfall), the impacts of environmental change on temporal variability in weather events are important, particularly in communities that have close relationships between seasonal patterns and livelihoods (Mainuddin, Kirby, & Hoanh, 2013; Poulton, Dalgliesh, Vang, & Roth, 2016). The research presented in this chapter seeks to understand these finer-scale variations in seasonal weather patterns, both within and between years, reflecting on 'typical' conditions as well as changes that may be outside the scope of 'normal' variability.

The ways in which communities have adapted historically and continue to adjust to environmental change are of significant importance to current research, with a strong emphasis on acknowledging and prioritising local knowledge and experience (Mainuddin et al., 2013). In recent years, mixed-method approaches incorporating both quantitative and qualitative means of gathering data have been employed to aid in understanding the dimensions of environmental change in areas that may be 'data-poor' but are also 'knowledge-rich' (Bernard, 2006). These methods often incorporate a gendered aspect to ensure that the data are representative of a wide range of experiences (Carr & Thompson, 2014). This investigation aims to explore the temporal variability in weather-related natural hazards and the subsequent adaptation strategies pursued by local communities in the LMB, with an emphasis on understanding strategies across a spectrum of village, livelihoods and individuals.

Environmental Change and Temporal Variation

Variations in the weather resulting from climate change have become an increasingly important focal point globally. This variability can be partitioned into temporal and spatial variation from established 'average' or typical conditions.

Temporal variation can be further divided into short- and long-term variation, or in other words, seasonal and inter-annual variation (Chen, Hu, & Yu, 2005). The temporal aspects of environmental change will likely be just as important as the overall magnitude of change (Sowjanya, Reddy, & Shashi, 2018). Understanding both the seasonal and inter-annual variation resulting from environmental change is a crucial aspect in quantifying the current and future impacts of change and planning for its management (Nam, Hong, & Choi, 2015). For instance, a recent analysis of rainfall and drought records in Southeast Asia stretching back over 350 years indicated a high degree of variability and uncertainty in the effects of the El Niño Southern Oscillation, with the authors recommending that future planning for climate change adaptation must embrace this uncertainty and complexity, and consider how societies have coped with, and persevered through, extreme conditions in the past (Räsänen, Lindgren, Guillaume, Buckley, & Kummu, 2016). Effective planning and management will likely result in the development of locally appropriate adaptation strategies, thus limiting the impacts felt by communities (Holzkämper, Calanca, & Fuhrer, 2011).

Adaptation and Environmental Change

Among many varied definitions, adaptation can be defined as the adjustment of natural or human systems to a new or changing environment and has come to the forefront of discussions surrounding the environmental change in recent years (Evers & Pathirana, 2018). Human adaptation to climate change encompasses the ability to change and adapt behaviours to meet current conditions, while simultaneously developing strategies to mitigate the impacts of expected environmental change in the foreseeable future (Evers & Pathirana, 2018). The concept of adaptation has become a focal point in global conversations, particularly with respect to the predicted impacts of climate change in developing countries, particularly within the agricultural sector (Sovacool, Amp, Agostino, Meenawat, & Rawlani, 2012).

The process of adaptation to environmental change can occur on different scales ranging from individual, regional, sectoral, national and global settings (Bryan, Deressa, Gbetibouo, & Ringler, 2009). Adaptive responses are also said to include autonomous responses and conscious adaptation (Dang, Li, Nuberg, & Bruwer, 2014). Autonomous responses can include irrigation, crop diversification or altering the agricultural calendar, while conscious adaptations are generally understood as government intervention strategies and public policies (Dang et al., 2014). Adaptive responses can also be categorised into short-term and long-term responses, and have been shown to be impacted by socio-economic factors and resource availability (Below et al., 2012).

To understand and record the impacts of environmental change and subsequent adaptation strategies developed by individuals and communities, it has become increasingly important to include components of scientific and local knowledge (Mercer, 2010). There are often areas of synergy and overlap between different forms of knowledge, as well as many ways in which different forms of knowledge may complement and support each other (Hiwasaki, Luna, Syamsidik, & Shaw 2014; Raymond et al., 2010). Research has indicated that when local communities are actively involved in research, the information gathered leads to a deeper understanding of the situation, particularly with respect to community adaptation (Fazey et al., 2010). Community involvement also has the potential to be beneficial in terms of future management, as the two-way relationships built during the process pave the way for future endeavours (Raymond et al., 2010).

The Mekong River and Cambodia

The Mekong River forms the largest river basin in Southeast Asia and spans six countries (Lauri et al., 2012). The resources provided by the Mekong are less understood and developed in comparison to other large river basins around the world (Evers & Pathirana, 2018). The LMB, which incorporates parts of Myanmar, Laos, Thailand, Cambodia and Vietnam, is said to be the most productive and ecologically diverse river basin in the world; supporting an estimated 60 million people (Mainuddin et al., 2013). By 2060, the total population in the LMB is predicted to reach 83 million (Evers & Pathirana, 2018).

The majority of the residents of the LMB are strongly dependent on the resources provided by the Mekong to sustain their livelihoods, as food security is closely tied to the river through agriculture, fisheries and hydropower (Sok & Yu, 2015). Over time, residents have adapted their livelihoods, particularly their agricultural systems, to the ebb and flow of the Mekong's seasonal flood regime (Sok & Yu, 2015). The health of the LMB is under threat due to significant flow regime changes resulting from the combination of anthropogenic stressors and climate change (Dugan et al., 2010). These anthropogenic factors include but are not limited to the development of hydropower stations, deforestation, unsustainable fishing practices and large-scale irrigation schemes (Eastham et al., 2008; Grumbine & Xu, 2011). These stressors are predicted to become more significant and result in more visible impacts on the Mekong over time.

The Mekong Basin is also predicted to be adversely impacted by climate change (Ziv, Baran, Nam, Rodríguez-Iturbe, & Levin, 2012). Modelling undertaken by Kingston et al. (2011) and Västilä, Kummu, Sangmanee, and Chinvanno (2010) projects that the discharge of the Mekong will decrease between 5.4% and 4.5% annually. An increase of 1°C in night temperatures could reduce rice grain yield by 10% (Peng et al., 2004), having a negative impact on the Mekong's residents who rely on rice-based agriculture (NCCC, 2013). The impacts of environmental change are influencing the LMB's weather and have resulted in significant flood regime shifts that are projected to continue into the future (Junk et al., 2006; Keskinen et al., 2010). Changes to the Mekong's flow regime are expected to have significant repercussions for the basin's major functions including reductions in aquatic productivity, inhibition of riverine transport, reduced availability of fresh water and lowered agricultural productivity (Eastham et al., 2008; Lauri et al., 2012; Mekong River Commission, 2010). Current projections for future environmental change highlight the vulnerability of rainfed rice agriculture in the LMB, with increased seasonal variability set to continue (Jiang et al., 2019).

Cambodia is predicted to be particularly adversely impacted by environmental changes due to low levels of resilience and adaptive capacity related to high levels of poverty (Doch et al., 2015). Cambodia's vulnerability to environmental change is predominantly driven by the combination of environmental and socio-economic factors. Exposure to natural hazards alongside poverty, inequality and a high dependence on natural resources aggravates the impacts of climate change on Cambodian households (Arias, Holtgrieve, Ngor, Dang, & Piman, 2019). In recent years, attaining food security has become challenging in many rural communities due to an increase in seasonal variability in combination with an increase in severe floods and droughts (Arias et al., 2019). In response to these predicted threats, the Cambodian government has developed a Climate Change Strategy Plan for 2014–2023, the aim of which is to:

> [...] Create a national framework for engaging the public and private sector, civil society organizations and development partners in a participatory process for responding to climate change to support sustainable development. (NCCC, 2013)

This plan also emphasises the importance of mainstreaming gender with respect to climate change planning, to ensure that women's experiences are taken into account in adaptation planning.

Gender Roles and Cambodia

Over the last two decades, the importance of gender equity has gained momentum worldwide, particularly in the agricultural sector in developing countries where women comprise half, or more than half, of the workforce (Ogawa, 2004). Women comprise 51.8% of the 13.8 million residents in Cambodia, representing 51.6% of the economically active residents, and heading 25.7% of households (NIS, 2013). Moreover, Resurrección and Boyland (2017) found that Cambodian women own approximately 65% of all registered businesses in the country.

Within rural Cambodia, women farmers comprise 55% of the farming population and their importance in rural development has long been emphasised by the government and in academic circles (Ogawa, 2004). The Cambodian Climate Change Strategic Plan (NCCC, 2013) denotes that the rural poor of Cambodia, the majority of whom are women, are most vulnerable to the impacts of environmental change due to their significant reliance on agriculture and natural resources. As women comprise more than 50% of the Cambodian population and in some circumstances may be disproportionately at risk to the impacts of environmental change, it is important to actively seek out and include women's experiences to inform future policies and plans to facilitate adaptation and gender mainstreaming.

Research Aim and Objectives

A number of studies have been undertaken in Cambodia, investigating the changes in the frequency and intensity of extreme climate events associated with environmental change (Jiang et al., 2019; Kingston et al., 2011; Lauri et al., 2012). However, the documentation and understanding of adaptation is still notably limited particularly on relatively small scales (Evers & Pathirana, 2018). It is for this reason that there is a need for research integrating both the scientific and local knowledge surrounding the adaptation strategies developed in response to continued environmental change in Cambodia. The overarching aim of this research is to investigate the impacts of temporal variation resulting from environmental change using the four villages in Kratie, Cambodia, as a case study. This research incorporates three main objectives, as follows:

(1) to assess historical temporal variability in rainfall and weather-related natural hazards for the region;
(2) to characterise seasonal and inter-annual variability in livelihood strategies and identify critical periods for decision; and
(3) to highlight strategies employed by community members and individuals to adapt to predicted changing environmental conditions.

METHODS

Study Site

This research focussed on a region south of the town of Kratie in the province of Kratie, approximately 300 km north-east of the capital Phnom Penh. Kratie Province is among the most disaster-prone provinces in the country and is frequently affected by damaging floods. Between 1996 and 2017, flooding in the province adversely affected over 500,000 people, damaging nearly 2,000 houses and destroying extensive areas of crops (Neef et al., 2020). In the most recent census, the population of the province was 344,195, with just over 70% living along the Mekong (NIS, 2013). The majority of residents obtain their livelihood from subsistence agriculture based predominantly on the cultivation of rice and corn, alongside raising livestock and fishing; all of which are highly impacted by changes in the flood regime (Mekong River Commission, 2010).

The communities in this region have adapted not only their agricultural practices but, moreover, their entire livelihoods around the seasonal monsoon. Plate 7.1 shows a traditional homestead for the region built on stilts to cope with the anticipated seasonal flooding. Historically, the first rice crop of the year is rainfed and grown at higher elevations to avoid damage from floods, and the second crop is grown after the floodwaters recede, relying predominantly on moisture stored within the fine-grained clay-rich soils, and supplementary irrigation from nearby wetlands and the Mekong River itself.

The four villages included in the study (Thma Reab, Ou Lung, Dei Doh Kraom and Kbal Kaoh, as shown in Fig. 7.1) are within Prek Prasob district, which is one of the most severely flood-impacted districts within Kratie Province. The district encompasses eight communes and 48 villages. The four study villages were located in close proximity to the Mekong, with Kbal Kaoh being situated on an island (Koh Tasuy) in the middle of the river. The villages were selected as a representative cross section of villages within the most severely flood-affected part of Prek Prasob district, covering a range of socio-economic and physiographic characteristics.

Plate 7.1. Traditional-Style Homestead in Thma Reab. *Source*: Authors' own.
The living areas for this house are elevated to give the residents and their
belongings a degree of protection if floodwaters enter the village.
Not all residents are able to construct elevated houses, as shown by the
house at right which is only slightly raised from the land surface.

As shown by the linear built-up areas mapped in Fig. 7.1, there are no distinct physical boundaries between villages; village boundaries are administrative and encompass a defined number of households within each village. Villages as a unit are closely linked to administrative goals from colonial and post-colonial periods (Oveson, Tranke, & Öjendal, 1996), although kinship and patronage relationships and networks are still central to village life (Ledgerwood & Vighjen, 2002; Thon, Ou, Eng, & Ly, 2010). In Cambodia, there are strong tendencies to work towards the collective good of the group or village (Chan & Chheang, 2008). Ledgerwood and Vighjen (2002) detail six complex, interlocking domains of influence and power that work together to make Khmer villages function as a unit, encompassing administration, religion, knowledge, spiritual leadership, wealth and development assistance, each of which has different patrons and power-brokers. With respect to administration, each village has a leader and deputy, appointed by the commune councillors. Commune council elections have been held since 2002 under the Cambodian programme of decentralisation (Thon et al., 2010). Village leaders play an important role as gatekeepers between the villagers (who are also voters) and the commune council, and hold influence in decisions concerning village and commune activities (Kim, 2012). Commune councils make decisions around administration and development goals, and are responsible for Commune Development Plans (Chhoeun, Sok, & Byrne, 2008), which are developed through village-level consultation and often include components around infrastructure and climate change adaptation (BenYishay et al., 2019; Carter & Sok, 2013).

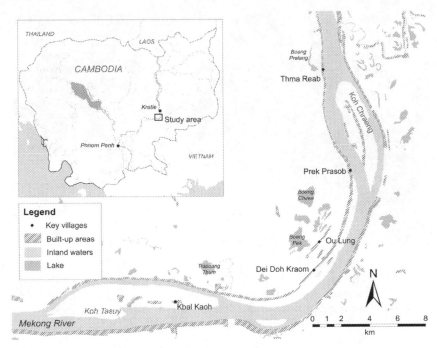

Fig. 7.1.   Map of the Study Area Showing Village Locations and Built-Up Areas.
Prek Prasob is the largest settlement in the district and location of the district
government. Numerous other villages are located within the regions marked
as built-up areas. *Source*: Williams, Pauli, and Boruff (2020, Chapter 6, Volume 22).

With regard to infrastructure, including electricity, access to clean water and
road access, Kbal Kaoh had the most developed infrastructure, and Ou Lung had
the least developed, with the other two villages intermediate. In Kbal Kaoh, all
residents had functioning solar panels and access to clean fresh water supplied by
a water treatment plant developed by the NGO Lien AID (Ye, 2017). Moreover,
Kbal Kaoh had a relatively well-maintained main road and access to a ferry port on
both the eastern and western sides of the island. Thma Reab and Dei Doh Kraom
demonstrated similar levels of infrastructure with some members of the community having access to power, water and the main road (which was reasonably well
maintained). Dei Doh Kraom was the largest community with diverse businesses,
markets and schools. Finally, Ou Lung was observed as the least developed in terms
of infrastructure, with almost no residents having access to electricity and only relatively wealthy residents having access to well water. Furthermore, Ou Lung was
also located a significant distance off the main road, which runs south along the
Mekong between Thma Reab and Dei Doh Kraom, thus making it less accessible.

These four villages are also notably variable with respect to topography, with
Thma Reab and Dei Doh Kraom situated at comparatively high elevation for the
region, on the natural levee of the Mekong. The village of Ou Lung was closer to

the backswamp and at a lower elevation away from the higher natural levee of the riverbank. Historically, Thma Reab and Dei Doh Kraom have not experienced flood inundation on an annual basis; however, Ou Lung floods almost every year. Finally, the village of Kbal Kaoh is also located on reasonably low-lying land on the island of Koh Tasuy in the middle of the Mekong, with the majority of this island submerged annually by floodwaters. The study villages consisted of approximately 100–200 households, with around three to four people per household, with the exception of Dei Doh Kraom which had around 350 households and an estimated 1,000 residents.

Research Approach

The methodology developed for this investigation combined local and scientific knowledge in the context of understanding the temporal variability in weather-related natural hazards and adaptation strategies pursued by local communities in the four study villages (Fig. 7.2 provides a graphical representation of the approach). The data required for this investigation were obtained using a mixed-methods approach, combining quantitative and qualitative approaches (Creswell & Plano Clark, 2017). This included a desktop analysis of relevant quantitative secondary biophysical data and a fieldwork component comprising qualitative seasonal calendar workshops and individual daily routine diaries. Interpretation of qualitative information was used to identify local adaptation strategies in line with Agrawal and Perrin's (2008) framework for understanding risks to rural live-lihoods, following the example of Neef et al. (2018).

Quantitative Biophysical Data

All hydrometeorological data analysed in this report were drawn from the PERSIANN-CDR; a global gridded (0.25° × 0.25°) data set of weather observations

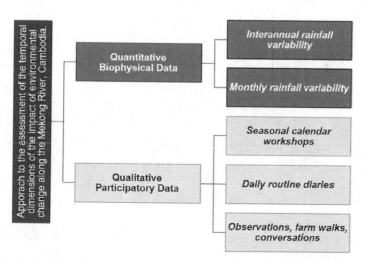

Fig. 7.2. An Overview of the Methodological Approach Adopted in the Research Presented in This Chapter.

developed by NOAA (Sorooshian, Hsu, Braithwaite, & Ashouri, 2014). This data set provides daily, modelled weather observations for the latitude band 60°S–60°N. We chose a location for the gridded data output concordant with the village of Dei Doh Kraom, Cambodia. Prior to analysis, all data were cleaned, and all subsequent analysis and graphics were created using RStudio (RStudio Team, 2015).

Qualitative Data Gathered through Participatory Processes

Seasonal Calendar Workshops
Workshops around the timing of key livelihood activities and hydrometeorological events were conducted in each of the four communities. Two workshops were conducted in Thma Reab, Ou Lung and Kbal Kaoh, and three workshops were conducted in Dei Doh Kraom. All workshops were conducted in Khmer, facilitated by Cambodian research assistants from the Royal University of Phnom Penh under the guidance of the authors. The workshops were run as semi-structured focus groups centred around an A0 size seasonal calendar, as illustrated in Fig. 7.3 (Bernard, 2006). To assist in the translation and accuracy of the information

Fig. 7.3. Seasonal Calendar Workshop Format and Example Output. The images within the composite area: (A) discussing the calendar during a focus group predominantly attended by women in Thma Reab; (B) a mixed-gender focus group in Kbal Kaoh; and (C) an example seasonal calendar developed during a workshop in the village of Dei Doh Kraom. *Source*: Authors' own.

gathered, small visual cards were used with an illustration or photo of a particular crop, animal or event, as well as both the English and Khmer words.

Each workshop had between 8 and 20 participants, and was usually conducted in or around the village leader or deputy leader's house. The majority of the workshops were held outside, either below the house or in an open area, and were therefore accessible to anyone passing by. A small number of workshops were held inside homes and typically had fewer attendees. The workshops ran for approximately 60–90 minutes, and participants were invited to attend by the respective village leader. At each workshop, there were a minimum of one researcher (the authors) and one Khmer-speaking research assistant. The researcher acted as a note taker and session facilitator, posing guiding questions to keep the group on task. The research assistant(s) acted as translators and filled in the seasonal calendars in Khmer based on instructions from the members of the focus group. Originally, the workshops were intended to be split along gender lines, with at least one workshop per village focussing on men and one on women. However, upon arriving in the villages there was a clear sense from participants that women and men worked together in many endeavours, and the researchers did not wish to exclude community members who wanted to participate in the workshops. In practice, this meant that some workshops where the invitation by the village leader was for a 'women's workshop' or 'men's workshop' ended up also including members of the opposite gender, with a bias in participant numbers towards either men or women (as advertised), while a small number of workshops ran with a more even split along gender lines. The seasonal calendars that were generated within sessions in each village were very similar, with no substantive differences noted among outputs from different sessions.

The semi-structured focus group technique was implemented with the aim of allowing the participants to steer the conversation in the direction they felt was most important for their own livelihood, while still allowing the researchers to redirect the group when necessary (Gero, Méheux, & Dominey-Howes, 2011). Each workshop commenced with a discussion surrounding the general rainfall and flood regime that participants expected and whether 2018 was notably different. The discussion was then focussed on important livelihood activities particularly with respect to agriculture, and when these activities were undertaken. Discussions around adaptation measures, coping strategies and noted changes in weather and climate were often raised during the focus group sessions. The responses from the focus group were reviewed for recurrent patterns and themes. A seasonal calendar was created for each village, by collating information from all workshops within a particular village.

Daily Routine Diaries

The fieldwork component of this research also included the creation of opportunistic daily routine diaries with women in three villages. This method was pursued as a means of gathering more detailed livelihood data, as the seasonal calendar sessions were not capturing as much gender-specific information as anticipated. Williams (2016) found that women in this region generally spoke more often about adaptation activities than men, prompting an interest to understand on a more individual level how women are affected by temporal environmental change. Moreover, these diaries were conducted with women due to the fact that most previous research in this area engaged in one-on-one conversations primarily with the village leaders and deputy leaders, of whom most, but not all, were men. The daily diaries were often undertaken directly after a seasonal calendar workshop if any participant was willing to stay behind for a further discussion. These were typically conducted on an individual basis and lasted under 30 minutes. In total, eight daily routine diaries were collected, two in Ou Lung and three in Dei Doh Kraom and Kbal Kaoh, respectively. The participants ranged from 28 to 60 years old, all having at least one child and having been married. The purpose of gathering the diaries was to gain a deeper understanding of the types of activities the residents participated in and how they were impacted by seasonal flooding and drought.

Observations, Farm Walks and Structured Conversations
Alongside the more formal qualitative methods used for gathering data, the authors also took part in farm walks and traversed with local community members, made observations during the time spent in the villages (data were collected over a two-week period where the researchers stayed in, or in close proximity to the study villages), and engaged in structured conversations with local leaders. Structured conversations took place at an opportune moment for the village elder, leader or deputy leader, and often included an overview of the village history, the impacts of recent floods or droughts, and views of what the future might hold.

FINDINGS I: A REGION OF INHERENT VARIABILITY IN RAINFALL PATTERNS

Temporal Analysis of Average Inter-Annual Rainfall

Over the last 34 years, the total annual rainfall (average: 2,167 mm) in Dei Doh Kraom, Cambodia, fluctuated from year to year, as expected for this region. Over time, the residents have shaped their livelihoods, particularly their agricultural systems, to take into account fluctuations in rainfall volume, developing various methods to aid in decision-making based on that year's conditions (Sok & Yu, 2015). However, from 2012 onwards, these fluctuations have become more prominent and have more regularly exceeded one standard deviation (380 mm) from the mean (Fig. 7.4). This is a notable amount of variation, particularly if one takes into account the relative frequency in which the average rainfall has exceeded one standard deviation in recent years. In particular, 2017 showed a substantive reduction in rainfall almost two and a half standard deviations from the mean, equating to a loss of over 40% of the region's annual rainfall (Fig. 7.4).

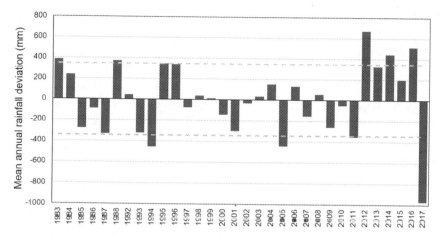

Fig. 7.4. Annual Average Rainfall Deviation from the Mean (2,167 mm) for the Study Area Near Kratie, Cambodia from 1983 to 2017. Dashed grey lines depict one standard deviation from the mean. Data for 1989–1991 were excluded due to anomalies in the data. *Data source*: Sorooshian et al. (2014).

Analysis of Temporal Monthly Rainfall Variation

While the wet monsoon falls between the beginning of May and late October, it is also important to note that this region experiences rainfall in most months of the year. Monthly rainfall is highly variable within each year, as well from year to year. Fig. 7.5 illustrates the variability in monthly rainfall for the study area. The average rainfall patterns follow a roughly unimodal distribution peaking in August and September. A more detailed examination of monthly rainfall for one of the driest years recorded (2017) indicated that there were still high levels of rainfall in May, August and September. However, there was a clear lack of rain in June and July contrary to the expected rainfall pattern for the region, changing the distribution to a bimodal one. The rainfall pattern for 2017 was highly variable and inconsistent with the expected rainfall flow for the region. In comparison, in the wettest year (2012) recorded between 1983 and 2017, there was a notable increase in rainfall in January and February due to a prolonged rainy season in 2011. There was also considerably more rain recorded for August and October relative to average conditions.

Significance and Interpretation

The quantitative data outlined previously support the predictions of environmental changes for the region, in that rainfall, flooding and drought-like conditions have increased in variability and are likely to increase in variability and intensity in the future (Dang et al., 2014; Dugan et al., 2010; Eastham et al., 2008; Evers & Pathirana, 2018). The increased variability in rainfall, timing of the wet season rains and reduction of rains outside this period were also noted by members in all four of the communities during field research. Many of the residents noted that changes in seasonal variability of the floods have already begun to impact their livelihoods. In

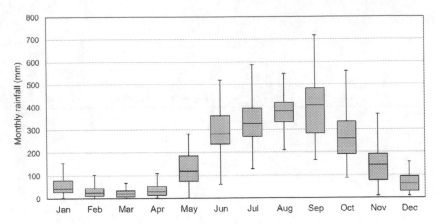

Fig. 7.5.   Representation of Average Monthly Rainfall Variability in the
Study Area Near Kratie, Cambodia Between 1983 and 2017. The boxes
represent the 25–75 percentile range of monthly precipitation values,
with the solid bar depicting the median value. 'Whisker' bars represent the
range; outliers have been removed. *Data source*: Sorooshian et al. (2014).

2018, the floods commenced early (mid-June) and rose rapidly in under two weeks
due to a dam failure upstream in Laos. Subsequently, members of the communities
in Thma Reab, Ou Lung, Dei Doh Kraom and Kbal Kaoh stated that they had lost
large proportions of their wet season crops, leading to a significant and detrimental
loss of income on both an individual and community scale. During the workshops
in all four villages, residents also highlighted that the floodwaters receded faster than
expected and indicated that they were currently (in November 2018) experiencing the
impacts of drought-like conditions, predicting that their dry season crop would also
show a decrease in yield. Previous research has also shown that continued changes
in the seasonality of major hydrometeorological events in the region will likely have
negative impacts on the number and variety of crops that can be cultivated in the
region (Chung, Takeuchi, Fujihara, & Oeurng, 2019). Overall, this desktop analysis
alongside supporting scholarly literature and community perceptions lends support
to the notion that the long-standing flood patterns on which residents of this region
rely have increased in variability both on a seasonal and inter-annual scale.

FINDINGS II: RURAL LIVELIHOODS ADAPT TO
SEASONAL VARIABILITY AND ENVIRONMENTAL
CHANGE

Seasonal Calendars and Key Decision-Making Periods

The seasonal calendars developed during focus group workshops were focussed
around a *typical* year for each location. Participants were invited to discuss major
hydrometeorological events, as well as different agricultural and fishing activities
undertaken during the year. In this section, we present the detailed calendars compiled for each of the four villages, together with an explanation of key points. This

level of detail, provided by the research participants, may be valuable to others working in the field, as well as a helpful reference for planning purposes. There are some similarities across the four villages, particularly those villages on the mainland that incorporate rice cultivation as a mainstay of agricultural production.

Thma Reab

The major hydrometeorological events depicted by the residents of Thma Reab closely follow the average rainfall patterns in the previous section (Fig. 7.5), similarly to residents in the other villages studied. Around 80% of the households in Thma Reab are involved in agriculture, which is focussed on the cultivation of rice, maize and cassava, with an expanding area of tree crops (particularly cashew and mango) in upland areas providing opportunities for income through sharecropping, as hired labour, or by owning trees. Special techniques are used to allow for two crops of mangoes during the year; mangoes command a higher price in the 'off-season' of November–December and can be sold to international buyers; the ordinary fruiting period is in March–April.

The seasonal calendar (Table 7.1) illustrates the timing of various agricultural activities in Thma Reab in a 'typical' year. In ideal conditions, two crops of rice and two crops of maize are grown per year. 'Wet rice' is planted with the onset of monsoon rains at higher elevations that are unlikely to flood, and is rainfed, with a similar pattern for 'wet maize'. The variety of rice that is planted depends on when the rains start; if the rains start early with planting possible from May, then a long-maturing rice variety can be grown, which fetches a higher price at the market than short-maturing varieties which could be planted in July. If there are heavy rains from the beginning of the wet season, people may decide not to plant much rice. The second crop of 'dry rice' and 'dry maize' is sown at lower elevations, after floodwaters have receded, and is harvested towards the end of the dry season. The 'dry' crops rely on retained soil moisture and on pumping of water into cultivated fields.

This fine balance in terms of the effects of rainfall on crops extended beyond rice and maize; for example, if rainfall is too heavy, then mango flowers will be destroyed, which affects yield, but with more rain, the fruits grow larger. Cassava takes a long time to mature compared with other crops; however, it can survive for one month without rain after planting. The risk inherent in reliance on seasonal weather patterns was brutally demonstrated in 2018, when farmers from Thma Reab lost much of their wet season crop due to rapid, early flooding in June, with many having to pick up off-farm labouring work to compensate for the loss.

Ou Lung

The timing of monsoon rains and floods given by residents of Ou Lung is similar to timing mentioned in Thma Reab (Table 7.2). Ou Lung is heavily reliant on rice cultivation, with at least six varieties of rice grown in the fields around the village covering some 140 ha. Transplanting of seedlings and direct seeding are both used for rice crops. The first crop of rice is sown with the wet monsoon, with villagers waiting until the rain starts and then choosing a rainy day to start planting. If the rains are delayed, then a short-maturing variety may be used.

Table 7.1.   Seasonal Calendar for a 'Typical Year' in the Village of Thma Reab, Cambodia.

Thma Reab	Jan	Feb	Mar	Apr	May	June	July	Aug	Sept	Oct	Nov	Dec
Hydrometeorological Events												
Rains			*Little rains*				*Heavy rain*					
Floods								*Flood*				
Drought	*Drought*										*Drought*	
Livelihood Activities												
Wet Rice						Preparation, sowing		Caring	Harvest		Drying	
Wet Maize					Prep, sowing		Harvest					
Dry Rice	Caring	Harvest			Drying							
Dry Maize	Caring	Harvest		Drying								
Cassava	Drying		Preparation, planting					Caring				
Soy	Caring		Harvest							Preparation, sowing		
Cashew		Fruit	Fruit								Preparation, sowing	
Mango									Flowering			
Off-Season Mango									Flowering / Harvest		Fruit	
Pig							Vulnerable to illness					
Buffalo/Cattle					Best	Sold						
Bamboo Shoots		Harvest										
Fish					Regular fishing					Best fishing		

Note: Not illustrated are crops grown only for household consumption, such as coconut, jackfruit and bananas, nor short-duration crops that are grown sporadically and opportunistically such as cucumber.

Table 7.2. Seasonal Calendar for 'Typical' Year for the Village of Ou Lung, Cambodia.

Ou Lung	Jan	Feb	Mar	Apr	May	June	July	Aug	Sept	Oct	Nov	Dec
Hydrometeorological Events												
Rains			*Little rains*			*Heavy rains*						
Floods							*Flood*		*Flood*			
Drought											*Drought*	
Livelihood Activities												
Wet Rice					Prep, sowing			Caring	Prep, sowing		Harvest	
Dry Rice	Harvest								Caring		Caring	
Sesame		Harvest				Preparation, sowing			Harvest			
Bamboo Shoots				Best								
Lotus			Harvest		Flowering							
Cashew		Harvest							Flower			
Mango		Harvest							Flower			
Off-Season Mango									Flower		Harvest	
Fishing					Regular fishing					Best fishing		

Note: Not illustrated are crops grown primarily for home consumption (home garden vegetables, herbs and fruits such as banana and coconut) nor sugar palm products.

During the flood of 2018, around 10% of the total rice crop was destroyed; wet season rice is normally planted at higher elevations so that it is not affected by floods. The rapid arrival of the flood at an earlier date than normal gave villagers little time to prepare; the village was inundated to a depth of around 1 m for two months. The drought was of greater concern than flooding at the time of the research in November 2018; little rain had fallen since September of that year, and there was concern for the second crop of rice, typically planted at the end of the wet season. Some irrigation channels have been dug near the village; however, farmers must pay the cost of the water hose and fuel for the pump in order to receive water for their fields. The concern over drought is demonstrated in the seasonal calendar, which highlights that drought can start even before the flood season is typically finished.

There were fewer alternative crops in Ou Lung compared with the other villages in the research. Cassava, soy and maize were not cultivated, as the village's land was low-lying and not suited to these crops. Fruit trees, sugarcane and other crops grow in and around the village; some young trees were badly damaged by flooding, and other crops have suffered from successive droughts and floods.

Dei Doh Kraom

The village of Dei Doh Kraom is the largest of the four villages and has the most diverse array of crops grown (Table 7.3). Preparation for the wet season rice tends to begin later here than in other villages. The floods of 2018 badly affected the wet rice crop around the village, with perhaps 80% of the crop destroyed. The dry rice crop was already suffering from the effects of drought in November 2018, with fears of a poor yield for that season. Other important crops include maize (with the potential for two crops per year), cassava, sesame, cashew, mango and rubber. Table 7.3 shows that many of the vegetable crops are planted or sown at the end of the rainy season, with harvests occurring from early to middle dry season. Some vegetable crops (e.g. cucumber, long bean) are grown intensively and opportunistically throughout the year owing to their short time to maturity and can be sold for income. Similarly, many of the fruit trees flower at the end of the rainy season, with fruits maturing through the dry season. Sugar palm and rubber trees can be harvested almost all year for their sap.

Dei Doh Kraom was the only village to identify a period of the year where fishing does not occur – during the breeding season of June and July. The 'best' fishing occurs at the end of the wet season, around September and October.

Kbal Kaoh

The island of Koh Tasuy floods in most years, with residents expecting some degree of inundation between July and October. In 2018, flooding of the island was severe and rapid, with a large proportion of crops destroyed. Although only a short distance from the mainland, livelihood activities on the island are quite distinct. Rice has not been grown on the island for more than 30 years. In the 1970s, tobacco was introduced as a cash crop, but this has gradually been replaced with maize as the major crop. The island produces around 5 tonnes of maize per year, which is sold as a cash crop. The periods for wet and dry maize cultivation are similar to those on the mainland, with the first crop sown at the start of the wet season around May and the second crop sown at lower elevations after floods have receded around

Table 7.3. Seasonal Calendar for the Village of Dei Doh Kraom, Cambodia.

Dei Doh Kraom	Jan	Feb	Mar	Apr	May	June	July	Aug	Sept	Oct	Nov	Dec
Hydrometeorological Events												
Rains			*Little rains*	*Little rains*	*Little rains*	*Heavy rains*	*Heavy rains*	*Heavy rains*	*Heavy rains*			
Floods								*Flood*	*Flood*			
Drought											*Drought*	*Drought*
Livelihood Activities												
Wet Rice						Prep		Caring			Harvest	Harvest
Dry Rice	Harvest									Prep	Caring	Caring
Wet Maize	Harvest			Prep	Caring		Harvest					Caring
Dry Maize	Caring	Harvest						Caring	Harvest	Prep	Harvest	Harvest
Cassava	Caring	Harvest			Preparation	Caring			Caring	Prep		
Sesame					Prep		Harvest			Prep		
Sweet Potato						Prep	Harvest			Prep	Harvest	Caring
Cucumber	Harvest			Harvest	Caring	Harvest				Prep	Harvest	Harvest
Pumpkin	Harvest			Prep		Harvest				Prep	Caring	Caring
Eggplant		Caring			Harvest					Harvest	Caring	Caring
Green Bean												
Tomato			Caring						Sept Prep	Harvest	Prep	Caring
Cabbage										Prep	Caring	
Sugarcane			Harvest									
Watermelon				Harvest	Harvest							
Peanut				Prep	Harvest						Prep	Harvest
Long Bean	Harvest		Harvest				Best			Harvest	Caring	
Gourds									Prep	Prep	Caring	
Morning Glory	Best					Best				Harvest	Best	
Bamboo Shoots							Harvest			Harvest		
Ginger					Fruits		Palm water (sap)	Harvest		Harvest		
Sugar Palm	Palm water (sap)										Best	Best
Rubber											Best	Best
Mango	Harvest	Fruit							Flower	Flowering		
Off-Season Mango												Fruit

a Cucumber
b Sugarcane

Table 7.3. (*Continued*)

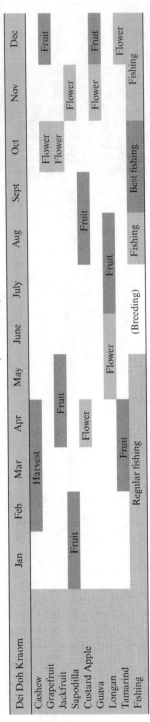

Dei Doh Kraom	Jan	Feb	Mar	Apr	May	June	July	Aug	Sept	Oct	Nov	Dec
Cashew										Flower		Fruit
Grapefruit										Flower	Flower	Fruit
Jackfruit											Flower	
Sapodilla			Harvest	Fruit								
Custard Apple				Flower				Fruit				
Guava	Fruit											
Longan					Flower		Fruit				Flower	Fruit
Tamarind			Fruit									Flower
Fishing		Regular fishing				(Breeding)		Fishing	Best fishing		Fishing	

[a]Cucumber takes 40 days from planting to harvest and can be grown at different times of the year. Long bean can be harvested every 30 days including at other times of the year from that shown. Okra (not shown) can be harvested every two months.
[b]Sugarcane takes around 12 months to grow before harvesting. Other: banana fruits throughout the year and is not depicted here.

Table 7.4. Seasonal Calendar for a 'Typical' Year for the Village of Kbal Kaoh, Cambodia.

Kbal Kaoh	Jan	Feb	Mar	Apr	May	June	July	Aug	Sept	Oct	Nov	Dec
Hydrometeorological Events												
Rains			*Little Rains*			*Heavy rains*						
Floods									*Flood*			
Drought											*Drought*	
Livelihood Activities												
Tobacco	Caring		Harvest							Preparation		Caring
Wet Maize		Caring			Prep	Harvest						
Dry Maize				Harvest	Prep. sowing	Harvest						
Sesame			Preparation		Prep. sowing						Prep. sowing	
Eggplant								Harvest				
Cucumber	Harvest									Prep	Caring	Harvest
Watermelon										Prep	Caring	Harvest
Pumpkin	Caring		Harvest							Preparation		Caring
Tomato	Harvest										Preparation	Prep
Lettuce									Prep	Harvest	Harvest	
Morning Glory				Harvest					Best		Harvest	
Bamboo Shoots				Harvest					Best		Harvest	
Mango			Fruit								Flowering	
Cashew		Fruit					Flowering					
Papaya				Fruit						Fruit	Flowering	
Banana			Flower								Flowering	Fruit
Wood Apple[a]				Fruit						Fruit		
Fishing				Fishing					Best fishing		Fishing	

[a]Wood apple refers to *Limonia acidissima* (Rutaceae), a tree related to the citrus species.

October (Table 7.4). Participants in one focus group commented that due to uncertainty around the impact of floods and droughts, some farmers are experimenting with intercropping corn and tobacco as a form of insurance in case one crop fails.

Some of the villagers from Kbal Kaoh have invested in land on the mainland, where cashew and mango are grown. Other crops include sesame, morning glory (also known as water spinach, *Ipomoea aquatica*) which can be harvested throughout the year and also grows wild, various other vegetables and bamboo. The latter has been planted to reduce erosion on the northern side of the island, and mature bamboo poles are also cut and sold.

Key Decision-Making Periods
Although the four villages reported slightly different timing of various livelihood activities, it is clear that significant agricultural decisions around when to plant crops, and which varieties of crops to plant, are made at the beginning of the wet monsoon and at the end of monsoon as floodwaters recede and rainfall declines. Projections indicate reduced rainfall at the beginning of the wet season under future scenarios of environmental change, which will negatively affect agriculture reliant on early wet season rain, such as long-maturing varieties of rainfed rice (Hoang et al., 2016; Yamamauchi, 2014). The importance of early-season rainfall is perhaps emphasised by comparing the seasonal calendars (Tables 7.1–7.4) with monthly rainfall records (Fig. 7.5). Rainfall for March and April is relatively low according to gridded data (Fig. 7.5), but focus group participants consistently said that 'little rains' fell in these months. By contrast, average rainfall in October and November is typically over 100 mm (higher in October), but these rains were not recorded on the seasonal calendars produced in focus groups. One explanation is that the calendars were more reflective of the most recent years' hydrometeorological events; another interpretation is that early wet season rainfall is a key indicator for agricultural decision-making and is closely monitored.

Rainfall, temperature, soil moisture, flood duration and a variety of other environmental factors all hold influence over the quality and quantity of many crops produced in the four villages. Farmers with access to irrigation are able to negate some of the risks of drought conditions for dry season crops, and even late wet season crops if rainfall is insufficient. The decision to plant rice in an area that may be flooded is risky. For instance, in Dei Doh Kraom, farmers who took a risk by planting rainfed rice in relatively low-lying areas were rewarded by a high price at the market when the predicted floods of 2016 did not eventuate. In other years, the same decision could lead to major crop loss. There was a recurring theme in focus groups of disbelief around flood projections and flood warnings, as many people no longer heed official warnings, and believe that flooding is now less predictable than in prior years.

Daily Routine Diaries: Experiences of Individual Women
During workshop discussions, women and men emphasised that they helped each other with the vast majority of livelihood activities conducted throughout the year. Daily activity diaries were collected only from women, in order to ensure

Hour ↓	Ou Lung — Seasonal daily routines, two women		Dei Doh Kraom — Daily routines reported by three women throughout the year			Kbal Kaoh — Daily routine, one woman	Kbal Kaoh — Seasonal daily routine, two women	
	Dry	Wet (floods)	All year			All year	Dry	Wet (floods)
4:00	Prepare food, eat	Prepare food		Sleep	Prepare food, clean, feed pigs	Prepare food, sell breakfast	Sleep	Prepare food
5:00		Travel by boat to gather forage, take feed to livestock (tended by husband), then take fish caught by husband to market	Cultivate land				Clean	
6:00	Tend to livestock			Prepare food, clean, feed pigs			Work in the fields	Travel by boat to tend to livestock, fetch feed for livestock and driftwood
7:00			Prepare food, clean		Work in the fields			
8:00			Tend to children					
9:00	Clean							
10:00	Rest			Go to market			Prepare food, eat	
11:00	Work in the fields		Prepare food	Prepare food	Rest in fields, eat	Sell food all day at the local school		Prepare food, rest
12:00								
13:00			Tend to house garden					
14:00	Prepare food, eat			Tend to children	Work in the fields		Tend to crops, pump water	Tend to livestock
15:00	Work in the fields	Return home and rest due to storms and waves						
16:00			Dinner					
17:00						Rest		
18:00	Prepare food, eat, rest		Clean		Prepare food, eat, clean, rest		Prepare food, eat, clean, rest	Prepare food, eat, clean, rest
19:00		Prepare food, eat		Prepare food, eat, rest		Prepare food, eat, clean, rest		
20:00			Tend to children, rest					
21:00								
22:00	Sleep	Sleep		Sleep	Sleep	Sleep	Sleep	Sleep
23:00			Sleep					

Fig. 7.6. Representation of Daily Activities Conducted by Seven Women Across Three Villages.

that their experiences were documented; this is not to negate or downplay the experiences of those who were not interviewed. At least one of the women interviewed stated that we should also note down her husband's daily activities, as he also worked very hard throughout the day and year.

The daily activities drawn from seven women across three villages are depicted in Fig. 7.6. Although there was variation in the income-producing activities undertaken by the women interviewed (including selling produce, running small businesses, working in their own fields and working as hired labour), most were also responsible for household food preparation (for daily consumption and for longer term preservation), cleaning, childcare (respondents with adult children were still involved in childcare for family members), tending to home gardens (vegetables may require daily watering especially in the dry season), providing feed and water for livestock, and collecting firewood.

In the villages of Ou Lung and Kbal Kaoh, where seasonal flooding signifi-cantly and regularly affects homes and fields, the daily activities carried out by women can differ greatly between seasons. During floods, women tend to stay at the primary residence, prepare food for themselves and their husbands (and any children staying in the house), collect and transport fodder for livestock (which are also kept on higher ground, tended to by the men, who stay with the livestock), and take fish to market, commonly travelling by boat. The days are very long and challenging; in addition, the women we spoke with could not swim, putting them in danger if the boat capsizes during storms and resultant choppy wave conditions that tend to occur from the middle to late afternoon in the wet season. With more frequent extreme flooding events predicted under climate change, there may be an increase in the length of time that families are physically separated and women remain in flooded villages, doing arduous work in difficult conditions and exposed to significant risks. Pumping water to irrigate fields during the dry season was another burdensome seasonal task undertaken by some of the women interviewed.

In the village of Dei Doh Kraom, the women's daily livelihood activities did not differ substantively between seasons. The village floods irregularly, having been flooded only three times since 2000 (2001, 2013 and 2018). The women inter-viewed in Dei Doh Kraom stated that during severe flood years, their daily lives were adversely impacted as they did not have mechanisms in place to cope with these conditions.

Adaptive Responses to Temporal Variability and Environmental Uncertainty

During fieldwork in the four communities, research participants and community members mentioned a number of strategies that could be described as ways of adapting to recent environmental change and uncertainty. The strategies were mentioned as an aside to, or in response to, discussions around the central research themes of temporal variability, and respondents were not specifically asked about all strategies used to cope with or adapt to environmental change. It is important to note that the extent and duration of flooding, along with the volume and seasonal distribution of rainfall, have varied from year to year within these communities over long periods of time, so that villagers are accustomed to variability. Many villagers perceive that the predictability of seasonal change has recently declined, so that new strategies are required to assist in overcoming these new challenges.

In this section, we reflect on how some of the strategies used by communi-ties in response to increased environmental uncertainty fit within Agrawal and Perrin's (2008) framework on adaptation practices that may alleviate risks to rural livelihoods posed by climate change. The framework highlights five classes of adaptation practice: mobility, diversification, storage, communal pooling and market exchange. We follow Neef et al.'s (2018) example by elaborating on com-munity-led adaptation practices that fit within social norms and cultural values at a particular place, as well as the environmental setting. Here, we do not seek to construct an exhaustive list of all adaptation practices used by the studied com-munities in the face of environmental change, but rather offer this interpretation as a way of bringing together different threads of practice and theory as a potential example for categorising and understanding adaptive responses to temporal change and environmental uncertainty.

Mobility as a strategy to alleviate risks to rural livelihoods across space was mentioned in a variety of contexts. At a very fine spatial and temporal scale, members of all four villages discussed the use of boats in times of flooding in order to move between homes, upland areas and markets, and highlighted boats as an important financial investment for families. Particularly in Kbal Kaoh, the most physically isolated of the four communities, almost all households reportedly owned or had access to a boat. In Thma Reab, mobility at a micro-scale was discussed, with children in the village now being taught how to swim after the drowning death of a child during the floods of 2013. Commonly, villagers (particularly the elderly and vulnerable, some children and men looking after livestock) may leave their homes if villages are inundated, and go to other towns, homes on higher ground, or to the nearest temple (see also Williams et al., 2020, Chapter 6, Volume 22). One family encountered in the fields inland of Thma Reab explained that they had bought 10 ha of land above the floodplain about 10 years prior and planted cashew trees. They no longer farm rice and stated that floods and droughts cannot affect their trees due to their elevated location.

The village of Thma Reab is the most well connected with the town of Kratie on the opposite bank of the Mekong, with a regular ferry service. Following the devastating floods of 2018, which destroyed much of the wet season rice crop in the village, there was an increase in residents from Thma Reab taking jobs as labourers and drivers outside of the village; Phnom Penh was a common destination but some international mobility also occurred with reports of work in Thailand and South Korea. In 2017, nearly 100,000 Cambodians went to work overseas (Mom, 2018). At the time of this research, a number of residents from across multiple villages stated that they believed that working in South Korea would lead to the best livelihood outcomes.

Diversification as a class of adaptation practice was mentioned frequently during focus group discussions, particularly with regard to agricultural activities. As highlighted by the seasonal calendars, there has been widespread growth in tree crops such as mango, cashew and rubber, as well as increased investment in high-value, intensively grown vegetables such as cucumber and tomato (several greenhouses planted to high-value vegetables were observed in the study area, along with areas of intensive seedling production). Examination of the seasonal calendars reveals that there are crops to be harvested (whether annual, perennial or wild-harvested) and fish caught in most months of the year, allowing for multiple income streams. During several focus group discussions, there was explicit mention of intercropping and consideration of different crop varieties to reduce risks and decrease the livelihood impact of failure in one particular crop. In Ou Lung, the village with the least access to infrastructure and the greatest reliance on agricultural activities, the village headman explained that he would like to see more government investment in irrigation in the province, so that farmers can have more opportunities to grow high-value crops that are reliant on regular water supplies just as in other provinces of the country.

Storage as an adaptation practice that reduces risks across time also arose in workshops and observations, with households storing large quantities of grains, livestock fodder and preserved fish (*prahok*) to last throughout the year (these are long-standing strategies that are related to the inherent seasonal variability that comes with living in the floodplain of the Mekong River). Storage locations for fodder and foodstuffs were often elevated on stilts to reduce the risk of damage by floodwaters, with many households with the economic means to do so opting to build higher stilts beneath houses due to the increased uncertainty around flood severity.

Members of all four villages also highlighted the importance of pooling of communal resources to help maintain their livelihoods. Residents from Ou Lung and Dei Doh Kraom highlighted the shared use and maintenance of water wells and irrigation ditches on a community level, while residents from Kbal Kaoh noted the shared use of water pumps and agricultural machinery. Communal investment was also seen in Kbal Kaoh, where residents planted bamboo to stabilise riverbanks and worked together to build up portions of elevated land to shelter livestock in times of flood. Temples have long been used as a place to house children and those without alternative accommodation during flood periods.

Adaptation practices related to 'market exchange' (such as crop insurance, new products for market and access to markets) were not explicitly mentioned during focus group workshops. However, many of the crops grown in the four villages were targeted strongly towards sale at market (including maize, tobacco, cashew, mango, rubber, sesame, vegetables, fruits and more), and participants were quick to highlight times of the year or situations that would lead to the highest or lowest price at market. Off-season mango was frequently mentioned as gaining a higher price at the market as it could be sold via Cambodian middlemen to Chinese buyers. Other locally produced or caught commodities (such as rice, poultry, fish and pigs) would be split between household consumption and sale at market, allowing for flexibility based on the situation in any particular year.

Household and community-level adaptation strategies have and will continue to play a significant role in rural livelihoods in the study region. However, an important level of structural support to aid in continued adaptation to environmental change depends on access to reliable infrastructure, particularly access to roads, electricity and clean water. Participants in all four villages explicitly stated that they were looking to the government to provide support to aid in their adaptation to environmental change, in terms of knowledge and guidance, hard infrastructure and economic funding.

CONCLUSION

This investigation explored the temporal aspects of environmental change, seasonality and adaptation strategies pursued by residents of four villages that have been severely impacted by seasonal flooding in the LMB. Our findings highlight that local communities use a variety of methods to manage the effects of seasonal and inter-annual variability, including growing a variety of crops at different times throughout the year, choosing appropriate varieties based on environmental conditions and investigating the potential of new methods to lessen the impact of reduced or more variable rainfall, such as irrigation. Local perceptions (see also Williams et al., 2020, Chapter 6, Volume 22) and rainfall records highlight that patterns in rainfall, flooding and dry spells have become less predictable in the study area. The increased climatic variability noted in the case study area is indicative of the projected direction of future environmental change across the Lower Mekong subregion (Jiang et al., 2019). As such, the adaptive responses by residents in the study area are likely to reflect the measures that other communities in this region will need to enact to sustain rural livelihoods into the future.

Beyond the four villages encompassed in this research, a substantial proportion of the rural population of the lower Mekong subregion draw livelihoods from agriculture and fisheries tailored to seasonal rainfall and the flood-pulse of the Mekong (FAO, 2011). The detailed seasonal calendars produced as part of this research highlighted two main decision-making periods, coinciding with the start (May June) and the end (September October) of the wet monsoon season; there are likely analogues in other villages of the region. These two periods of the year are also among the most likely to be affected by projected changes in precipitation patterns under climate change (Hoang et al., 2016; Yamamauchi, 2014). The predicted temporal impacts of climate change combined with alterations in flow from the development of hydropower dams upstream will likely hold adverse impacts (if unmitigated) for many communities in the Lower Mekong subregion, due to their strong reliance on seasonality for their agriculture-based livelihoods.

The residents of the Lower Mekong have long been accustomed to environmental variability, with a variety of strategies available to adjust to years that are dryer or wetter than usual. The experiences and knowledge of community members documented in this research suggest that there has been an acceleration or intensification in variability over recent years, so that an increasing repertoire and extent of coping and adaptation strategies are needed. Our findings highlight the importance of ensuring an accurate representation of experiences when researching environmental change. This investigation also clearly illustrated that drawing on communities' experiences and knowledge through participatory processes can add substantial value to scientific research, resulting in a more accurate understanding of the temporal effects of environmental change.

NOTE

1. In this chapter, 'environmental change' refers to the combined effects of climate change and other anthropogenic drivers such as (but not limited to) land-use change and alterations to river flow regimes through dam construction and reservoir operation. Hydropower dams are leading to significant biophysical change along the Mekong River (Piman, Lennaerts, & Southalack, 2013; Pokhrel et al., 2018).

ACKNOWLEDGEMENTS

The authors wish to thank the communities of Thma Reab, Ou Lung, Dei Doh Kraom and Kbal Kaoh for participating in this research and hosting the authors. The authors thank the Kratie Provincial Government, Prek Prasob District

Governor, commune leaders and village heads who allowed and assisted in the organisation of the fieldwork and accommodated the research team. We thank our two research assistants and translators from the Royal University of Phnom Penh (RUPP), Ms Hak Thidameas and Mr Eom Nakhem, and acknowledge the support and constructive advice from Dr Kimlong Ly and Dr Nyda Chhinh (both RUPP), Mr Touch Siphat (Ministry of Rural Development, Cambodia), Dr Chanrith Ngin and Prof. Andreas Neef (both University of Auckland), Dr Bryan Boruff (University of Western Australia), and Floris van Ogtrop (University of Sydney). The research was made possible through funding and support provided by the Asia-Pacific Network for Global Change Research (CAF2017-RR01-NMY-Neef, 'Climate Change Adaptation in Post-Disaster Recovery Processes: Flood-Affected Communities in Cambodia and Fiji') and the UWA School of Agriculture and Environment at the University of Western Australia.

REFERENCES

Agrawal, A., & Perrin, N. (2008). *Climate adaptation, local institutions, and rural livelihoods.* Working Paper No. W081-6. International Forestry Resources and Institutions Program, University of Michigan, Michigan. Retrieved from http://www.umich.edu/~ifri/Publications/W0816%20Arun%20Agrawal%20and%20Nicolas%20Perrin.pdf

Arias, M. E., Holtgrieve, G. W., Ngor, P. B., Dang, T. D., & Piman, T. (2019). Maintaining perspective of ongoing environmental change in the Mekong floodplains. *Current Opinion in Environmental Sustainability, 37,* 1–7. doi:10.1016/j.cosust.2019.01.002

Below, T. B., Mutabazi, K. D., Kirschke, D., Franke, C., Sieber, S., Siebert, R., & Tscherning, K. (2012). Can farmers' adaptation to climate change be explained by socio-economic household-level variables? *Global Environmental Change, 22*(1), 223–235. doi:10.1016/j.gloenvcha.2011.11.012

BenYishay, A., Parks, B., Trichler, R., Baehr, C., Aboagye, D., & Prum, P. (2019). *Building on a foundation stone: The long-term impacts of a local infrastructure and governance program in Cambodia.* EBA Report 2019:04. The Expert Group for Aid Studies (EBA), Stockholm. Retrieved from https://eba.se/wp-content/uploads/2019/06/2019-04-Infrastructure-and-Governance-Program-in-Cambodia.pdf

Bernard, H. R. (2006). *Research methods in anthropology: Qualitative and quantitative approaches.* Lanham, MD: AltaMira Press.

Bryan, E., Deressa, T. T., Gbetibouo, G. A., & Ringler, C. (2009). Adaptation to climate change in Ethiopia and South Africa: Options and constraints. *Environmental Science & Policy, 12*(4), 413–426. doi:10.1016/j.envsci.2008.11.002

Carr, E. R., & Thompson, M. C. (2014). Gender and climate change adaptation in agrarian settings: Current thinking, new directions, and research frontiers. *Geography Compass, 8*(3), 182–197. doi:10.1111/gec3.12121

Carter, J., & Sok, V. (2013). *Cambodia community based adaptation programme (CCBAP) programme review.* Final Report. Retrieved from https://info.undp.org/docs/pdc/Documents/KHM/CCBAP%20Review%20Final%20Report_February%202013.pdf

Chan, R., & Chheang, V. (2008). Cultural challenges to the decentralization process in Cambodia. *Ritsumeikan Journal of Asia Pacific Studies, 24,* 1–16.

Chen, X., Hu, B., & Yu, R. (2005). Spatial and temporal variation of phenological growing season and climate change impacts in temperate eastern China. *Global Change Biology, 11*(7), 1118–1130. doi:10.1111/j.1365-2486.2005.00974.x

Chhoeun, T., Sok, P., & Byrne, C. (2008). 'Citadel of women': Strengthening female leadership in rural Cambodia. *Gender & Development, 16*(3), 535–547. doi:10.1080/13552070802465433

Chung, S., Takeuchi, J., Fujihara, M., & Oeurng, C. (2019). Flood damage assessment on rice crop in the Stung Sen River Basin of Cambodia. *Paddy and Water Environment, 17*(2), 255–263. doi:10.1007/s10333-019-00718-1

Creswell, J. W., & Plano Clark, V. L. (2017). *Designing and conducting mixed methods research.* Thousand Oaks, CA: SAGE Publishing.

Dang, H. L., Li, E., Nuberg, I., & Bruwer, J. (2014). Understanding farmers' adaptation intention to climate change: A structural equation modelling study in the Mekong Delta, Vietnam. *Environmental Science & Policy, 41*, 11–22. doi:10.1016/j.envsci.2014.04.002

Doch, S., Diepart, J.-C., & Heng, C. (2015). A multi-scale flood vulnerability assessment of agricultural production in the context of environmental change: The case of the Sangkae River watershed, Battambang province. In J.-C. Diepart (Ed.), *Learning for resilience: Insights from Cambodia's rural communities* (pp. 19–49). Phnom Penh: The Learning Institute.

Dugan, P. J., Barlow, C., Agostinho, A. A., Baran, E., Cada, G. F., Chen, D., ... Winemiller, K. O. (2010). Fish migration, dams, and loss of ecosystem services in the Mekong Basin. *Ambio, 39*(4), 344–348. doi:10.1007/s13280-010-0036-1

Eastham, J., Mpelasoka, F., Mainuddin, M., Ticehurst, C., Dyce, P., Hodgson, G., ... Kirby, M. (2008). *Mekong River Basin water resources assessment: Impacts of climate change.* Canberra: CSIRO Water for a Healthy Country National Research Flagship. Retrieved from http://hdl.handle.net/102.100.100/120292?index=1

Evers, J., & Pathirana, A. (2018). Adaptation to climate change in the Mekong River Basin: Introduction to the special issue. *Climatic Change, 149*(1–11). doi:10.1007/s10584-018-2242-y

FAO. (2011). *Mekong River Basin.* Water Report (Vol. 37). Rome: Food and Agriculture Organisation of the United Nations, AQUASTAT.

Fazey, I., Kesby, M., Evely, A., Latham, I., Wagatora, D., Hagasua, J.-E., ... Christie, M. (2010). A three-tiered approach to participatory vulnerability assessment in the Solomon Islands. *Global Environmental Change, 20*(4), 713–728. doi:10.1016/j.gloenvcha.2010.04.011

Gero, A., Méheux, K., & Dominey-Howes, D. (2011). Integrating community based disaster risk reduction and climate change adaptation: Examples from the Pacific. *Natural Hazards and Earth System Sciences, 11*(1), 101–113. doi:10.5194/nhess-11-101-2011

Grumbine, R. E., & Xu, J. (2011). Mekong hydropower development. *Science, 332*(6026), 178–179. doi:10.1126/science.1200990

Hiwasaki, L., Luna, E., Syamsidik, & Shaw, R. (2014). Process for integrating local and indigenous knowledge with science for hydro-meteorological disaster risk reduction and climate change adaptation in coastal and small island communities. *International Journal of Disaster Risk Reduction, 10*(Pt. A), 15–27. doi:10.1016/j.ijdrr.2014.07.007

Hoang, L. P., Lauri, H., Kummu, M., Koponen, J., van Vliet, M. T. H., Supit, I., ... Ludwig, F. (2016). Mekong River flow and hydrological extremes under climate change. *Hydrology and Earth System Science, 20*, 3027–3041. doi:10.5194/hess-20-3027-2016

Holzkämper, A., Calanca, P., & Fuhrer, J. (2011). Analyzing climate effects on agriculture in time and space. *Procedia Environmental Sciences, 3*, 58–62. doi:10.1016/j.proenv.2011.02.011

Jiang, Z., Raghavan, S. V., Hur, J., Sun, Y., Liong, S.-Y., Nguyen, V. Q., & Van Pham Dang, T. (2019). Future changes in rice yields over the Mekong River Delta due to climate change – Alarming or alerting? *Theoretical and Applied Climatology, 137*(1), 545–555. doi:10.1007/s00704-018-2617-z

Junk, W. J., Brown, M., Campbell, I. C., Finlayson, M., Gopal, B., Ramberg, L., & Warner, B. G. (2006). The comparative biodiversity of seven globally important wetlands: A synthesis. *Aquatic Sciences, 68*(3), 400–414. doi:10.1007/s00027-006-0856-z

Keskinen, M., Chinvanno, S., Kummu, M., Nuorteva, P., Snidvongs, A., Varis, O., & Västilä, K. (2010). Climate change and water resources in the Lower Mekong River Basin: Putting adaptation into the context. *Journal of Water and Climate Change, 1*(2), 103–117. doi:10.2166/wcc.2010.009

Kim, S. (2012). *Democracy in action: Decentralisation in post-conflict Cambodia.* Ph.D. dissertation, University of Gothenburg, Gothenburg, Sweden.

Kingston, D., Thompson, J. R., & Kite, G. (2011). Uncertainty in climate change projections of discharge for the Mekong River Basin. *Hydrology and Earth System Sciences, 15*, 1459–1471. doi:10.5194/hess-15-1459-2011

Lauri, H., de Moel, H., Ward, P. J., Räsänen, T. A., Keskinen, M., & Kummu, M. (2012). Future changes in Mekong River hydrology: Impact of climate change and reservoir operation on discharge. *Hydrology and Earth System Sciences, 16*(12), 4603–4619. doi:10.5194/hess-16-4603-2012

Ledgerwood, J., & Vighjen, J. (2002). Decision making in rural Khmer villages. In J. Ledgerwood (Ed.), *Cambodia emerges from the past: Eight essays* (pp. 109–150). DeKalb, IL: Centre for Southeast Asian Studies, Northern Illinois University.

Mainuddin, M., Kirby, M., & Hoanh, C. T. (2013). Impact of climate change on rainfed rice and options for adaptation in the Lower Mekong Basin. *Natural Hazards, 66*, 905–938. doi:10.1007/s11069-012-0526-5

Mekong River Commission. (2010). *State of the basin report 2010*. Vientiane, Lao PDR: Mekong River Commission. Retrieved from http://www.mrcmekong.org/assets/Publications/basin-reports/MRC-SOB-report-2010full-report.pdf

Mercer, J. (2010). Disaster risk reduction or climate change adaptation: Are we reinventing the wheel? *Journal of International Development, 22*(2), 247–264. doi:10.1002/jid.1677

Mom, K. (2018, March 13). Spike in migrant worker numbers. *Khmer Times*. Retrieved from https://www.khmertimeskh.com/113661/spike-in-migrant-worker-numbers/

Nam, W.-H., Hong, E.-M., & Choi, J.-Y. (2015). Has climate change already affected the spatial distribution and temporal trends of reference evapotranspiration in South Korea? *Agricultural Water Management, 150*, 129–138. doi:10.1016/j.agwat.2014.11.019

NCCC. (2013). *Cambodia climate change strategic plan 2014–2023*. Phnom Penh: National Climate Change Committee, Royal Government of Cambodia. Retrieved from http://extwprlegs1.fao.org/docs/pdf/cam143041.pdf

Neef, A., Benge, L., Boruff, B., Pauli, N., Weber, E., & Varea, R. (2018). Climate adaptation strategies in Fiji: The role of social norms and cultural values. *World Development, 107*, 125–137. doi:10.1016/j.worlddev.2018.02.029

Neef, A., Boruff, B., Bruce, E., Ngin, C., Pauli, N., Davies, K., … Weber, E. (2020). Climate change adaptation in post-disaster recovery processes: Evidence from flood-affected communities in Cambodia and Fiji. *APN Science Bulletin* (in press).

NIS. (2013). *Cambodia inter-censal population survey 2013: Final report*. Phnom Penh: National Institute of Statistics. Retrieved from https://www.stat.go.jp/info/meetings/cambodia/pdf/c13_np02.pdf

Ogawa, Y. (2004). Are agricultural extension programs gender sensitive? Cases from Cambodia. *Gender, Technology and Development, 8*(3), 359–380. doi:10.1177/097185240400800303

Oveson, J., Tranke, I. B., & Öjendal, J. (1996). *When every household is an island: Social organisation and power structures in rural Cambodia*. Uppsala Research Reports in Cultural Anthropology No. 15. Uppsala University and Sida, Uppsala, Sweden.

Peng, S., Huang, J., Sheehy, J. E., Laza, R. C., Visperas, R. M., Zhong, X., … Cassman, K. G. (2004). Rice yields decline with higher night temperature from global warming. *Proceedings of the National Academy of Sciences, 101*(27), 9971–9975. doi:10.1073/pnas.0403720101

Piman, T., Lennaerts, T., & Southalack, P. (2013). Assessment of hydrological changes in the Lower Mekong Basin from basin-wide development scenarios. *Hydrological Processes, 27*, 2115–2125. doi:10.1002/hyp.9764

Piya, L., Maharjan, K. L., & Joshi, N. P. (2019). Climate change and rural livelihoods in developing countries. In L. Piya, K. L. Maharjan, & N. P. Joshi (Eds.), *Socio-economic issues of climate change: A livelihood analysis from Nepal* (pp. 11–33). Singapore: Springer.

Pokhrel, Y., Burbano, M., Roush, J., Kang, H., Sridhar, V., & Hyndman, W. D. (2018). A review of the integrated effects of changing climate, land use, and dams on Mekong River hydrology. *Water, 10*(3), 266. doi:10.3390/w10030266

Poulton, P. L., Dalgliesh, N. P., Vang, S., & Roth, C. H. (2016). Resilience of Cambodian lowland rice farming systems to future climate uncertainty. *Field Crops Research, 198*, 160–170. doi:10.1016/j.fcr.2016.09.008

Räsänen, T. A., Lindgren, V., Guillaume, J. H. A., Buckley, B. M., & Kummu, M. (2016). On the spatial and temporal variability of ENSO precipitation and drought teleconnection in mainland Southeast Asia. *Climate of the Past, 12*, 1889–1905. doi:10.5194/cp-12-1889-2016

Raymond, C. M., Fazey, I., Reed, M. S., Stringer, L. C., Robinson, G. M., & Evely, A. C. (2010). Integrating local and scientific knowledge for environmental management. *Journal of Environmental Management, 91*(8), 1766–1777. doi:10.1016/j.jenvman.2010.03.023

Resurrección, B. P., & Boyland, M. (2017). *Gender equality in renewable energy in the Lower Mekong: Assessment and opportunities*. Prepared by Stockholm Environment Institute for USAID Clean Power Asia. Retrieved from https://pdf.usaid.gov/pdf_docs/PA00SVKB.pdf

RStudio Team. (2015). *RStudio: Integrated development for R*. Boston, MA: RStudio Inc. Retrieved from http://www.rstudio.com

Sok, S., & Yu, X. (2015). Adaptation, resilience and sustainable livelihoods in the communities of the Lower Mekong Basin, Cambodia. *International Journal of Water Resources Development, 31*(4), 575–588. doi:10.1080/07900627.2015.1012659

Sorooshian, S., Hsu, K., Braithwaite, D., & Ashouri, H. (2014). *NOAA climate data record (CDR) of precipit*ation estimation from remotely sensed information using artificial neural networks (PERSIANN-CDR) (1983–2018), version 1 revision 1.* Silver Spring, MD: National Oceanic and Atmospheric Administration. doi:10.7289/V51V5BWQ

Sovacool, B. K., Amp, A., Agostino, A. L., Meenawat, H., & Rawlani, A. (2012). Expert views of climate change adaptation in least developed Asia. *Journal of Environmental Management, 97*, 78–88. doi:10.1016/j.jenvman.2011.11.005

Sowjanya, P. N., Reddy, K. V., & Shashi, M. (2018). Spatial and temporal variations of climate variables over a river basin. *Journal of Rural Development, 37*(2), 383–398. doi:10.25175/jrd/2018/v37/i2/129705

Thon, V., Ou, S., Eng, N., & Ly, T. (2010) *Leadership in local politics of Cambodia: A study of leaders in three communes of three provinces.* CDRI Working Paper 42. Phnom Penh: Cambodia Development Resource Institute. Retrieved from https://cdri.org.kh/wp-content/uploads/wp42e.pdf

Väätilä, K., Kummu, M., Sangmanee, C., & Chinvanno, S. (2010). Modelling climate change impacts on the flood pulse in the Lower Mekong floodplains. *Journal of Water and Climate Change, 1*(1), 67–86. doi:10.2166/wcc.2010.008

Williams, M. (2016). *Participatory GIS and community based adaptation to climate change and environmental hazards: A Cambodian case study.* Master of Environmental Science thesis, The University of Western Australia, Perth, Australia.

Williams, M., Pauli, N., & Boruff, B. (2020). Participatory GIS and community based adaptation to climate change and environmental hazards: A Cambodian case study. In A. Neef & N. Pauli (Eds.), *Climate-induced disasters in the Asia-Pacific region: Response, recovery, adaptation* (pp. 113–134). Bingley: Emerald Publishing.

Yamamauchi, K. (2014). Climate change impacts on agriculture and irrigation in the Lower Mekong Basin. *Paddy and Water Environment, 12*(S2), 227–240. doi:10.1007/s10333-013-0388-9

Ye, W. (2017). *Lien AID partners with UNICEF Cambodia to bring affordable clean water to more than 27,000 villagers in Kratie and Kandal Provinces.* Singapore: Lien AID. Retrieved from http://www.lienaid.org/lien-aid-partners-with-unicef-cambodia-to-bring-affordable-clean-water-to-more-than-27000-villagers-in-kratie-and-kandal-provinces/

Ziv, G., Baran, E., Nam, S., Rodríguez-Iturbe, I., & Levin, S. A. (2012). Trading-off fish biodiversity, food security, and hydropower in the Mekong River Basin. *Proceedings of the National Academy of Sciences, 109*(15), 5609–5614. doi:10.1073/pnas.1201423109

CHAPTER 8

THE EFFECTS OF PRIVATE HOUSEHOLD INSURANCE ON CLIMATE CHANGE ADAPTATION STRATEGIES IN SAMOA

Ashley Bartlett, Meg Parsons and Andreas Neef

ABSTRACT

Private household insurance has been relatively uncommon among households in Samoa to date. Meanwhile, numerous other adaptation interventions are also being implemented, including community-based adaptation (CBA) projects which draw on the skills of the community to address the climate change-related hazards that are expected to affect local communities. Through semi-structured interviews with community members from the urban/peri-urban area around Apia (with and without insurance) and an insurance company representative, this research explores private household natural perils insurance uptake in Samoa and the effect that the uptake of this insurance has on household engagement in other climate change adaptation (CCA) strategies such as CBA projects. Findings suggest that individuals whose homes are already insured with natural perils insurance are more likely to express more individualistic values or beliefs than those without natural perils insurance. Insured homeowners commonly framed adaptation as a technical challenge, with insurance being part of the technical and expert-led approach to prepare for, manage and recover from extreme events. In contrast, householders without insurance perceived CCA as less of a technical task and more of a social process. Those individuals with private household natural perils insurance coverage (in keeping with their more individualistic values) reported that they were less engaged in CBA projects compared to participants without insurance (who held more communalistic

Climate-Induced Disasters in the Asia-Pacific Region: Response, Recovery, Adaptation
Community, Environment and Disaster Risk Management, Volume 22, 167–191
ISSN: 2040-7262/doi:10.1108/S2040-726220200000022007

values). Given the importance of household participation in CBA projects, an increased uptake of insurance may have problematic outcomes for the adaptive capacity of the broader community.

Keywords: Community-based climate adaptation; disaster risk management; household insurance; social contract; Samoa; South Pacific

INTRODUCTION: INSURANCE AS CLIMATE ADAPTATION STRATEGY

International organisations, such as the United Nations (UN) and the Intergovernmental Panel on Climate Change (IPCC), have been increasingly promoting the use of insurance in developing countries in order to support climate change adaptation (CCA). The Alliance of Small Island States (AOSIS) first raised the idea of a regional-based insurance programme in 1991 (McGee, Phelan, & Wenta, 2014). However, after decades of discussions, it was not until the 2013 Warsaw Conference of the Parties (COP 19) meeting that the vision of the AOSIS was realised in the form of the 'Warsaw International Mechanism for Loss and Damages', which was established to manage risk at a national level (McGee et al., 2014). In 2012, the year prior, the IPCC released a special report: *Managing the Risks of Extreme Events and Disasters to Advance Climate Change Adaptation (SREX)* which recommended the use of risk-sharing tools, such as insurance, at all levels, including the local (household) level (IPCC, 2012). In 2014, the IPCC released the Fifth Assessment Report which also clearly identified the key role of insurance for supporting communities, especially in developing countries, to adapt to climate change (IPCC, 2014).

Despite the enthusiasm of international organisations for insurance at the local level, this strategy is relatively new to households in developing countries such as small island developing states (SIDS). Lucas (2015) estimates that among Pacific SIDS, the mean insurance penetration rate is as low as 1.6%. According to Munich Re, a global reinsurance provider, currently only 1% of households in low-income and middle-income countries have insurance coverage against catastrophe risks, compared to 30% in high-income countries (Ramachandran & Masood, 2019). Scholars have previously optimistically suggested that within a few decades, developing nations will 'constitute half of the global market' (Mills, 2005, p. 1040).

Private household natural perils insurance is a strategy that will join an existing repertoire of strategies that households within SIDS have already been using in order to adapt to climate change. Much of the scholarship exploring household adaptation to climate change in developing countries, such as SIDS, have identified that households are implementing strategies to respond to the environmental changes they are facing. In addition to diversifying their livelihoods (Béné et al., 2016; Campbell, Barker, & McGregor, 2011) and relocating their household to respond to environmental hazards, such as sea level changes (Kelman, 2018), scholars recognise that many households also participate in community-based adaptation (CBA) projects to address climate change-related hazards (Gero, Méheux, & Dominey-Howes, 2011; McNamara & Buggy, 2017). CBA projects come in many forms, and examples can include community awareness programmes, community tree-planting programmes, community-built seawalls (Plate 8.1) and other activities that involve members across a community.

When successfully implemented, CBA strategies draw on and utilise a broad range of skills, resources and opinions across communities to collectively address local issues and increase community 'ownership of the adaptation' (Klöck & Nunn, 2019, p. 206). Yet household insurance is a more individual and private approach to adaptation, and is not a form of CBA, as households choose to invest in a policy to secure their own home and possessions from being damaged or lost by natural perils risks. Given the importance of household participation in CBA projects, it is crucial to understand if, and how, the introduction of private household insurance will shape household engagement in CBA. With a better understanding of how private household insurance affects household adaptation behaviour, policymakers and adaptation practitioners can make more informed decisions regarding adaptation planning and avoid encouraging adaptation interventions that may be maladaptive.

This research is based on fieldwork undertaken in Samoa, a small South Pacific island nation. This country was chosen because of the greater availability of information on Samoa's adaptation actions compared to other Pacific nations, including details about insurance penetration and the prevalence of CBA projects. Eight members of the Samoan public, selected from the urban/peri-urban area close to Apia, two with natural perils insurance and six others without natural perils insurance, and one insurance company representative took part in this exploratory research. The major research question that this study addressed is: How does the use of household insurance as a CCA strategy influence household engagement in CBA strategies in Samoa?

Plate 8.1. Community-built Seawall in Samoa's Capital Apia. Photo by A. Bartlett.

COMMUNITY-BASED CLIMATE ADAPTATION AND PRIVATE NATURAL PERILS INSURANCE IN SIDS: A BRIEF REVIEW

Relevance of CBA Strategies in SIDS

In the context of SIDS, where communities are vulnerable to a host of climatic and other hazards, CBA has been described as an essential strategy for communities to address both climate change issues and underlying social and economic challenges that exist across these nations (McNamara & Buggy, 2017). NGOs have promoted CBA as it may be a means of 'demonstrating the importance of participatory and deliberative methods within climate change adaptation ... and the role of longer-term development and social empowerment as a means to reducing vulnerability' (Forsyth, 2017, p. 1). As there is no standard formula for CBA, communities can draw upon different types of adaptation interventions to reach a range of beneficial outcomes appropriate to their own situation.

Academics recognise that the presumed suitability of CBA in SIDS is due to the relatively small scale of the projects and how these projects typically address the local impacts of climate change (McNamara & Buggy, 2017; Westoby et al., 2020). Scholars have argued that community-based methods foster the development of appropriate local solutions (Ayers & Forsyth, 2009; Heltberg, Siegel, & Jorgensen, 2009), which challenges the command-and-control approach to environmental problems that is driven from 'above' (Rojas Blanco, 2006). Therefore, practical initiatives that tangibly address and improve societal adaptive capacity, thereby reducing vulnerability, are commonly expected to be evident at the community scale (Ford & Smit, 2004; Kates, 2000; Kelly & Adger, 2000). This benefit of CBA effectively allows communities to identify their own vulnerabilities and design solutions that are appropriate for their needs.

CBA projects have also been recognised as important for supporting development within SIDS as they reframe adaptation and guide projects that have multiple benefits. As Schipper (2007) observed, this reframing is occurring as communities want projects that address underlying social issues in order to reduce their vulnerability. As a result, there have been significant attempts to design projects that tie in development aims with CCA. Given that SIDS are all at various stages in their development, as McNamara and Buggy (2017) noted, it is assumed that CBA projects also include opportunities that would support sustainable development outcomes.

McNamara and Buggy (2017) note, for CBA projects to be successful, they need to draw on the skills of a broad range of community members. Despite the apparent suitability of CBA projects in developing countries like SIDS, many CBA projects have been considered unsuccessful. Scholars such as Barnett (2008) have suggested that the cause of many of the failures has been the way projects have been implemented by elite actors to the community, rather than by the community. For instance, many donor-funded projects have also become donor-directed, or directed by elite members within a community, without consulting with other members of the community. Betzold (2015) argues that this common practice has resulted in the exclusion of many parts of the community from the project, and the outcomes of the initiatives not adequately addressing the concerns affecting the majority of the community. Therefore, Klöck and Nunn (2019) contend that the success of CBA projects is dependent upon the integration of the broader community, as this allows the projects to be community-owned and genuinely address the issues that are of concern to them. However, Westoby et al. (2020) argue that CBA projects also fail when they are designed by foreign experts and delivered back to the community. According to the authors, this results in CBA projects that cannot be continued by the community, especially once funding ceases. Thus, Westoby et al. (2020, p. 1) argue that the key to successful adaptation is that the interventions are 'locally-led', rather than being just 'community-based' in order to maximise the likelihood that they address the needs of, and can be sustained by, the community.

The focus on 'locally-led' projects means that local community members will be required to participate in CBA. Given that successful CBA projects require the engagement of the broader community, it follows that these community members must be available and able to participate in CBA. However, as Dodman and Mitlin (2013, p. 647) noted, communities are not homogeneous entities, which the CBA literature 'tends to assume'. Rather, there are power relations based upon age, gender and socio-economic positions within these communities which may work to exclude people from participating (Dodman & Mitlin, 2013). Furthermore, various factors constrain individual and household participation in CBA projects such as income and available time (Dodman & Mitlin, 2013). While Hagedoorn et al. (2019) recognise that household participation in community-based activities enhances adaptive capacity within communities, there are many barriers that can prevent individuals from being involved in community projects, such as social exclusion, time preferences and high opportunity costs.

Private Household Insurance and Individual Responsibility for Adaptation

Despite the increasing recognition of the importance of CBA, private insurance is also being increasingly emphasised by international organisations as a useful adaptation strategy. Schäfer, Warner, and Kreft (2019, p. 318) contend that 'insurance has been a cornerstone in climate impact related discourses of the United Nations Framework Convention on Climate Change (UNFCCC) from its establishment in 1992'. The potential of insurance to support adaptation was also outlined in several UN reports, including SREX (IPCC, 2012) and the Fifth Assessment Report (IPCC, 2014). Most recently, the UN Climate Action Summit held in September 2019 discussed how developed nations including the UK and Germany could work towards increasing insurance coverage, including the provision of microinsurance products in developing countries for the benefit of the most vulnerable members of society (United Nations, 2019). As a result, the benefits and critiques of insurance as an adaptation strategy have been increasingly explored throughout the CCA, risk management and insurance literature.

In the context of climate change, risk management scholars have emphasised the positive role insurance companies could play in reducing household exposure to climate change risks. Since the role of insurance started to be discussed in CCA discourse, scholars from the risk management and insurance fields have emphasised the value of insurance as they argue it can encourage 'the adoption of measures designed to minimise damages' (Freeman & Kunreuther, 2002, p. 202). Similarly, Herweijer, Ranger, and Ward (2009, p. 379) argued that private insurance can 'incentivise and enable adaptation'. Scholars also emphasised the role that insurance could have in increasing the adaptive capacity of communities, particularly in developing countries (Hecht, 2008; Mills, 2007; Starominski-Uehara & Keskitalo, 2016). Specifically discussing SIDS, Campbell and Barnett (2010, p. 9) stated that insurance has the potential to increase adaptive capacity as 'people with insurance coverage are better able to recover from an extreme event than those without insurance cover'. This would increase adaptive capacity as communities could recover more quickly from a single impact climate change event, such as a cyclone, and prepare for the next potential climate change event.

However, the limited short-term adaptation benefit of insurance is a key critique that has emerged within the recent literature on insurance. O'Hare, White, and Connelly (2016) first began to challenge the usefulness of insurance as an adaptation strategy in the case of flood insurance in low socio-economic communities in Europe. These scholars argue that insurance merely serves to uphold the status quo by reinstating damaged property in a 'like for like' fashion, which means that the original materials that were damaged are what is replaced by the insurers. Accordingly, O'Hare et al. (2016, p. 1) argue that this serves to 'embed risky behaviours' and inhibit change after an event as the original structure which was destroyed is reconstructed in the same way, which supports a non-progressive form of resilience that maintains the status quo. For O'Hare et al. (2016), household natural perils insurance is therefore a form of maladaptation because it only addresses sudden and single event environmental hazards and does not adequately support long-term adaptation to a changing climate. This is an important critique to consider in the context of SIDS, which face both sudden and single event climate change risks (such as cyclones) and slow-onset risks (such as sea level rise).

An additional critique of insurance focusses upon the accessibility of insurance schemes for vulnerable people within a population. Drawing on social justice principles, O'Hare and White (2018, p. 389) stated that because some individuals 'might lack the resources required to ... participate in insurance schemes', encouraging the increased uptake of insurance as a method of individual adaptation may be inappropriate. For these scholars, as the high costs of insurance premiums exclude households from taking out insurance coverage, this strategy would not be suitable for members of the community unless the policies were subsidised. This is an important critique as international organisations, scholars and commercial organisations are increasingly promoting insurance as a suitable adaptation method for households, including those in low socio-economic communities, around the world.

Within SIDS, due to the high costs associated with insurance, scholars have also directly questioned the practicality of insurance as an adaptation strategy within these nations. Baarsch and Kelman (2016) argue that as a result of exclusionary clauses and premium costs, private insurance policies are likely to be of limited value in Pacific SIDS. Parsons, Brown, Nalau, and Fisher (2018) also note that business people in developing countries struggle with affording insurance;

therefore, it seems unlikely that members of the community, who are typically in a lower socio-economic bracket, would be capable of affording insurance as they may have less disposable income to take out an insurance policy and meet any required preconditions. Combined, the contributions of these authors suggest that there are many limitations of insurance as a form of adaptation in SIDS due to the high costs associated with this strategy.

In addition to the high costs associated with insurance, scholars have also critiqued insurance as an adaptation strategy in SIDS as only some community members will be eligible for coverage. Surminski and Oramas-Dorta (2013) questioned the role of insurance as a form of adaptation across the region due to the range of climate change threats expected to affect SIDS. As many states across the Pacific region will face increasing climate variability and more exposure to specific climate change risks, insurance companies will not be able to offer insurance to all of society for all climate change risks. Insurance will not be available to all members of society due to the issue of 'insurability' whereby many climate change-induced risks are not insurable from a commercial perspective (Savitt, 2017). This issue of insurability is problematic because as the risks of climate change become more certain with time, it is more likely that areas and communities that were once insurable become uninsurable. Therefore, as the risks of climate change increase for SIDS, it is likely that in the future a lower share of the population will be eligible for an insurance payout despite investing in this type of adaptation in the present due to insurance companies progressively withdrawing coverage for increasingly high-risk areas.

Despite historically low levels of insurance penetration within SIDS, financial institutions are increasingly attempting to gain further penetration at the household level within the region. According to Lassa, Surjan, Caballero-Anthony, and Fisher (2019), insurance uptake in the Asia-Pacific region is among the lowest in the world. This runs counter to Mills' (2005) earlier predictions that insurance coverage for natural perils insurance will increase significantly in the developing world, accounting for over half of policies in the global market in a few decades. In Samoa, a report produced by the University of the South Pacific (USP) (2016) outlined the results of a financial programme, which included a module on insurance, administered by a commercial bank. The report noted that all individuals who attended the programme run by the bank felt more confident about the insurance options that would work for them (University of the South Pacific, 2016). While there is limited research available about the frequency of these programmes in SIDS, the report from USP exemplifies how insurance providers are trying to educate potential customers on the benefits of insurance coverage and expand the insurance market throughout SIDS within the Pacific.

Potentially as a result of insurance companies seeking to expand into new markets, a significant part of the scholarship on insurance is focussed on exploring the design of insurance products for developing countries, especially designing out the risk of 'moral hazard' (Linnerooth-Bayer et al., 2009). Moral hazard refers to human behaviour that intentionally increases the exposure of insured individuals (Mcleman & Smit, 2006). Miranda and Vedenov (2001) argued that insurers have tried to manage this issue by creating index-based insurance products that reduce the incentives for insured households to intentionally destroy their property (i.e. crops) in order to receive an insurance payout. For household insurance policies, the establishment of strict prerequisites households must meet in order to be eligible for insurance coverage can also be described as a way in which insurers are working to prevent moral hazard.

Morale hazard is also a significant hazard generated by insurance coverage which has received little attention in the literature focussed on climate change insurance. Similar to moral hazard, morale hazard also refers to human behaviour that increases the exposure of individuals to potential perils, but it differs because it is a result of unintentional rather than intentional actions. The outcomes of morale hazard can be equally as damaging as the outcomes of moral hazard. A notable exception to the dearth of literature on morale hazard and CCA is the work of Mcleman and Smit (2006) who reconceptualised the standard approach to vulnerability into the language of insurance and risk management and developed a new conceptual model of vulnerability. The authors applied their model to crop insurance products (designed to reduce losses from climate change) to determine the effect of insurance on the level of risk the farmers faced. Through their novel approach, Mcleman and Smit (2006) found that morale hazard due to insurance coverage caused individuals to unintentionally make decisions that increased their exposure to climate change risks, for example, by choosing to grow a less diverse range of crops. Therefore, this finding exposed that in addition to moral hazard, research should also explore how insurance may result in morale hazard and the extent to which this hazard might offset the potential benefits of insurance for reducing risk.

Discussions about the role of insurance also feed into a larger debate about the responsibilities of different actors within society for managing environmental issues such as climate change. Pretty and Ward (2001) argued that the responsibility for the environment, traditionally managed by the State, was increasingly shifting to individuals through government policies. Several scholars have argued that this shift in the traditional division of responsibilities between the State and society is a result of the governing regime of neoliberalism, which advocates for the elimination of price controls, deregulation of capital markets and increased privatisation (Blythe et al., 2018; Joseph, 2013). In the context of CCA, Adger et al. (2013) argue that unclear social contracts between States and communities may be problematic, and therefore should be made explicit in order to promote effective and consistent long-term CCA.

If the social contract, the division of responsibilities between the State and society, becomes explicitly clear, individual community members may become abruptly responsible for adapting to environmental changes. Vilcan (2017) has drawn on the governance concept of 'responsibilisation' to describe the process where responsibility shifts, or appears to shift, from governments to individuals within adapting communities. According to Vilcan (2017), this process of responsibilisation is driving individuals and communities to manage adaptation themselves, despite largely not being responsible for the issues causing the changes to their environment. Explored largely in the context of flood risk management, the responsibilisation of the community requires citizens to manage and implement their own risk management initiatives, though there is doubt regarding their ability, or adaptive capacity, to do so (Walker, Whittle, Medd, & Watson, 2010). Research conducted by Bergsma, Gupta, and Jong (2012) on the use of insurance to manage flood events in the Netherlands suggested that the increasing use of this individualistic strategy has caused fragmentation in society. This breakdown of social ties within the community has resulted in a reduction in the overall capacity of Dutch society to manage the risks and adapt to flooding as households are acting autonomously, rather than collectively. This suggests that there is a strong link between a changing social contract (real or perceived), increasing individual responsibilisation, individual insurance coverage and a reduced capacity in the community to respond to environmental issues, like flooding.

Customary Forms of Insurance in SIDS

Scholars in the field of anthropology, economics and rural sociology have identified that in many developing country contexts, individuals and communities are more likely to rely on traditional relationships of reciprocity and mutual assistance to avoid losses rather than engaging with Western forms of insurance (Fafchamps & Lund, 2003; Platteau, 1997). Reciprocity essentially functions as a form of insurance as there is a strong belief by community members that if goods, such as money or food, are shared with others, they will be returned to a similar value in times of need. In many instances, if a community member wants to leave the informal system without having to claim back their goods, the goods will be returned to them in their entirety (Platteau, 1997). Evidently, this is very different from the way in which Western insurance companies operate.

Scholarship on traditional forms of insurance exploring the use of these socio-cultural forms of insurance against climate-induced hazards within SIDS remains scant. Despite the recognition that in developing countries, communities are more likely to use reciprocity as a form of protection against loss than commercial forms of insurance, there has been little systematic research exploring such social mechanisms within SIDS nations in terms of their role as a form of insurance against the risks of climate change. Notable exceptions include the work of Perkins and Krause (2018) and Hofmann (2017) who have explored traditional forms of insurance used to protect communities from environmental changes in the Federated States of Micronesia (FSM). Perkins and Krause (2018) identified how the Sawei system operating in Yap State has enabled the local communities to adapt to climate change. The Sawei system is a 'bicultural system of tribute offerings, gift exchange, and disaster relief' between MI [main island] and OI [outer island] cultures (Hunter-Anderson & Zan, 1996, p. 1, as cited in Perkins & Krause, 2018). As Perkins and Krause (2018) noted, the structured movement of goods between the main and outer islands of Yap ceased long ago, but the legacy of the system continues to shape the relations between people living on the islands. Perkins and Krause (2018, p. 73) have described the practice as an 'adaptation of mutual reciprocity' since one set of islands provided the other set of islands with the resources they needed in order to survive. Hofmann (2017, p. 88) similarly identified the movement of individuals and communities between islands in Chuuk State,

FSM, as a socio-cultural activity that served as a form of 'insurance' for the local communities. The ongoing use of these systems in Yap State and Chuuk State during periods of environmental change indicates that they have a history of success in protecting the communities from loss.

While not directly referring to a form of mutual reciprocity, Le De, Gaillard, Friesen, and Smith (2015) recognised that Samoan households consider the transfer of money, or remittances, from family living abroad as a form of 'self-insurance' during post-hazard periods. Underpinning Samoan society and all aspects of Samoan life, including their economy, is *fa'asamoa*, or the 'Samoan way of life'. *Fa'asamoa* comprises three key aspects which include *matai* (chief system), *aiga* (family) and religion (Thornton et al., 2010, p. 1). Parsons et al. (2018) argue that *fa'asamoa* plays a key role in driving decisions, including around CCA. In addition to attending religious services, households within Samoa have a cultural obligation to donate generously to the church. As part of *fa'asamoa*, there is an expectation held within the community that each household will give financial donations to the church in their village. As noted by Thornton et al. (2010, p. 7), this type of kinship obligation carries a significant financial burden which 'presents a dilemma for those who are struggling to cope with increasing hardship'. However, the movement of money and other goods between families and the church can also be seen as a form of 'community insurance', as there is an expectation that social-cultural networks will support families in the aftermath of disasters. Clearly, given the recognition that societies in SIDS are utilising traditional and communal forms of insurance to protect themselves against losses, it is important to consider the extent to which this may impact the uptake of private insurance coverage.

In conclusion, despite the growing amount of literature focussing on adaptation, significant gaps still remain. There is a dearth of studies that have sought to explore different people's perceptions of insurance within developing countries through qualitative methodologies, and little is known about the uptake of household insurance as an adaptation strategy in the Pacific. Furthermore, of the scholarship that has addressed potential maladaptation caused by insurance, no research has explored the effect insurance coverage may have on CBA strategies. Therefore, this study seeks to contribute to filling this gap by exploring how individuals in urban and peri-urban households in Samoa perceive household insurance as a CCA strategy and how this influences their engagement in CBA strategies.

METHODOLOGY

Given the exploratory nature of the research project, semi-structured, conversational interviews were considered as the most culturally appropriate method in the context of the fieldwork location of Samoa. *Talanoa*, which translates to storytelling, is a means of communicating that is appropriate in the Pacific context, particularly in Samoa, Tonga and Fiji (Vaioleti, 2006). This form of communication allows meaning to be co-created in the interview process between the participant and the interviewer through the use of personal stories. This simultaneously develops a sense of trust between the researcher and the participant which allows for sensitive or personal topics and information to be discussed safely.

Research participants were recruited through a third party, a Samoan research assistant. In accordance with ethics regulations, particular emphasis was given to informed consent and non-disclosure of research participants' identity. Interviews were conducted face-to-face by the first author, with a total of nine participants who represented the Samoan public (referred to as CM1-8 in the findings section) and a Samoan representative from a major insurance company (IC1) in Samoa. All participants agreed to have the interview recorded. Interview transcripts were coded with NVivo 12 software and thematically analysed.

FINDINGS

This section presents the results obtained from interviews with community members and an insurance company representative in Samoa. Three critical themes emerged from the interviews and are used to organise the results. The three key themes are: (1) a shared and strong sense of individual responsibility for adaptation; (2) the technical and self-oriented approach to adaptation taken by households with natural perils insurance coverage; and (3) household insurance as a new challenge to the existing socio-cultural 'insurance' networks in Samoa.

Strong Sense of Individual Responsibility for Adaptation within the Community

The first theme evident in the primary data concerns how different people (insurance company representative, community members) perceived who was responsible for planning for, and enacting, adaptation at the household level. In this section, we present the different perceptions the research participants held on the topic of individual responsibility for climate change in Samoa.

Research participants frequently raised the topic of responsibility for adaptation. They questioned who was responsible for implementing CCA actions. The insurance company representative suggested that people in Samoa did not possess a strong sense of responsibility for taking individual actions to reduce their vulnerability to environmental hazards, including those related to climate change, due to the Samoan identity. Samoan community members were perceived by the insurance company representative to 'take things lightly' and underestimate their risks:

> I know our people. They just joke about everything and anything, [they] take things lightly. If they see a wave, you know, a big tsunami coming, they're probably going to make a joke right before the tsunami hits them ... but that's just how our people are .... People can probably see those aids and people coming in to help build something. And then to them its 'Oh, we're settled. Nothing to worry about. This is awesome.' (IC1, 2019)

With this obviously paternalistic statement, the insurance company representative suggested that this attitude made the Samoan community dependent on external assistance. This comment also implied that the insurance company representative is of the opinion that Samoan people are resistant to taking on the responsibility for enacting disaster risk reduction and CCA strategies. He also characterised Samoans as lacking motivation for change and void of a sense of personal responsibility for adaptation. Instead, he considered Samoan people to be reactive (responding to environmental hazards following extreme events) rather than proactive in their actions and mostly dependent on foreign (outside) knowledge, skills and financial support in times of crisis. However, as the following paragraphs will show, this characterisation of Samoan community members as dependent was not represented in most responses obtained from participants representing the community.

The majority of community members interviewed as part of this research expressed a strong sense of individual responsibility for adapting to the impacts of climate change, which included the desire to receive training in how to do so. When the topic of responsibility was raised with participant CM7, for instance, she declared that 'I think everybody should get involved.' Similarly, when participant CM5 was reflecting on the responsibility of individuals to implement adaption strategies, she expressed a clear desire to take on more responsibility for CCA:

> So, I think, I think whichever – governments, local governments or someone from overseas – should, what's it called, empower our communities to do projects for climate resilience. (CM5, 2019)

The above quote, which was representative of the views of most of the community members interviewed in this research, highlights their view of shared responsibility for CCA. Rather than being merely dependent on outside assistance, CM5 articulated a more nuanced depiction of the relationships between external actors (international, national and local government institutions) and local communities. The adaptation policies and projects should empower community members (and communities) to be able to take responsibility for addressing the impacts of climate change. Community members did not appear unwilling to take on more responsibility at the community level for adapting to the impacts of climate variability, including extreme weather events, and ongoing changing climate conditions. Instead, community members were constrained to take on personal and collective responsibilities for climate adaptation due to existing power dynamics and institutional arrangements. Recognition of the need for community members to take responsibility for CCA and their desires to be given more responsibility through CCA policies and projects in the future was further emphasised by participants' expressions of disapproval about other organisations being given responsibility for adaptation.

When discussing the role of the Church (which includes a diverse range of different Christian denominations) within Samoan society, one community participant (CM6) spoke about her opposition to Samoans being dependent on such organisations for assistance with adaptation (and in post-hazard periods). In Samoa, CM6 noted, religious groups as well as NGOs and international aid agencies were involved in projects to assist Samoan communities to adapt to climate change. Several research participants spoke disapprovingly about such organisations, sources of foreign aid and the ongoing pattern of receiving aid from external sources as a way to cope with extreme events.

> But I would never expect the church to come help, which is why as you can see, I put a lot of effort into doing what I think [is important] and that is for my own safety, for my own future. (CM6, 2019)

For CM6, individuals were (or should be) taking responsibility for adaptation, rather than relying on outside assistance (including insurance companies). The sense of individual responsibility and the emphasis on individuals' agency (and capacities to enact changes) were strongly expressed by the Samoan community members who participated in this study, which contrasted with the insurance company representative's depiction of Samoans as being dependent on foreign assistance and unmotivated to take actions to reduce their vulnerability and adapt to climate change.

Technical and Self-oriented Approach to Adaptation by Households with Natural Perils Insurance

The second theme developed from the interviews reflects the way in which households with natural perils insurance engage in adaptation in a more self-oriented and technical manner compared to non-insured participants. In this section, different strategies that households implement or engage with in order to adapt to climate change are explored. The strong sense of responsibility that community member participants in this research feel towards CCA is clearly evident in their reported behaviour and engagement with adaptation strategies. Five out of the six participants that did not have natural perils insurance coverage were involved in implementing or engaging with strategies at both the household and community level. The other two participants, who had natural perils insurance, did not report engagement in CBA strategies, such as growing community crops inland, planting community trees or attending community seminars.

When participants discussed whether they were using household natural perils insurance to adapt to climate change, the two households with the natural perils insurance coverage focussed on describing the logical nature of their behaviour to take out an insurance policy. Both participants indicated that investing in an insurance policy with natural perils coverage was a logical decision considering they were living in Samoa, an environment exposed to climatic and other hazards. For these participants, it was logical because they trusted that their insurance policies would cover the value of their properties in the instance of an environmental hazard linked to climate change. Both participants also highlighted that their households have been a big investment for them, and thus, they are 'worth' protecting:

> I grew up in New Zealand so if you want to protect your investment, it's not a stupid thing to do, especially when you're in an area which does have cyclones. (CM1, 2019)

> So, when I moved back to Samoa, we bought a cemented concrete double storey building, injected a lot of money for renovation, making sure we get everything done. Insurance on the house, insurance for both businesses, the coffee shop and the [restaurant], insurance on the cars, dogs, … everything. (CM2, 2019)

Clearly from the perspective of these householders, the use of this strategy in Samoa was a rational choice to protect the financial value of their investment, their household. The participants also indicated that their decision to take out household insurance was significantly shaped by their international experiences. CM1 directly noted that their experience living in New Zealand shaped their thoughts on insurance. This participant alluded to the importance of accumulating wealth and protecting it, through the purchase of property, which, according to the participant, is symbolic of the culture in New Zealand. Additionally, throughout the interview with CM2, the participant also described how experiences of living in Europe and New Zealand shaped their worldview, which included their opinions on the importance of insurance. These comments strongly reflect how participants have brought the concept of insurance and ways of thinking about this strategy back to Samoa.

Unlike the participants who use natural perils insurance as a form of adaptation, other research participants perceived insurance as an illogical waste of money. The one participant who had household insurance without natural perils insurance and the two participants who no longer had insurance coverage expressed far more critical opinions of insurance as a suitable adaptation strategy compared to the participants with natural perils coverage. Instead, these participants claimed that insurance was an illogical choice for economic reasons. A major concern of these participants was that in the instance of an environmental hazard that caused damage to their property, the amount of compensation they would receive after making a claim with the insurance company would be less than the amount of money they had paid the insurance company in premium fees:

> If I add all the premiums that they can ask me to pay them on a yearly basis, and then compare it to any damages that would occur, whether it be from climate change or strong winds or whatever, I think I would much rather fork out the money and it will cost less. (CM3, 2019)

This attitude was expressed as a result of previous personal experiences and stories of other people within the community who had experienced difficulty when making claims with insurance companies. Another participant also demonstrated her scepticism of insurance, stating 'like I said, I'm very wary of their small print that they have' (CM7, 2019) due to a past experience trying to gain compensation from an insurance company after a cyclone struck her property. Clearly, these critical reflections on insurance reveal there are very different perceptions of the value of insurance and experiences with the trustworthiness of insurance companies among the participants interviewed in this research project within Samoa.

Participants with natural perils insurance had homes that were built to a higher technical standard than participants without insurance. When discussing the resilience of their household, three participants identified that they had built or purchased a home that was resilient to the effects of climate change. Two of these participants also had the natural perils insurance to adapt to climate change, while the other participant did not. Despite all three participants identifying that they had built or purchased a resilient house, there was a marked difference between the insured participants and the participant without insurance. The insured participants focussed on how their home had been built to a specific standard, such as a 'Kiwi Build' (CM2, 2019) standard, or designed by a certified 'engineer' (CM1, 2019) to be resilient to climate change. However, when the participant without insurance was explaining how they were building a new house with concrete in order to be 'stronger and cooler' (CM8, 2019), they mentioned that it was not designed by an engineer, but a friend of the family, a builder. When discussing the construction of the home, this participant reflected on how the quality of the workmanship had occasionally been poor. As a result, several contractors had been used to build the home. These responses suggest that there was likely to be a difference in the quality and resilience of the homes of the insured participants compared to the uninsured participants – probably due to the wealth differences – despite the three participants identifying that they were implementing the same strategy.

The insurance company representative indicated that in order to obtain insurance certain building requirements (such as an engineer's report) specific to the insurance company must be met. According to the insurance company representative, many households in Samoa are still living in traditional housing situations, such as 'huts, with coconut leaves as roofing' (IC1, 2019). The insurance company representative acknowledged that this was a problematic situation for these households as it would be a barrier preventing them from obtaining insurance coverage. The insurance company indicated that these households would be excluded from coverage as the risk of damage to their household would be too high, and therefore, the insurance company would be unwilling to provide insurance coverage. The insurance company representative described how their process of assessing households to determine whether they are insurable excludes many types of buildings, in favour of buildings which are constructed to a higher technical standard:

> And so, if we go to see a building and it's a rundown building, I would say, uh … it's made out of timber [for example], it's a risk that we probably would not want to take, and therefore we will probably have to decline [their request for insurance]. And so, [because of that], I'm sure people won't bother to insure, unless they have a brand-new house or very solid building. (IC1, 2019)

Additionally, the participants with household insurance had more technical strategies to prepare for the post-hazard period. Drawing on an experience with Cyclone Evan in 2012, when most of the electricity in Apia was down for months, participant CM2 described why it was necessary to install a generator and a water tank. The participant emphasised the practicality of this adaptation strategy, as it would allow them to remain 'functional' if another devastating event should occur, unlike in the aftermath of Cyclone Evan:

> So, making sure you have a water tank and making sure you have a generator and the generator to run electricity for the property. For example, we have a generator here, at home, at the restaurant, just to make sure that you know, you know, you can keep the food cool. Then, if you need maybe a place to go, then you know everything is functional. (CM2, 2019)

During the interview, the participant also mentioned how other community members seemed to challenge the participant's decision to invest in this strategy. The participant described how other people in the community had questioned his decision to replace the existing generator, 'And people will say, well, why are you buying a new generator?' (CM2, 2019), rather than expressing support for the decision. Despite this, the participant stated that they proceeded with the generator as they felt that in Samoa 'you just need to be in the state of mind of always being on the safe side' (CM2, 2019). Considered in the context of the interviews with the community members, this further represents the self-oriented behaviour of the insured participant as they spent money on their own adaptation strategy, rather than giving it to CBA projects which would benefit the broader community.

When non-insured members of the community discussed how they were adapting to the anticipated losses from an environmental hazard, they identified less technical strategies. One participant without household insurance mentioned that her household has a basic 'preparation kit' (CM4, 2019) which contains simple emergency supplies, such as a torch and non-perishable food, that they can use in the event of an environmental hazard, such as a cyclone. Compared to the participant using generators and water storage, this strategy allows this participant to cope, rather than remain functional. There is clearly a big technical difference in the strategies that the household with natural perils insurance and the one without natural perils insurance are using in preparing for climate change events.

Furthermore, the adaptation strategy that was most frequently discussed by participants within the interviews was ongoing basic do-it-yourself (DIY) maintenance to their home in order to make it secure and ready for weather events which may be aggravated by climate change. Conducting ongoing DIY maintenance to their house was the strategy that most participants identified implementing in order to adapt to climate change at the household level. For most participants, this meant 'nailing down' (CM7, 2019) or 'buckling down' (CM6, 2019) the surface material of their home in order to make it more stable before cyclone season. This strategy was also suggested by one of the participants with natural perils insurance coverage as a strategy that would be most appropriate for other people within the community to implement. Despite having insurance for their own home, this participant said that 'tying down their roofs' (CM1, 2019) would be the most appropriate adaptation strategy that other members of the community should do, rather than purchase household insurance. This suggests that less technical solutions are considered unsuitable for households that have insurance. However, this may be because insured households are built to a higher standard than those without natural perils insurance.

The participants without natural perils insurance expressed a strong sense of awareness and involvement in community adaptation events that were occurring in their village, and more broadly across Samoa. Many participants spoke of their awareness about local initiatives that they could participate in, such as community meetings, through to nation-wide initiatives, like tree planting. Research participants without insurance coverage for natural perils described themselves as being 'very busy' in their day-to-day lives in Samoa, but despite their busy schedules, they discussed their involvement in community-based strategies. These participants identified that these initiatives were successful because people across the community were all doing their part:

> I think tree planting is one of the best ways that we're all doing. (CM6, 2019)

Furthermore, these participants without natural perils insurance also discussed the collective benefits that participating in these projects could have for community resilience. Attending seminars, meetings and participating in community-based emergency drills were strategies and adaptation events that several participants reported actively engaging in. Three participants identified that their communities were implementing these CBA strategies, such as engaging in community seminars or emergency drills, in order to ensure that people within the community were prepared for environmental hazards associated with climate change, such as cyclones and other hazards like earthquakes and tsunamis. The importance of these events was emphasised by these participants as they bring the community together and ensure that everyone is aware of what to do in the case of an emergency:

> Yeah, I think with our church community we actually had like a session where the pastor would make sure that we understand, especially with the cyclones, and when we had the earthquake. They actually gave a little session about, you know, preparing and being prepared. When there would be a cyclone we would have to evacuate, the numbers to call, you know we have 911 now, and where a centre would be for our church community to actually come and gather together, say if something happened. So, we have the church community hall that actually caters if a disaster came up and people who have their houses destroyed or something. They can actually be, they are supposed to come there for shelter. (CM3, 2019)

Additionally, the important environmental and social outcomes that participating in CBA strategies could have on the environment were also highlighted by participants without insurance. The participants without insurance spoke about how strategies such as the community planting initiatives directly help to address the cause of climate change by reducing atmospheric carbon dioxide, while simultaneously helping to enable community members to adapt to rising temperatures because it provides shade for people. Of all the adaption strategies mentioned by participants, this strategy was the one that resonated most strongly with the majority of participants:

> To plant trees to save the, uh, the climate. [They] will help with all the changing of the weather. So, I think everybody's aware of trying to plant, and don't cut down those trees, but leave some .... Yeah, everybody goes out and plants some. It's called conservation day. They have it on a Monday, usually it's on a Monday and it's a day off ....That's what we're doing. (CM7, 2019)

However, when the topic of CBA was raised with participants during the interviews, participants with natural perils insurance did not have many comments to share about strategies being implemented within their communities. An exception to this was one participant expressing their awareness about community seminars being held in order to help with CCA. However, they stated that they were too busy at work to attend community events of this nature:

> Well, actually, not much. I am pretty much busy with my two family businesses that I don't get much time to go to events or conferences. (CM2, 2019)

These reactions clearly reflect how attending community events, like seminars, is of a low priority to these insured participants as they were unable to spare time to attend the events. This is particularly clear when compared to the responses of the participants without natural perils insurance, as they described being similarly busy in their everyday lives.

Furthermore, when discussing CBA projects, participants with natural perils insurance chose to highlight that they perceived the actions of other community members as irresponsible. These participants highlighted that they felt community members made poor personal choices as they did not take proactive action to adapt. One of the participants with insurance focussed on the choice of individuals within the community to live in vulnerable areas, while the other participant focussed on the reactive nature of people within the Samoan community:

> Um … because, you know, a lot of it is up to personal choice because a lot of people choose to live in vulnerable areas, because of their family connection. Sometimes they feel they have nowhere else to go. So, you know, they have made themselves more vulnerable to climate change by choice. Not because they want to be vulnerable, but because that's where they decided to live, and they are well aware of the risks of living there. (CM1, 2019)

> What I think, Samoa has never been a very proactive country … it's kind of a last-minute rush to the shops and trying to buy candles, some canned food, or try to fix the house, everything happens very last minute. (CM2, 2019)

These criticisms emphasise how the participants who have natural perils insurance believe that individuals are responsible for managing risks associated with climate change-related hazards. This approach reflects a self-oriented approach to adaptation and helps to explain why they may not be engaging as actively as people without insurance in community-based initiatives.

Clearly, despite the active and meaningful participation and engagement in community strategies reported by most participants, there was a distinct lack of engagement in these strategies reported by the two participants who were using insurance as a household adaptation strategy. As shown, the participants with natural perils insurance did not report engaging in adaptation strategies beyond the household level, unlike other participants without natural perils insurance. The focus of these participants on their own households reflects a self-oriented approach to adaptation.

Private Household Insurance as a New Challenge to Existing Socio-Cultural Security Networks in Samoa

The third major theme that emerged from the data concerns the way in which insurance is perceived as a new challenge to the existing socio-cultural security networks that operate in Samoa. This section explores how participants without insurance perceived it as a foreign concept and an expensive form of adaptation that challenges the existing cultural obligations of Samoa. Participants also identified an existing form of socio-cultural insurance in Samoa, which the introduction of Western insurance products appears to be challenging.

For most participants, the alien nature of insurance was identified as the reason why insurance penetration was so low in Samoa. Some participants suggested that only people living in the capital city, Apia, would be aware of insurance, and that the community members living further from the nation's capital would be unaware of the concept. One participant directly stated that insurance is a concept from abroad:

> With all due respect from the Samoan community, this concept of insurance … it comes from overseas. (CM4, 2019)

The perspective of the insurance company representative confirmed these views, emphasising that this was an issue that needed to be addressed. He described an awareness-raising initiative which involved speaking to children in several schools. However, it was acknowledged that this initiative would exclude the vast majority of the population. The response from the insurance company shows that insurance is currently not a widely used strategy within Samoa, but attempts are being made by the industry to promote the strategy in places beyond the capital Apia in order to increase the uptake of coverage:

> Well, we did once get involved with something that was arranged with the Central Bank of Samoa, where we did speak to about 100+ students from different schools and talk about insurance. But as you know, those types of programs and workshops would really help [promote insurance] not only for students, but to the public in general. We get a lot of profiles for commercial risk and these people understand the importance of insurance, but it's the other maybe 80% of the community who don't understand is the concern for us. And it's them that are the target. Not so much that we want their money .... (IC1, 2019)

Many participants also highlighted that fulfilling cultural obligations was of a higher priority than purchasing insurance in the Samoan context. Most of the participants interviewed raised the cultural obligations towards which they are expected to contribute as a major barrier limiting their financial capacity to take out insurance coverage. Donations to the Church and financial support to family members are expected and some participants identified that this was due to the competitive culture that existed between households, where they needed to donate more money than other families, especially to the Church, in order to retain a high social standing:

> I'm not sure if it's culture but you know how we do fa'alavelave [funeral, wedding, other life-altering event]. We have obligations to do like funeral, family bestowments and also we have obligations when we become chief. So, most of the family have to give money to church, to the village, and fa'alavelave. I think the mentality is that when it comes to fa'alavelave, when it comes to funeral and things like that it becomes the priority for most of Samoan families give a lot of money to funerals and stuff. (CM5, 2019)

Evidently, the cultural traditions and obligations within Samoa place a large financial burden on households, which plays an important role in shaping household uptake of insurance. While the insurance company representative agreed that insurance is expensive, he also emphasised that it was an attainable form of CCA for members of the broader Samoan community. When discussing the considerable costs of insurance coverage including natural perils coverage in Samoa, the insurance company representative acknowledged that it was expensive for the average family in Samoa. Similar to participants from the community, he also noted that cultural events are a priority for many families which limits their financial resources. Yet he also suggested that if a household wanted to ignore these cultural obligations in order to take out insurance, it would be possible:

> Because if it's important, if you understand and if you know what's important, regardless, you put money into it. I think money will come second or third to being the issue. But if your mind is set to something, and you know how important it is, then regardless if it's expensive or unaffordable, you make, you make an effort to, to get there and do something about it. (IC1, 2019)

Yet the insurance company also acknowledged that they were considering potential strategies to assist households in overcoming the financial barriers that prevent Samoan families from taking out insurance coverage. The representative expressed that it was difficult for households to take out insurance coverage due to high premium costs and the prerequisites they must meet, such as an engineering certificate of the property. As a result, the company was exploring potential ways they could assist households in taking out coverage.

When discussing the topic of choosing whether insurance was necessary in Samoa, many participants expressed that there is an existing system that serves as a form of insurance against losses in Samoa. Many participants talked about how they felt that Western insurance was not necessary in Samoa. In particular, participant CM8, who had spent more than 50 years living in New Zealand and had had household insurance coverage for his home there, reflected on the decision to return back to Samoa and to not take out insurance coverage for the family home in Samoa:

> But it did arise in my mind that this is home and there is no need for insurance. (CM8, 2019)

Taking time to think about the reasoning for this response, this participant expressed that there was a culture of reciprocity that already existed in Samoa before the concept of insurance was introduced.

> I'm finding that insurance maybe is a foreign idea that gets pushed and slowly creeps in.... And, it takes away that openness to compensate for (imitates the voice of a young boy) 'Fa'amolemole (please), can I please have some money or some mangos to eat because our crops aren't going too well?'. (CM8, 2019)

This response highlights how people in Samoa have managed difficulties and hard times by drawing on their social network. While the participant was sharing this opinion, he also shared a story of an interaction with a young boy that had occurred during the morning, just prior to our interview. The young boy from a neighbouring house in his village had come over to ask for some mangos to eat because his family was hungry. This story helped to emphasise how close social relationships are between people within the community in Samoa, literally and physically, and that they serve as a form of insurance for many people within the community.

DISCUSSION AND CONCLUSION

Given that CBA strategies are an essential part of Samoa's approach to adaptation, there is a risk that increased insurance coverage may have a significant impact on the adaptation outcomes of Samoa. Within the scholarship, there is consensus that CBA strategies are an essential way in which SIDS, including Samoa, can successfully adapt to climate change. This is due to how CBA strategies allow for CCA to be implemented from the 'bottom up', with interventions and projects designed at the grassroots level to address climate change impacts that will be of concern to people at the local level. Within Samoa, participants in this research confirmed that CBA projects are addressing a range of climate change effects affecting the community at the local level. However, despite the relative success of CBA in Samoa, there is also a parallel push by insurance providers, development agencies and government to increase the number of people taking out private household insurance across the country as a way to reduce the risks to their properties posed by climate change-related natural hazards. Yet, if there is indeed a tendency of insured households to become more self-oriented, the success of CBA projects may be reduced due to a decrease in the level of participation of insured households in CBA strategies.

Furthermore, the eligibility criteria that prevent many members of the Samoan community from gaining insurance challenge the assumption that insurance coverage can be a widely adopted adaptation strategy by households. As shown within the literature on CCA, there is some confidence that insurance can support adaptation efforts in communities in developing countries. However, a growing portion of the literature has identified that there are several social justice and equity issues that act as barriers preventing large parts of the population from gaining coverage. Scholars have identified the costs of insurance premiums and the location of households as two significant barriers preventing the uptake of insurance (Baarsch & Kelman, 2016; Parsons et al., 2018; Phelan, 2011; Picard, 2008). As identified in the findings section, insurance companies are addressing the cost issue by considering subsidised premiums for households. However, it was also revealed by the insurance company representative that insurance companies require households to confirm the structural integrity of their homes before they can be insured. It was acknowledged by the insurance company that many households in Samoa are constructed with traditional building materials such as coconut husks, rather than the materials used in modern Western homes, and consequently, these households would be unable to take out insurance.

Given the collective nature of Samoan society, the socio-cultural system, *fa'asamoa*, can be understood as a traditional form of insurance as it helps to prevent loss across society. As demonstrated in the results from this research, many community members interviewed for this research expressly referred to how the Samoan way of life, or *fa'asamoa*, has played a significant role in shaping their actions, including those around adaptation. As many participants noted, because *fa'asamoa* promotes the generous sharing of resources, including money, food and gifts, within family and the wider community, in times of hardship it is likely that these resources will flow back to those who give generously. The role that *fa'asamoa* has on providing community members with a sense of protection from loss is important because it clearly demonstrates that a traditional form of insurance is already in use in Samoa. Therefore, efforts to increase the penetration of Western insurance products within Samoa, and potentially other SIDS nations, must be cognisant of existing cultural systems that may already be providing this protection to the community. It is important to recognise the role of traditional socio-cultural systems as it is crucial to support adaptation strategies that are culturally relevant to communities in order to ensure that adaptation effects are successful.

The importance of non-Western knowledge is becoming increasingly more appreciated within the literature on environmental management issues. Increasingly, scholars, policymakers and adaptation practitioners are recognising the importance of local knowledge in discussions about direct actions to address climate change, including adaptation policies and practices. Political and community leaders from SIDS nations themselves are demanding that the leading Western nations consider the value of local knowledge and embed it within climate adaptation policies and projects. To date, aside from the research conducted by Perkins and Krause (2018) and Hofmann (2017) in FSM, and Le De et al. (2015) in Samoa, there is a dearth of studies explicitly exploring traditional insurance systems in the context of CCA in Pacific SIDS nations including Samoa. This research adds to the growing body of literature that is seeking to emphasise the value of non-Western approaches to environmental issues, including CCA. Therefore, recognising the role of *fa'asamoa* in Samoa is an important contribution to the adaptation literature as it further confirms that traditional socio-cultural systems based on reciprocity are valuable non-Western forms of insurance that are proven to play a vital role in protecting communities from loss during times of environmental change.

Without understanding the impacts of introducing Western adaptation strategies into non-Western nations, tensions may develop that limit the social cohesiveness of the community. Rather than providing improved human security for the wider community, the introduction of insurance may create some tension or social disparity within Samoan society between those households with insurance and those without insurance. The tension could intensify as households without insurance continue to give the majority of their resources to their family or church (for the collective benefit). In contrast, those with insurance are, or may in the future, reduce their donations in order to pay their insurance premium and implement adaptation strategies to their household. This highlights how the introduction of insurance might support adaptation to climate change on the one hand, yet may also simultaneously disrupt existing social-cultural practices on the other. In the case of Samoa, the existing socio-cultural system has already been shown to be considered a traditional form of insurance for many people within the community. Given the importance of social networks in Samoa, this is an important finding that must be considered when insurance is encouraged as a form of adaptation in SIDS such as Samoa.

A growing amount of literature has been published by academics on the imperialist nature of the approach to CCA led by Western nations. Scholars such as Sealey-Huggins (2017) have suggested that the CCA industry is a new form of imperialism as it forces developing countries to adopt particular strategies for the benefit of a developed nation. According to Sealey-Huggins (2017), the capacity of people to survive is recast as a commodity and thus something that can be financialised and traded by agencies who claim the authority of having resources to help alleviate their vulnerability. This critical view is supported by Moulton and Machado (2019) who argued that the damage caused by Hurricanes Irma and Maria was problematised as a physical issue that required a technical response which could be solved by fossil fuel imports and hard solutions, which further embedded the historical debt issues faced by the Caribbean SIDS. The concerns raised by participants about the extractive nature of insurance companies can be understood in this way as foreign-owned insurance companies offer insurance to vulnerable members of the community, and similar to colonists before them, are actively engaged in extracting resources from the nation.

The results from this exploratory study with a small sample size illustrate that there is a need for further empirical research to determine whether this pattern of insured households not engaging in CBA is observable at a broader scale. If future studies determine that this pattern is evident across the nation, increasing penetration of private insurance products in Samoa may lead to a fragmentation across the Samoan community which may have a noticeable impact on Samoa's adaptive capacity, and thus adaptation outcomes.

REFERENCES

Adger, W. N., Quinn, T., Lorenzoni, I., Murphy, C., & Sweeney, J. (2013). Changing social contracts in climate-change adaptation. *Nature Climate Change, 3*(4), 330–333.

Ayers, J., & Forsyth, T. (2009). Community-based adaptation to climate change. *Environment: Science and Policy for Sustainable Development, 51*(4), 22–31.

Baarsch, F., & Kelman, I. (2016). Insurance mechanisms for tropical cyclones and droughts in Pacific Small Island Developing States. *Jàmbá: Journal of Disaster Risk Studies, 8*(1), 1–12.

Barnett, J. (2008). The effect of aid on capacity to adapt to climate change. Insights from Niue. *Political Science, 60*(1), 31–45.

Béné, C., Al-Hassan, R. M., Amarasinghe, O., Fong, P., Ocran, J., Onumah, E., ... Mills, D. J. (2016). Is resilience socially constructed? Empirical evidence from Fiji, Ghana, Sri Lanka, and Vietnam. *Global Environmental Change, 38,* 153–170.

Bergsma, E., Gupta, J., & Jong, P. (2012). Does individual responsibility increase the adaptive capacity of society? The case of local water management in the Netherlands. *Resources, Conservation and Recycling, 64,* 13–22.

Betzold, C. (2015). Adapting to climate change in small island developing states. *Climatic Change, 133*(3), 481–489.

Blythe, J., Silver, J., Evans, L., Armitage, D., Bennett, N. J., Moore, M.-L., ... Brown, K. (2018). The dark side of transformation: Latent risks in contemporary sustainability discourse. *Antipode, 50*(5), 1206–1223.

Campbell, D., Barker, D., & McGregor, D. (2011). Dealing with drought: Small farmers and environmental hazards in southern St. Elizabeth, Jamaica. *Applied Geography, 31*(1), 146–158.

Campbell, J., & Barnett, J. (2010). *Climate change and small island states: Power, knowledge and the South Pacific.* London: Routledge.

Dodman, D., & Mitlin, D. (2013). Challenges for community-based adaptation: Discovering the potential for transformation. *Journal of International Development, 25*(5), 640–659.

Fafchamps, M., & Lund, S. (2003). Risk-sharing networks in rural Philippines. *Journal of Development Economics, 71*(2), 261–287.

Ford, J. D., & Smit, B. (2004). A framework for assessing the vulnerability of communities in the Canadian Arctic to risks associated with climate change. *Arctic, 57*(4), 389–400.

Forsyth, T. (2017). Community based adaptation. In H. von Storch (Ed.), *Oxford research encyclopaedia of climate science* (pp. 1–22). Oxford: Oxford University Press.

Freeman, P. K., & Kunreuther, H. (2002). Environmental risk management for developing countries. *The Geneva Papers on Risk and Insurance-Issues and Practice, 27*(2), 196–214.

Gero, A., Méheux, K., & Dominey-Howes, D. (2011). Integrating community based disaster risk reduction and climate change adaptation: Examples from the Pacific. *Natural Hazards and Earth System Sciences, 11*(1), 101–113.

Hagedoorn, L. C., Brander, L. M., van Beukering, P. J. H., Dijkstra, H. M., Franco, C., Hughes, L., ... Segal, B. (2019). Community-based adaptation to climate change in small island developing states: An analysis of the role of social capital. *Climate and Development, 11*(8), 723–734.

Hecht, S. B. (2008). Climate change and the transformation of risk: Insurance matters. *UCLA Law Review, 55*(6), 1559–1619.

Heltberg, R., Siegel, P. B., & Jorgensen, S. L. (2009). Addressing human vulnerability to climate change: Toward a 'no-regrets' approach. *Global Environmental Change, 19*(1), 89–99.

Herweijer, C., Ranger, N., & Ward, R. E. T. (2009). Adaptation to climate change: Threats and opportunities for the insurance industry. *The Geneva Papers on Risk and Insurance Issues and Practice, 34*(3), 360.

Hofmann, R. (2017). Experiencing environmental dynamics in Chuuk, Micronesia. In E. Dürr & A. Paascht (Eds.), *Environmental transformations and cultural responses: Ontologies, discourses, and practices in Oceania* (pp. 75–101). New York, NY: Palgrave Macmillan.

IPCC. (2012). Summary for policymakers: Managing the risks of extreme events and disasters to advance climate change adaptation. In C. B. Field, V. Barros, T. F. Stocker, D. Qin, D. J. Dokken, K. L. Ebi, … P. M. Midgely (Eds.), *A special report of working groups I and II of the Intergovernmental Panel on Climate Change* (pp. 1–19). Cambridge: Cambridge University Press.

IPCC. (2014). Annex II: Glossary. In J. Birkmann, M. Campos, C. Dubeux, Y. Nojiri, L. Olsson, B. Osman-Elasha, … A. L. St Clair (Eds.), *AR5 climate change 2014: Impacts, adaptation and vulnerability* (pp. 1757–1776). Geneva: IPCC. Retrieved from https://www.ipcc.ch/site/assets/uploads/2018/02/WGIIAR5-AnnexII_FINAL.pdf

Joseph, J. (2013). Resilience as embedded neoliberalism: A governmentality approach. *Resilience, 1*(1), 38–52.

Kates, R. (2000). Cautionary tales: Adaptation and the global poor. *Climatic Change, 45*(1), 5–17.

Kelly, P., & Adger, W. (2000). Theory and practice in assessing vulnerability to climate change and facilitating adaptation. *Climatic Change, 47*(4), 325–352.

Kelman, I. (2018). Islandness within climate change narratives of small island developing states (SIDS). *Island Studies Journal, 13*(1), 149–166.

Klöck, C., & Nunn, P. D. (2019). Adaptation to climate change in small island developing states: A systematic literature review of academic research. *The Journal of Environment & Development, 28*(2), 196–218.

Lassa, J. A., Surjan, A., Caballero-Anthony, M., & Fisher, R. (2019). Measuring political will: An index of commitment to disaster risk reduction. *International Journal of Disaster Risk Reduction, 34*, 64–74.

Le De, L., Gaillard, J. C., Friesen, W., & Smith, F. M. (2015). Remittances in the face of disasters: A case study of rural Samoa. *Environment, Development and Sustainability, 17*(3), 653–672.

Linnerooth-Bayer, J., Warner, K., Bals, C., Höppe, P., Burton, I., Loster, T., & Haas, A. (2009). Insurance, developing countries and climate change. *The Geneva Papers on Risk and Insurance Issues and Practice, 34*(3), 381–400.

Lucas, B. (2015). *Disaster risk financing and insurance in the Pacific.* Birmingham: University of Birmingham.

McGee, J., Phelan, L., & Wenta, J. (2014). Writing the fine print: Developing regional insurance for climate change adaptation in the Pacific. *Melbourne Journal of International Law, 15*(2), 444–472.

Mcleman, R., & Smit, B. (2006). Vulnerability to climate change hazards and risks: Crop and flood insurance. *Canadian Geographer/Le Géographe Canadien, 50*(2), 217–226.

McNamara, K. E., & Buggy, L. (2017). Community-based climate change adaptation: A review of academic literature. *Local Environment, 22*(4), 443–460.

Mills, E. (2005). Insurance in a climate of change. *Science, 309*(5737), 1040–1044.

Mills, E. (2007). Synergisms between climate change mitigation and adaptation: An insurance perspective. *Mitigation and Adaptation Strategies for Global Change, 12*(5), 809–842.

Miranda, M., & Vedenov, D. V. (2001). Innovations in agricultural and natural disaster insurance. *American Journal of Agricultural Economics, 83*(3), 650–655.

Moulton, A., & Machado, M. (2019). Bouncing forward after Irma and Maria: Acknowledging colonialism, problematizing resilience and thinking climate justice. *Journal of Extreme Events, 6*(1), 1–22.

O'Hare, P., & White, I. (2018). Beyond 'just' flood risk management: The potential for – and limits to – alleviating flood disadvantage. *Regional Environmental Change, 18*(2), 385–396.

O'Hare, P., White, I., & Connelly, A. (2016). Insurance as maladaptation: Resilience and the 'business as usual' paradox. *Environment and Planning C: Government and Policy, 34*(6), 1175–1193.

Parsons, M., Brown, C., Nalau, J., & Fisher, K. (2018). Assessing adaptive capacity and adaptation: Insights from Samoan tourism operators. *Climate and Development, 10*(7), 644–663.

Perkins, R. M., & Krause, S. M. (2018). Adapting to climate change impacts in Yap State, Federated States of Micronesia: The importance of environmental conditions and intangible cultural heritage. *Island Studies Journal, 13*(1), 65–78.

Phelan, L. (2011). Managing climate risk: Extreme weather events and the future of insurance in a climate-changed world. *Australasian Journal of Environmental Management, 18*(4), 223–232.

Picard, P. (2008). Natural disaster insurance and the equity-efficiency trade-off. *Journal of Risk and Insurance, 75*(1), 17–38.

Platteau, J.-P. (1997). Mutual insurance as an elusive concept in traditional rural communities. *The Journal of Development Studies, 33*(6), 764–796.

Pretty, J., & Ward, H. (2001). Social capital and the environment. *World Development, 29*(2), 209–227.

Ramachandran, V., & Masood, J. S. (2019). Are the Pacific Islands insurable? Challenges and opportunities for disaster risk finance. Retrieved from Center for Global Development website: https://www.cgdev.org/sites/default/files/WP516-Ramachandran-Are-The-Pacific-Islands-Insurable_0.pdf

Rojas Blanco, A. V. (2006). Local initiatives and adaptation to climate change. *Disasters, 30*(1), 140–147.

Savitt, A. (2017). Insurance as a tool for hazard risk management? An evaluation of the literature. *Natural Hazards, 86*(2), 583–599. https://doi.org/10.1007/s11069-016-2706-1

Schäfer, L., Warner, K., & Kreft, S. (2019). Exploring and managing adaptation frontiers with climate risk insurance. In R. Mechler, L. Bouwer, T. Schinko, S. Surminski, & J. Linnerooth-Bayer (Eds.), *Loss and damage from climate change. Climate risk management, policy and governance* (pp. 317–341). Cham: Springer.

Schipper, E. L. F. (2007). *Climate change adaptation and development: Exploring the linkages.* Working Paper No. 107. Norwich: Tyndall Centre for Climate Change Research, 13. Retrieved from https://www.sei.org/publications/climate-change-adaptation-development-exploring-linkages/

Sealey-Huggins, L. (2017). "1.5°C to stay alive": Climate change, imperialism and justice for the Caribbean. *Third World Quarterly, 38*(11), 2444–2463.

Starom+-ski-Uehara, M., & Keskitalo, E. C. H. (2016). How does natural hazard insurance literature discuss the risks of climate change? *Journal of Insurance Regulation, 35*(6), 1–26.

Surminski, S., & Oramas-Dorta, D. (2013). *Do flood insurance schemes in developing countries provide incentives to reduce physical risks?* IDEAS Working Paper Series from RePEc. Retrieved from http://search.proquest.com/docview/1698743178/?pq-origsite=primo

Thornton, A., Kerslake, M. T., & Binns, T. (2010). Alienation and obligation: Religion and social change in Samoa. *Asia Pacific Viewpoint, 51*(1), 1–16.

United Nations. (2019, November). Efforts to make communities safer from climate change to be launched at Climate Action Summit include insurance, early warning, and investment in small-scale farmers [Press release]. Retrieved from https://www.un.org/en/climatechange/assets/pdf/release_resilience_adaptation.pdf 108

University of the South Pacific. (2016). Money minded in Samoa impact report 2016. Retrieved from https://www.anz.com.au/content/dam/anzcomau/documents/pdf/aboutus/money-minded-report-samoa-2016.pdf

Vaioleti, T. M. (2006). Talanoa research methodology: A developing position on Pacific research. *Waikato Journal of Education, 12*(1), 21–34.

Vilcan, T. (2017). Articulating resilience in practice: Chains of responsibilisation, failure points and political contestation. *Resilience, 5*(1), 29–43.

Walker, G., Whittle, R., Medd, W., & Watson, N. (2010). *Risk governance and natural shazards.* CapHaz-Net WP2 Report. Lancaster: Lancaster Environment Centre, Lancaster University. Retrieved from http://caphaz-net.org/outcomes-results/caphaz-net_WP2_risk-governance.pdf

Westoby, R., McNamara, K. E., Kumar, R., & Nunn, P. D. (2020). From community-based to locally led adaptation: Evidence from Vanuatu. *Ambio, 49,* 1466–1473.

CHAPTER 9

PLANNED RELOCATION AS A CONTENTIOUS STRATEGY OF CLIMATE CHANGE ADAPTATION IN FIJI

Lucy Benge and Andreas Neef

ABSTRACT

'Planned relocation' has emerged in the international climate policy arena as an 'adaptation' solution with the potential to enhance resilience, address underdevelopment and debunk age-old narratives around migration as a risk to peace and security. In 2018, Fiji became one of the first countries to develop Planned Relocation Guidelines, with upwards of 80 villages thought to require relocation over the coming years due to the impact of climate change. Through interviews carried out with representatives from organisations involved in planning for community relocations in Fiji, this chapter explores the creation of planned relocation as a form of climate change adaptation and development. Looking specifically at the value-based challenges of implementation in Fiji, this research provides insight into what happens when dominant international policy narratives play out in practice. Through the presentation of culturally nuanced ways of understanding the problem of climate-induced migration, this chapter invites policymakers to seek out these voices when devising displacement solutions.

Keywords: Climate-induced migration; climate change adaptation; planned relocation; forced displacement; development opportunity; Fiji

Climate-Induced Disasters in the Asia-Pacific Region: Response, Recovery, Adaptation
Community, Environment and Disaster Risk Management, Volume 22, 193–212
Copyright © 2021 by Emerald Publishing Limited
All rights of reproduction in any form reserved
ISSN: 2040-7262/doi:10.1108/S2040-726220200000022008

INTRODUCTION: VOLUNTARY PLANNED RELOCATION AS AN ALTERNATIVE TO FORCED DISPLACEMENT

In 1990, the Intergovernmental Panel on Climate Change (IPCC) argued that forced displacement may be set to become one of the 'most severe effects of climate change', with the potential to create tens of millions of environmental refugees (Tegart, Sheldon, & Griffiths, 1990, p. 10). More recently, the Internal Displacement Monitoring Centre (2015) indicated that approximately 26.4 million people were annually displaced from their homes between 2008 and 2014 due to weather-related hazards. Forced displacement, as a result of sea level rise and the increased frequency of extreme weather events, is therefore predicted – according to António Guterres, then High Commissioner for Refugees – to 'unseat conflict as the main driver of mass migration in coming years' (Guterres as cited in Hall, 2011, p. 108). This is of particular concern for low-lying countries at risk of losing their ability to sustain human habitation and cultural identity (Barnett & Adger, 2003).

The occurrence of migration in response to sudden-onset disasters and slow-onset environmental change has been seen to place pressure on food security, livelihoods, infrastructure and social services. Furthermore, as the IPCC (2014) Synthesis Report suggests: 'populations that lack the resources for planned migration experience higher exposure to extreme weather events, particularly in developing countries with low income' (p. 16). In response to this, international organisations and local governments are increasingly looking for ways to manage and *plan* for voluntary migration so as to avoid the threat posed by mass displacement (Petz, 2015). In this way, the ability to adequately plan for migration has become a way of both reducing vulnerability and enhancing development opportunity (IPCC, 2014).

In an effort to avoid loss of land, livelihoods and rights, the 2010 Cancùn Adaptation Framework[1] established planned relocation as a form of 'adaptation'. This move encouraged states to design frameworks to appropriately manage relocation to harness its benefits *before* disasters occurred. In accordance with this, the International Organization for Migration (IOM, 2014) defined relocation as: 'permanent voluntary migration, with an emphasis on rebuilding livelihoods in another place' (p. 16). Through a focus on enhancing livelihoods elsewhere, 'planned' or properly 'managed' relocation was constructed as a solution to anticipated displacement and redefined as a 'feature' of adaptation rather than a 'failure' to adapt.

Following extensive vulnerability and risk mapping exercises, the Fijian government has compiled a list of villages expected to require relocation due to climate-induced land degradation and coastal erosion. While population mobility is not new to Fiji – with migration for employment and education being an established practice throughout the Pacific – climate change is intersecting with these drivers, leading to the new possibility of permanent community relocations (Hugo, 2010). In response to this, in 2012 Fiji started drafting its own national Planned Relocation Guidelines in order to facilitate relocation for communities that lodge a formal request for it. Fiji was chosen as a case study for the research presented in this chapter given its leading role internationally in the establishment of such guidelines. This, combined with the large-scale devastation caused by Tropical Cyclone (TC) Winston in February 2016, makes Fiji an important case for understanding how planned community relocation might be used as a strategy of climate change adaptation and of community development.

Understanding the Political Shift towards Planned Relocation as a Form of Climate Change Adaptation

The link between climate change and migration was first highlighted in 1985 with Essam El-Hinnawi's seminal paper for the United Nations Environment Programme, which popularised the term 'environmental refugee'. This term contributed to the construction of climate-induced migration as a threat to international peace and security, fostering an alarmist narrative among local and international NGOs, UN organisations and governments which continued well into the 2010s (Hall, 2016).

Although helping to draw international attention to the link between climate change and migration, alarmist narratives have been criticised for their negative depiction of climate refugees (Farbotko, Stratford, & Lazrus, 2016), their overly deterministic understanding of the triggers of migration (Campbell, 2010; Farbotko & Lazrus, 2012), and their limited recognition of the benefits migration may offer (Barnett & Webber, 2010; Black, Bennett, Thomas, & Beddington, 2011). This has led to a move away from alarmist state-centric security narratives, towards a stronger emphasis on human security and resilience (Methmann & Ocls, 2015). Efforts to protect against climate-induced migration have eventually been replaced by an acceptance that migration might be used as a form of protection against the impacts of climate change, and as a way of empowering migrants to take control of their own mobility. This is based on the idea that 'voluntary migration [...] can provide an opportunity to seek employment and reduce the risk of displacement in times of humanitarian crisis' (Kälin, 2015, p. 6).

While much work has been carried out on the link between climate change and migration, this has largely focussed on a rejection of the 'environmental refugee' concept, given its ability to 'entrench vulnerable communities in inequitable power relations; further redirecting their fate from their' (Farbotko & Lazrus, 2012, p. 383; Ransan-Cooper, Farbotko, McNamara, Thornton, & Chevalier, 2015). The rejection of alarmist narratives has led to a distinct body of literature looking at how migration might be used as a form of climate change adaptation and as a tool of self-determining, self-responsible actors (Barnett & O'Neill, 2012; Barnett & Webber, 2010; Black et al., 2011, Burson, 2010; Campbell, 2010). While this has enabled a move away from security-driven efforts at shutting down migration pathways, a number of scholars have recently started to look at how the 'adaptive migration' narrative is contributing to the establishment of subtler liberal modes of governance (Bettini, 2014; Bettini & Gioli, 2016; Felli & Castree, 2012; Felli, 2013; Grove, 2010; Methmann & Oels, 2015; Oels, 2005).

This new body of literature looks at how framing migration as a form of 'adaptation' has failed to acknowledge the global inequalities which make some groups more susceptible to climate change impacts (Bettini, 2014; Methmann & Oels, 2015). By focussing on the adaptive capacity of migrants, scholars have expressed concern that this might remove accountability from the international sphere. As McNamara and Gibson (2009) have suggested, framing migration as 'adaption' provides 'no premise to persuade the major polluters to mitigate and prevent further damage' (p. 481). Similarly, Methmann and Oels (2015) argue that by constructing a resilient subject, adaptive migration narratives are able to couch 'loss and vulnerability in the language of progress and transformation' (p. 62). Consequently, there is concern that 'adaptive migration' narratives might be used as a political tool for justifying failed climate change mitigation efforts (Fair, 2015; Gemenne, 2015; Warner, 2012). These authors look at how framing migration as a form of adaptation has become a technique for concealing environmental injustice. For example, Bettini (2014) suggests,

> [t]he smoother tones and the association of CM [climate-induced migration] to adaptation do not result (solely) from analytical advancements [....] They also relate to political conveniences and circumstances. Within the UNFCCC framework, the transition from 'climate refugees' to 'climate migrants' has allowed CM to be couched 'as a low controversy issue within adaptation'. (p. 185)

This chapter adds to this body of literature, looking at how planned relocation – specifically relocation within borders – has been constructed as a necessary form of climate change adaptation. Furthermore, by examining the political effects of framing planned relocation in these terms, this chapter helps to draw attention to the way in which solutions such as planned relocation are immersed in geopolitical relations of power.

Planned Relocation as a Pathway to 'Transformative Development'

Climate change is increasingly understood as having the ability to entrench inequality in material and social well-being, given its disproportionate effect on the socially, economically and politically vulnerable (Dow, Kasperson, & Bohn, 2006; Tanner & Allouche, 2011). Dow et al. (2006) recognise how the risks of climate change will 'settle primarily upon people already beset by other existing or future environmental and economic stresses – people who possess inadequate coping resources and limited adaptive capacities' (p. 82). Addressing the impacts of climate change, therefore, requires initiatives to support a 'broader development agenda' (Dow et al., 2006, p. 84).

The link between natural hazards, climate change and underdevelopment has come about through the recognition of vulnerability as an expression of deeper socioecological relationships (Hewitt, 1983; O'Keefe, Westgate, & Wisner, 1976). This has led towards the integration of climate change adaptation and development projects, with action upon social vulnerabilities – including livelihood insecurity and poverty – becoming an essential part of disaster risk reduction strategies. Ferris (2012) argues that rather than simply using relocation as a form of risk reduction, resettlement planning, preparation and implementation activities should be conceived and executed as sustainable development programs. In this regard, special attention should be directed toward those whose pre-displacement standard of living is below their country's poverty line to ensure that their standard of living is raised. (p. 29)

The Advisory Group on Climate Change and Human Mobility[2] (AGCCHM, 2015) also suggests that:

[s]olutions exist and can be further developed to minimise risks of displacement, with a potential to deeply transform societies through a right-based participatory approach with co-benefits on poverty and sustainable development objectives'. (p. 2)

In this way, planned relocation – when carried out in a participatory manner – attempts not only to reduce risk but also to improve the overall quality of life for relocated persons by ensuring their resettlement promotes new livelihood opportunities and economic prosperity.

In response to this narrative shift, the United Nations Refugee Agency (UNHCR) began working with states to include planned relocation within their National Adaptation Plans and to create a consensus on how planned relocation might be used as a form of protection against displacement. In 2015, this led to the development of a guide for states on how to carry out planned relocation in the context of climate change. The UNHCR (2015) guide envisions planned relocation as an opportunity to improve the livelihoods of relocated persons 'as both a matter of right and as an essential component in preventing impoverishment' (p. 20). This demonstrates how planned relocation increasingly corresponds with an idea of adaptation that not only moderates harm but also works to transform communities by enhancing their 'agency, resilience, and empowerment' (UNHCR, 2015, p. 12).

The idea that planned relocation could be used as a form of adaptation with transformational development benefits resembles something close to Pelling's (2011) idea of 'transformational adaptation'. Transformational adaptation is defined by Pelling (2011) as: 'the deepest form of adaptation indicated by reform in overarching political economy regimes and associated cultural discourses on development, security and risk' (p. 50). Transformational climate change adaptation is closely connected to development narratives, which offer an 'opportunity for social reform, for the questioning of values that drive inequalities in development and our unsustainable relationship with the environment' (Pelling, 2011, p. 1).

Despite the shift away from alarmist international policy discourses – which depicted the migrant as a threat to peace and security – the transformational adaptation narrative still relies on the creation of a subject falling short of capacity and resilience (a subject in need of 'development'). Consequently, and despite the opportunities planned relocation might offer for 'development', this narrative may fail to question the 'underlying assumptions or power asymmetries in society' (Pelling, 2011, p. 50). Through an analysis of how planned relocation is understood by government officials and development actors in Fiji, this research begins to unpack the unseen sociocultural and political effects of constructing planned relocation as a form of climate change adaptation and as a tool of transformational development.

UNDERSTANDING THE CONTEXT OF PLANNED RELOCATION IN FIJI

The Sudden and Slow-onset Triggers of Relocation in Fiji

In 2011, the Fiji Meteorological Service (FMS) released a report – 'Current and future climate of the Fiji Islands' under the Australian Government's International Climate Change Adaptation Initiative. This report noted several key changes in climate, most notably an increase in observed temperature of 0.15 °C per decade since 1950 and a rise in sea levels of approximately 6 mm per year since 1993 – a figure that is substantially greater than the 2.8–3.6 mm per year global average (Fiji Meteorological Service (FMS), Australian Bureau of Meteorology, & Commonwealth Scientific and Industrial Research Organisation, 2011, p. 4). Sea level around the Fiji Islands is anticipated to rise within the range of 30–160 mm by 2030 relative to the average of the period between 1980 and 1999 (FMS et al., 2011, p. 7). The report further notes that: 'sea-level rise combined with natural year-to-year changes will increase the impact of storm surges and coastal flooding' (FMS et al., 2011, p. 7). Consequently, while coastal erosion and saltwater intrusion slowly make coastal lands uninhabitable, severe weather events will often speed up the process.

It was estimated by the Fijian government in 2014 that 676 villages will likely be affected by the impacts of climate change and may require relocation in the future (Leckie & Huggins, 2016). More recently, Piggott-McKellar, McNamara, Nunn, and Sekinini (2019) noted that 80 communities have been recognised by the Fijian government as currently in need of relocation. The need for relocation was exacerbated by TC Winston – which struck Fiji on the 20th of February 2016. Following TC Winston media reports cited the Minister for Rural and Maritime Development and National Disaster Management's claim that 63 villages would need to be relocated as a direct result of the cyclone (Swami, 2016). Hon. Minister Seruiratu described how relocation was a consequence of climate change and would take time to implement given the need for approval from the community as well as the process of finding suitable land for relocation (Swami, 2016).

In the four years since TC Winston, there is no official number available to tell us how many villages have been relocated as a result of the cyclone. However, research suggests that several villages may be in the process of relocation (Nichols, 2019; Piggott-McKellar, McNamara, Nunn, & Sekinini, 2019). With the release of Fiji's Planned Relocation Guidelines in December 2018, and the establishment of a process for villages to formally request relocation, the number of government-recognised relocations in Fiji may be set to rise significantly over coming years.

The Land and Livelihood-based Challenges of Relocation in Fiji

Understanding the challenge of planned relocation in Fiji requires an effort to understand Fijian relationships to the land and the way land is connected to identity, social well-being and cultural cohesion. Tuwere (2002, p. 94) describes the land as an integral part of people and their identity – leading to a 'strong sense of belonging to the land rather than the land belonging to the people as a tradable commodity'. This relationship between the land and the people, their culture, history and beliefs creates a holistic interconnectivity between the physical, social, spiritual and economic dimensions of life, a universal whole known as *vanua*. Nabobo-Baba (2008, p. 143) has defined *vanua* as more than simply 'the land' but instead a concept inclusive of 'a chief [...] their people and their relationships, their land, spiritualties, knowledge systems, cultures and values'. The strong link *vanua* creates between people and their environment has meant that Fijian identity is often expressed through the land: 'their land is an extension of themselves' (Ratu Mosese Volavola as cited in Crosetto, 2005, p. 71).

If land is understood as an extension of the self, then relocation will have impacts not only upon material well-being but also upon spiritual and cultural health. Understanding the likely impact of relocation in Fiji, therefore, entails a way of understanding its holistic impact by giving greater weight to 'community, stability and wellbeing rather than materialism and "progress"' (Batibasaqa, Overton, & Horsley, 1999, p. 106). This does not mean that planned relocation should be seen as incompatible with *vanua*, but instead suggests that *vanua* may offer an alternative way of understanding the effects of climate-induced relocation.

In 2014, Vunidogoloa village on the island of Vanua Levu became the first in Fiji to officially relocate due to the slow-onset effects of climate change. The community of 26 households made the decision to relocate after in situ attempts at adaptation – including the building of a seawall and the raising of houses – became ineffective (McNamara & Des Combes, 2015). After requesting assistance for relocation from the Fijian government in 2007, the village was eventually relocated within its own customary land boundaries – 2 km from the original village site (McNamara & Des Combes, 2015). The relocation of Vunidogoloa within their own *mataqali*[3] land was seen by government officials as a key factor contributing to the success of their relocation.

The inalienability[4] of Indigenous land in Fiji and the potential for a growth in tension over land ownership between Indigenous (*iTaukei*) communities and Fijians of Indian descent[5] may become one of the key inhibitors of successful relocation in Fiji. The inalienability of land makes it difficult for *iTaukei* Fijians to leave their land, as they are unable to sell it and they receive only small rents for leasing it to Fijian farmers of Indian descent. Furthermore, as tourism, agriculture and commerce continue to grow, the utilisation and demand for *iTaukei* land also increases (iTaukei Land Trust Board, 2014), making land a major source of social tension. With the relocation of communities facing the impacts of climate change, the issue of land and its accessibility will raise further questions around who will be able to relocate, and how relocation might be negotiated between communities in a way that both protects Indigenous ownership and prevents further entrenching tensions over land ownership.

An additional challenge facing the successful planned relocation of communities in Fiji relates to the ability for communities to maintain or re-establish suitable livelihoods (cf. Neef et al., 2018). Ensuring Planned Relocation offers communities *improved* livelihood opportunities is a thought to be a key factor in deeming planned relocation a form of successful 'adaptation'. For instance, the Asian Development Bank (ADB, 2012) argues that when 'properly managed and supported, migration [...] can often improve livelihoods, reduce poverty, meet labor force needs, bolster economies, and strengthen links between communities and countries' (p. VII). Similarly, the UNHCR 2015 Planned Relocation Guidelines envision planned relocation as a tool for the enhancement of living standards, 'ideally through the improvement [...] of livelihoods of Relocated Persons as a matter of right and as an essential component in preventing impoverishment' (p. 20).

In Fiji, the majority of communities facing relocation due to the impact of climate change are those living in coastal villages and whose livelihoods depend in part on access to the ocean and waterways for fishing. Although villages often have multiple livelihood sources including agriculture, livestock rearing and increasingly tourism, planned relocation risks dislocating villages from their traditional fishing grounds. While planned relocation may come with opportunities for new livelihood ventures such as the planting of alternative crop varieties and better access to roads for work in towns and cities, it is not obvious that this constitutes an 'improvement' to livelihoods or simply the loss of a traditional livelihood repackaged as a 'development opportunity'.

Fiji's Relocation Guidelines and Their Link to Long-Term Development Objectives

In response to the increasing need for relocation, the drafting of relocation guidelines began in Fiji in 2012, and in 2018, the final Planned Relocation Guidelines (hereafter the Guidelines) were published under the guidance of the Ministry of Economy with support from the Deutsche Gesellschaft für Internationale Zusammenarbeit GmbH (GIZ). The Guidelines were intended to provide

> guidance for the Government of the Republic of Fiji and all Other Stakeholders present in Fiji, to consider planned relocation solutions for the affected communities as part of their *adaptation* strategies in relation to disasters and climate change related slow-onset events .... [emphasis added] (Government of the Republic of Fiji, 2018a, p. 3)

Interestingly Fiji's Planned Relocation Guidelines are linked to their 5-year and 20-year development goals and are intended to further accelerate Fiji's progress in meeting its Sustainable Development Goals and other national, regional and global commitments. The connection between the Guidelines and Fiji's development objectives is further evidenced in the Guideline's definition of relocation as

> the voluntary, planned and coordinated movement of climate-displaced persons within states ... where they can enjoy the full spectrum of rights including housing, land and property rights and all other livelihood and related rights. (Government of the Republic of Fiji, 2018a, p. 6)

In utilising planned relocation as a strategy of climate change adaptation, the intention is not only to moderate the harm facing communities but to exploit relocation for its 'beneficial opportunities' (Government of the Republic of Fiji, 2018a).

The Guidelines (Government of the Republic of Fiji, 2018a, p. 7) also make a link between the need for relocation and pre-existing developing pressures such as 'overcrowding, unemployment, infrastructure, pollution and environmental fragility'. This allows planned relocation to become a solution to social as well as environmental challenges by ensuring a 'progressive standard of living for the affected communities, in accordance with their cultural and basic human rights' (Government of the Republic of Fiji, 2018a, p. 14). In this way, the Guidelines attempt to establish Planned Relocation not only as a reaction to climate change but also as a rational livelihood and development strategy. Despite understanding planned relocation as a strategy for climate change adaptation, it should be noted that the Guidelines only allow for planned relocation as a 'last resort, after all other adaptation options have been explored' (2018a, p. 1).

RESEARCH METHODOLOGY

Through semi-structured interviews with actors involved in planning for relocation in Fiji, it was possible to analyse the way in which the narrative of 'planned relocation as a form of climate change adaptation' has been appropriated, reinterpreted and resisted by those at the forefront of implementation. Interviews were conducted in July 2016 by the first author with representatives from key government departments, international development organisations, regional non-government faith-based and science-based organisations, as well as international funding agencies involved in planning for, facilitating and implementing planned relocation in Fiji. It should be noted that these interviews were carried out while Fiji's Planned Relocation Guidelines were in the process of being drafted, and at that point in time, interviewees were not directly referring to or responding to the Guidelines themselves. Despite this, these interviews provide an interesting and still highly relevant commentary on the dissidence that sits behind the seemingly rational narrative of 'planned relocation as a form of climate change adaptation' presented in the Guidelines. Furthermore, many of the representatives interviewed worked for agencies who were at the forefront of the Guidelines development. This provided us a unique insight into the 'behind the scenes' uncertainty involved in the creation of planned relocation as a form of climate change adaptation and tool for community development.

Participants were identified largely through the help of gatekeepers and snowball sampling. Recruitment involved making contact through email with a small group of relevant organisations. This initial process of desk-based recruitment resulted in two key interviews: one with a representative of the Climate Change Division of the Ministry of Finance (CDD) and the other with a representative from the Pacific Conference of Churches (PCC) – an organisation active in the accompaniment of communities facing relocation. These initial interviews facilitated the use of snowball sampling, whereby interviewees nominated other participants relevant to the study.

This process led to seven face-to-face interviews with key informants from different organisations, including two government agencies, three international development organisations and two regional non-government organisations. Of these seven participants, three were *iTaukei* Fijians and four were expats. While most participants were directly involved in relocation plans either through their contribution to the drafting of Fiji's Planned Relocation Guidelines, consultation with communities facing relocation, procurement of funding for relocation, or assessment of risk and vulnerability, two participants spoke more generally about the role of the organisation they worked for and Fiji's plans for community relocation. In this way, it was possible to gather perspectives on relocation and its relationship to Fijian ideas of identity, as well as more practical action-oriented perspectives on how and when relocation should be implemented. Interviews were semi-structured to allow interviewees to speak about the aspects of planned relocation most relevant to their work. Despite the open format of interviews, interviewees tended to focus on the risks facing communities and the reasons relocation was needed, questions of responsibility around facilitating relocation and the adaptive opportunities and place-based challenges relocation was thought to pose in Fiji.

All interviews were digitally recorded, apart from one interviewee who preferred not to be recorded, and notes were also taken during interviews. Interviews were later transcribed verbatim and analysis was carried out focussing on three key themes: (1) the cause of relocation (i.e. environmental hazards, social vulnerably and under-development, poor governance/planning, global injustice); (2) the responsibility for planned relocation (i.e. individuals, households, communities, states, organisations); and (3) the intent or purpose of planned relocation (i.e. risk reduction, livelihood guarantees, development opportunities) and whether relocation could be understood as a form of 'adaptation'. While interviews were analysed according to these three themes, it became apparent that a significant amount of overlap existed between them. For instance, how interviewees understood the cause of relocation often cor-related with where they attributed responsibility and whether they felt it reasonable to label planned relocation as a form of climate change adaptation.

The analysis focussed on the language participants used as well as the key tensions and uncertainties they identified around when, how and in whose inter-est relocation occurs. The analysis was less concerned with an evaluation of the success or limitations of planned relocation in Fiji and more interested in how the dominant narrative around planned relocation as an 'adaptation solution' has been understood, justified or resisted.

FINDINGS

The findings presented here have been divided into three sections. The first sec-tion broadly addresses the first two themes outlined above and examines how interviewees understood the drivers (or cause) of community relocations as well as what this says about who should ultimately be held responsible; the second and third sections then address the larger issue of how interviewees understood the opportunities and challenges posed by planned relocation and whether planned relocation could be seen as a form of climate change adaptation with develop-ment benefits (these sections broadly correspond with the third theme outlined previously but also link back to the first and second themes regarding causality and responsibility). These findings demonstrate how planned relocation has been both constructed and resisted as a form of climate change adaptation and provide insight into the place-based complexities that the narrative of 'planned relocation as a climate change adaptation' conceals.

Perspectives on Causality and Responsibility

On the question of what causes communities to require relocation, several interviewees steered away from environmentally deterministic answers and looked instead at the intersecting social, political and economic development factors which have combined with environmental causes to make planned relocation necessary. An interviewee from the Secretariat of the Pacific Community, responsible for carrying out risk and vulnerability assessments, spoke, for example, about the difficulty of carrying out these assessments due to the cultural, social, economic and political factors which could never be adequately captured in scientific risk assessments (interview, 13 July 2016). Similarly, an interviewee from the United Nations Development Program (UNDP) suggested that more emphasis should be placed on understanding the local-level causes of relocation. Cautioning against environmental determinism, he called for a closer look at the local social, political and historical factors that contribute to migration. Focussing on the need for local-level change, he pointed to the difficulty of identifying a root cause:

> there are a plethora of factors that are causing a specific community to be exposed to risk, and those can be environmental, they can be economic, political and cultural [...] Nadi, for example, nearly every year there is flooding, but is that due to climate change ... natural variability, or lack of planning? (UNDP, interview, 12 July 2016)

While the interviewee at UNDP advocated for a greater focus on government accountability, other participants recognised planned relocation as a consequence of global inequality and spoke of how local efforts at adaptation and sustainable living 'fail in comparison to the effects of what others are doing' (IOM, interview, 15 July 2016). The difficulty of ensuring large-scale emitters are held accountable was thought to be in part because of the challenge of isolating climate change as the key determining factor in decisions to relocate. Echoing this, the Fiji Climate Change Division continues to push for global accountability and recognition of relocation as a 'loss and damage'[6] despite its international reframing as a form of 'adaptation' – 'we [bear] the brunt of the issue because of big emitting countries, [so] they are liable to pay us and increase financial support ' (CDD, interview, 11 July 2016). The interviewee from PCC reiterated this position, suggesting that while we must recognise the multiple factors that contribute to migration, this can enable emitters to conceal their accountability. It is therefore essential to push for global accountability – 'it is only right, because it's caused by something and it's certainly not [caused by] the communities that are affected' (PCC, interview, 12 July 2016). This demonstrates an effort to focus on questions of global environmental justice, while at the same time not undermining the need for practical local-level efforts to plan for and address climate impacts.

Perspectives on Planned Relocation as 'Adaptation'

When asked whether relocation should be understood as a form of adaptation, participants usually referred to the opportunities relocation could offer. Aside from ensuring the physical security of people, relocation was seen to offer the benefit of accessibility – bringing communities closer to schools, hospitals and other social services, as well as better access to communication networks. Relocation was also understood as offering the possibility of access to better, more fertile land, alternative livelihood options and better accessibility to markets. Despite recognising the potential benefits of relocation, there was noticeable reservation around labelling relocation as a successful adaptation strategy:

> the immediate response would be 'well, they are out of harm's way' [...] so, yes, it is positive, but I think given what I know about our land, the complexities of land in Fiji, I would say we have a better understanding [of the challenges] now. (IOM, interview, 15 July 2016)

In the context of Fiji, the impact of relocation upon land and identity was a key factor contributing to a reluctance to label relocation as an 'adaptation' strategy. One interviewee from GIZ said that despite their funding for relocation coming under the banner of 'adaptation', 'I don't think this is a strategy of adaptation. This is an answer to some of the issues, but in Fiji this is very personal' (interview, 15 July 2016). This indicates concern over how labelling relocation as a form of 'adaptation' might undermine the personal and cultural implications of leaving one's home. The interviewee from the National Disaster Management Office also made this point, suggesting that relocation might be met with resistance given the attachment to land and burial sites and the risk of social and cultural disturbance that it poses (NDMO, interview, 15 July 2016). Therefore, despite the potential for relocation to offer protection from physical risks, this approach was also seen as being unable to recognise the 'very real spiritual, cultural traditional connections with the actual place that *iTaukei* people have' (IOM, interview, 15 July 2016). Compounding these concerns is a fear that relocation might exacerbate tension over land ownership, particularly if the land required for relocation belongs to a different *mataqali*.

It is largely for this reason that planned relocation in Fiji has been conceived as a 'last resort', adopted only when all other in situ adaptation options have been attempted (Government of the Republic of Fiji, 2018a). However, while not actively promoting the idea of relocation as a form of 'adaptation', participants were also reluctant to label relocation as 'failed adaptation': 'I think failed adaptation is the wrong way to put it, because we have actually tried, we just haven't managed to curb the problem' (PCC, interview, 12 July 2016). Another participant spoke about how relocation would require adaptation to the new environment, so in that sense despite having exhausted all in situ adaptation options, relocation 'does not take you away from the term itself' (CDD, interview, 11 July 2016).

While the debate around planned relocation has tended to swing between viewing climate-induced relocation as either an 'opportunity' or 'impact', 'form of adaptation' or a 'failure to adapt', in practice the distinction between these positions seems less clear. In Fiji, the planned relocation of communities is seen as having the potential to both reduce vulnerability to environmental degradation and increase vulnerability to cultural loss. In acknowledgement of this, Fiji's Planned Relocation Guidelines attempt to mitigate the risks associated with relocation by ensuring decisions to relocate are made under voluntary conditions, with full knowledge of the risks and with the participation of all stakeholders. Ensuring relocation enables opportunities while minimising losses requires – according to the Guidelines – a lengthy process of consultation and consensus building among affected communities. Through consultation, and the communication of risk, it is hoped that decisions to relocate can be made voluntarily because, according to the Climate Change Division – 'we would not want to go in and forcefully remove the community because we see them in danger, the important thing is to get their consensus' (CDD, interview, 11 July 2016).

The 2018 Planned Relocation Guidelines (Government of the Republic of Fiji, 2018a, p. 12) strongly reiterate this position, suggesting that relocation could be done voluntarily when effort is made to:

> Collaborate with the affected communities, ensuring the diverse needs of the community are integrated in preparing and elaborating the relocation plan, in accordance with conserving traditions, cultural practices, and human rights standards, by initiating a real dialogue with the affected population and put[ting] in place measures to remove obstacles to participation and to capture the views of differently affected groups.

Despite this, there was doubt among interviewees on the question of whether relocation could ever be truly 'voluntary'. While consultation with community members meant that relocation could fall under the government's definition of 'voluntary', 'it would be forced from the perspective that they had no choice post TC Winston' (IOM, interview, 15 July 2016). Similarly, other interviewees recognised that despite communities often putting themselves forward to relocate, they were still 'forced' in the sense that they were motivated to relocate due to circumstances outside their control or in contexts of limited alternatives. In this sense, relocation is forced – 'but it is not forced by government ... it is necessary because of climate change' (GIZ, interview, 15 July 2016).

The question of whether relocation should be understood as a form of adaptation eventually came back to notions of causality, responsibility and justice. There was concern that by labelling relocation as an 'adaptation strategy', this might conceal the way people are 'adapting to something [they] didn't actually cause' (UNDP, interview, 12 July 2016). This underlying sense of injustice seemed to perpetuate a reluctance to talk about relocation as a form of 'adaptation'. Even when relocation was acknowledged as necessary, there was nonetheless a desire to have it recognised as a 'loss and damage' within UNFCCC negotiations. Despite ambivalence about framing relocation as a form of adaptation, current relocation projects in Fiji continue to be funded under its banner, demonstrating the way in which power can define possibilities for action. The European Union is responsible for a large portion of funding for relocation in Fiji; however, as one participant pointed out, 'the EU wouldn't dare fund anything under the banner of loss and damage – so relocation becomes talked about as an extreme form of adaptation' (PCC, interview, July 12, 2016). This demonstrates the political motive embedded in labelling techniques such as 'adaptation', and comments on the way in which narratives such as 'planned relocation as a form of adaptation' are utilised to meet political ends – such as the need to work within donor requirements for funding.

Awareness around the way in which international and local policy narratives have constructed planned relocation as a form of adaptation – and moreover as an adaptation solution with 'development benefits' – was evident among participants interviewed for this research. One participant reflected on how certain terminology and 'buzzwords' influence people's understanding of the problem (UNDP, interview, 12 July 2016). This interviewee explored the way in which certain problems have been constructed as 'real' – despite being a 'reflection of society, and power and who speaks, and who has an opinion' and how certain solutions have been legitimised due to the 'Eurocentric ... belief in rationality and scientific method and also the belief that you can plan' (UNDP, interview, 12 July 2016).

This interviewee called for more awareness of how these 'truths' are the product of society, power structures and vested interests – 'from down at the community level all the way up to when they negotiate at Paris' (UNDP, interview, 12 July 2016). Becoming aware of the politics of problem construction involved, for this interviewee, greater recognition of the diversity of meaning attached to mobility and an attempt to better link the knowledge and needs of affected communities to the practices and programmes of the organisations who offer 'solutions'.

Perspectives on the Place-based Impacts of Relocation: De-bunking the Dominant Narrative

While planned relocation has arisen as a form of climate change adaptation and protection against forced displacement in Fiji, this is curtailed by the recognition that relocation poses serious challenges around land accessibility, community cohesion and sociocultural well-being, including *vanua*.

In one example, discussing the lessons learnt from the relocation of Vunidogoloa, the interviewee from IOM spoke of how the traditional healers of the village had returned to the original site a year after the relocation, because 'moving to the new site meant they lost their traditional healing powers that were tied to the old land' (IOM, interview, 15 July 2016). This demonstrates how in the context of Fiji the success of relocation depends not only on the ability to protect people from environmental hazards but also on the ability to protect what is valued socially, culturally and historically. Therefore, while scientists and policymakers may legitimise relocation through the establishment of 'sound risk predictions' and appropriate consultation, there is a need to look more closely at the diversity of factors that contribute to the success of relocation.

For this reason, participants interviewed for this research recognised that relocation was never simply a 'positive' or 'negative' response to climate change, but rather a response that is highly contingent upon Fijian ideas of identity, belonging and mobility. Interviewees tended to agree that planned relocation could be a 'climate justified measure', but could not always be considered a 'no or low regret option'. Fiji's 'National Adaptation Plan' – which was in the process of being drafted when these interviews took place – defines a 'no regret' adaptation option as one that has environmental, social and economic co-benefits (Government of the Republic of Fiji, 2018b, p. 14).

Despite this, practitioners continue to look for ways to reconcile the need for relocation with Fijian ideas of identity and belonging. For example, the *iTaukei* representative from IOM spoke of the need to transform what it means to belong to Fiji and to identify as Fijian, in order to facilitate a freer movement between the land of different *mataqali*. This involved advocating for 'a real civic education around what it means to be Fijian' in order to foster the idea that: 'I belong to Fiji regardless of where I live and that I am not so tied to the land...that I will not accept another clan moving onto that land' (IOM, interview, 15 July 2016). This practitioner understood that relocation was going to start changing ideas of what it means to belong to a particular place, but looked for a way to incorporate this change into *iTaukei* epistemology.

In an effort to make displacement solutions more relevant to the Fijian context, practitioners often found alternative ways of framing, labelling and identifying the problem. For example, the interviewee from PCC spoke about the value of the Moana Declaration[7] (2009) and its attempt to bring about a 'new consciousness on climate change' (p. 1). This Declaration, which brought together Pacific church leaders to formulate a statement on resettlement as a consequence of climate change, called for

> projects that demonstrate an alternative economic model reflecting faith based values of: justice, equity, and sustainability – in challenge to the values inherent in the neo-liberal economic model dominant in the world today. (Moana Declaration, 2009, p. 2)

In this way, the Moana Declaration demonstrated an attempt to find solutions to displacement that are more culturally suitable, faith-based and value-driven – thereby recognising that the right of protection extends beyond physical and material security. Acknowledging that relocation impacts upon a holistic idea of well-being in which physical, social, economic and environmental health are highly interdependent helps to problematise solutions which privilege the protection of a single dimension of well-being. Through reference to the Moana Declaration, this practitioner attempted to understand the impacts relocation and resettlement might have upon Fijian identity, belonging and faith and to integrate these considerations into her assessment of the viability and success of planned relocation.

These examples demonstrate how practitioners in Fiji occupy an intermediary position: at once aware of the increasing need for planned relocation (especially post TC Winston), while at the same time recognising the challenges relocation poses around land-based identity, belonging, faith and well-being in Fiji.

CONCLUSION

The findings presented in this chapter demonstrate how dominant narratives never transition neatly between policy sites and implementation contexts. These findings reveal gaps between 'the world conveyed in the [policy] texts and the world to be transformed' (Li, 2007, p. 123). They demonstrate how – despite attempts to manage risk through vulnerability assessment, risk mapping, adaptation, resilience building and proper planning – place-based realities will always pose challenges to generalised solutions. Although international policy discourse (such as UNHCR 2015 Planned Relocation Guidelines) has framed planned relocation as a form of adaptation with development benefits, practitioners in Fiji expressed uncertainty over the way 'adaptation' might conceal the specific challenges Fiji faces – in particular the impacts of relocation upon identity and land ownership.

In an effort to move away from alarmist 'environmental refugee' narratives, planned relocation emerged as a way of offering protection to those who risked forced displacement. Through accurate risk predictions and the transfer of risk knowledge, planned relocation became a way of enabling retreat before forced displacement occurred, offering 'opportunities' for relocated populations to demonstrate their resilience and adaptive capacity. In other words, the adverse impacts of relocation were legitimised, and global accountability for relocation as a 'loss and damage' concealed, through the framing of planned relocation as a form of adaptation and tool for development.

This emphasis on community-level adaptation leaves little room to consider the larger political and economic structures that have made some places and people more vulnerable to climate change. Focussing on the development and livelihood benefits of planned relocation has worked to reframe the migration of people in response to climate change as an expression of 'resilience' and 'adaptation', thus avoiding the accountability and financial compensation that comes with acknowledging relocation as a 'loss and damage'. Although interviewees recognised the growing need for relocation in Fiji, there was hesitancy around labelling it as a form of adaptation given concerns that this would reduce the need for political action. Most practitioners agreed that the inclusion of planned relocation within Fiji's National Adaptation Strategy served a political purpose, ensuring that Fiji could apply for international funding to relocate communities that request it.

This chapter has shown how efforts to address climate-induced displacement are increasingly characterised by the assertion of generalised solutions over placed realities. While planned relocation attempts to provide protection against the threat of forced displacement, this research has drawn attention to its less obvious sociocultural and political effects. By couching planned relocation in the language of climate change 'adaptation' and development 'opportunity', relocation is made to appear 'voluntary' – a tool of self-determining, resilient subjects. Though this narrative has helped to debunk alarmist depictions of 'vulnerable' climate refugees, it also has the effect of placing responsibility upon communities and thus of concealing global political accountabilities.

While Fiji is most certainly leading the way towards implementing the planned relocation of communities in response to climate change, there is noticeable caution among practitioners around its use as a form of 'transformative adaptation' or 'development opportunity'. This is largely due to the sociocultural losses and tensions relocation is likely to bring about in Fiji, as well as the global accountability concealed through the language of 'transformation' and 'opportunity'. By drawing attention to the gap between dominant global narratives and local implementation realities, greater weight has been given to the diversity of narratives surrounding climate-induced displacement. In doing so, this research hopes to inform action that recognises situated interests and values, while at the same moving towards genuinely 'transformative' approaches to adaptation within global economic and political structures.

NOTES

1. In 2010, the UNFCCC's (2010) Conference of Parties in Cancún, Mexico, marked a turning point in climate change negotiations by agreeing that adaptation must be addressed with the same priority as mitigation. This commitment saw migration included as a form of adaptation, with paragraph 14f of the Cancún Adaptation Framework suggesting the need for 'measures to enhance understanding, coordination and cooperation with regard to climate change induced displacement, migration and planned relocation [...] at the national, regional and international levels' (UNFCCC, 2010, p. 5). The Cancún Framework replaced the demand for an international legal protection mechanism inclusive of 'climate refugees', looking instead towards international cooperation and ways of planning for migration in the face of climate change.

2. The Advisory Group on Climate Change and Human Mobility (AGCCHM) comprises the United Nations High Commissioner for Refugees (UNHCR), the International Organisation for Migration (IOM), the United Nations University Institute for Environment and Human Security, Refugees International and the Norwegian Refugee Council.

3. *Mataqali* is the term for the most significant landholding unit in Fiji. A *Mataqali* is composed of family groups that live in close proximity and are related to each other through marriage. Approximately 89.75% of land in Fiji is *iTaukei* (Indigenous) land held by the *Mataqali* (iTaukei Land Trust Board, n.d.).

4. In 1875, the colonial administration in Fiji created a prohibition on land sales, ensuring that Indigenous land could not be alienated for foreign commercial interest. This was in an effort to avoid repeating the land wars that had occurred in New Zealand (Lashley, 2011).

5. Arriving from India as indentured labourers between 1879 and 1884, Fijians of Indian descent today make up the majority of commercial agricultural workers in Fiji, forming just under 40% of the population (Tanner, 2007).

6. The Warsaw International Mechanism for Loss and Damage (UNFCCC, n.d.) associated with Climate Change Impacts was established at COP19 in 2013 to address loss and damage associated with impacts of climate change, including extreme events and slow-onset events, in developing countries that are particularly vulnerable to the adverse effects of climate change. The Loss and Damage Mechanism can provide countries with finance, technology and capacity building initiatives to help address the loss and damage associated with climate change.

7. The Moana Declaration sought a binding agreement to protect the rights of those displaced by environmental change or climate disasters. The Moana Declaration also appealed regionally to other Pacific nations to start looking for land for the resettlement of migrants both within and across domestic borders (Kempf, 2012).

ACKNOWLEDGEMENTS

We are indebted to all research participants in Fiji who generously shared their knowledge, perspectives and insights. Funding and support for this research was provided by the Asia-Pacific Network for Global Change Research (CAF2016-RR05-CMY-Neef, 'Climate Change Adaptation in Post-Disaster Recovery Processes: Flood-Affected Communities in Cambodia and Fiji').

REFERENCES

Advisory Group on Climate Change and Human Mobility (AGCCHM). (2015). *Human mobility in the context of climate change UNFCCC – Paris COP21*. Recommendations from the Advisory Group on Climate Change and Human Mobility. Retrieved from https://environmentalmigration.iom.int/sites/default/files/Research%20Database/Paris_COP21-Human_Mobility-AdvisoryGroup.pdf

Asian Development Bank. (2012). *Addressing climate change and migration in Asia and the Pacific*. Final Report. Asian Development Bank, Manila.

Barnett, J., & Adger, W. N. (2003). Climate danger and atoll countries. *Climate Change, 61*, 321–337.

Barnett, J., & O'Neill, S. (2012). Islands resettlement and adaptation. *Nature Climate Change, 2*, 8–10.

Barnett, J., & Webber, M. (2010). Migration as adaptation: Opportunities and limits. In J. McAdam (Ed.), *Climate change and displacement: Multidisciplinary perspectives* (pp. 37–55). Oxford: Hart Publishing.

Batibasaqa, K., Overton, J., & Horsley, P. (1999). Vanua: Land, people and culture in Fiji. In J. Overton & R. Scheyvens (Eds.), *Strategies of sustainable development* (pp. 100–106). London: Zed Books.

Bettini, G. (2014). Climate migration as an adaptation strategy: De-securitising climate-induced migration or making the unruly governable? *Critical Studies on Security, 2*(2), 180–195.

Bettini, G., & Gioli, G. (2016). Waltz with development: Insights on the developmentalization of climate-induced migration. *Migration and Development, 5*(2), 171–189.

Black, R., Bennett, S. R. G., Thomas, S. M., & Beddington, J. R. (2011). Climate change: Migration as adaptation. *Nature, 478*, 447–449.

Burson, B. (Ed.). (2010). *Climate change and migration: South Pacific perspectives*. Wellington: Milne Print.

Campbell, J. (2010). Climate change and population movement in Pacific Island countries. In B. Burson (Ed.), *Climate change and migration: South Pacific perspectives* (pp. 29–50). Wellington: Milne Print.

Crosetto, J. (2005). The heart of Fiji's land tenure conflict: The law of tradition and vakavanua, the customary 'way of the land'. *Pacific Rim Law & Policy Journal, 14*(1), 71–101.

Dow, K., Kasperson, R., & Bohn, M. (2006). Exploring the social justice implications of adaptation and vulnerability. In N. Adger, J. Paavola, S. Huq, & M. J. Mace (Eds.), *Fairness in adaptation to climate change* (pp. 79–96). London: The MIT Press.

Fair, H. (2015). Not drowning but fighting: Pacific island activists. *Forced Migration Review, 49*, 58–59.

Farbotko, C., & Lazrus, H. (2012). The first climate refugees? Contesting global narratives of climate change in Tuvalu. *Global Environmental Change, 22*, 382–390.

Farbotko, C., Stratford, E., & Lazrus, H. (2016). Climate migrants and new identities? The geopolitics of embracing or rejecting mobility. *Social and Cultural Geography, 17*(4), 533–552.

Felli, R. (2013). Managing climate insecurity by ensuring continuous capital accumulation 'climate refugees' and 'climate migrants'. *New Political Economy, 18*(3), 337–363.

Felli, R., & Castree, N. (2012). Neoliberalising adaptation to environmental change: Foresight or foreclosure? *Environment and Planning A: International Journal of Urban and Regional Research, 44*(1), 1–4.

Ferris, E. (2012). *Protection and planned relocations in the context of climate change*. Legal and Protection Policy Research Series. Geneva: UNHCR.

Fiji Meteorological Service (FMS), Australian Bureau of Meteorology, & Commonwealth Scientific and Industrial Research Organisation. (2011). Current and future climate of Fiji Islands. Retrieved from https://www.pacificclimatechangescience.org/wp-content/uploads/2013/06/1_PCCSP_Fiji_8pp.pdf

Gemenne, F. (2015). One good reason to speak of 'climate refugees'. *Forced Migration Review, 49*, 70–71.

Government of the Republic of Fiji. (2018a). *Planned relocation guidelines. A framework to undertake climate change related relocation*. Suva: Ministry of the Economy.

Government of the Republic of Fiji. (2018b). *Republic of Fiji national adaptation plan. A pathway towards climate resilience*. Suva: Ministry of Economy.

Grove, K. (2010). Insuring "our common future?" Dangerous climate change and the biopolitics of environmental security. *Geopolitics, 15*(3), 536–563.

Hall, N. (2011). Climate change and institutional change in UNHCR. In M. Leighton, X. Shen, & K. Warner (Eds.), *Climate change and migration: Rethinking policies for adaptation and disaster risk reduction* (pp. 102–114). Bonn: United Nations University.

Hall, N. (2016). *Displacement, development, and climate change: International organizations moving beyond their mandates*. New York, NY: Routledge.

Hewitt, K. (1983). *Interpretations of calamity from the viewpoint of human ecology*. Boston: Allen & Unwin.

Hugo, G. (2010). Climate change-induced mobility and the existing migration regime in Asia and the Pacific. In J. McAdam (Ed.), *Climate change and displacement: Multidisciplinary perspectives* (pp. 9–35). Oxford: Hart Publishing.

Intergovernmental Panel on Climate Change. (2014). *Climate change 2014: Synthesis report.* Contribution of working groups I, II and III to the Fifth Assessment Report of the Intergovernmental Panel on Climate Change. IPCC, Geneva.

Internal Displacement Monitoring Centre. (2015). *Global estimates 2015: People displaced by disasters.* IDMC and Norwegian Refugee Council, Geneva.

International Organization for Migration. (2014). *Migration, environment and climate change: Evidence for policy, glossary.* Geneva: IOM.

iTaukei Land Trust Board. (2014). TLTB history. Retrieved from https://www.tltb.com.fj/history/

iTaukei Land Trust Board. (n.d.). Land ownership in Fiji. Retrieved from https://www.tltb.com.fj/getat-tachment/Media/Brochures/Land-Ownership-in-Fiji-Booklet-(1).pdf.aspx?lang=en-US

Kälin, W. (2015). The Nansen Initiative: Building consensus on displacement in disaster contexts. *Forced Migration Review*, *49*, 5–7.

Kempf, W. (2012). Climate change, migration and Christianity in Oceania. In K. Hastrup and K. F. Olwig (Eds.), *Climate change and human mobility: Global challenges to the social sciences* (pp. 235–257). Cambridge: Cambridge University Press

Lashley, M. E. (2011). Strange bedfellows? Customary systems of communal land tenure and indig-enous land rights in New Zealand, Fiji and Australia. *Pacific Studies*, *34*(2/3), 103–141.

Leckie, S., & Huggins, C. (Eds.). (2016). *Repairing domestic climate displacement: The peninsula princi-ples.* New York, NY: Routledge.

Li, T. M. (2007). *The will to improve: Governmentality, development and the practice of politics.* London: Duke University Press.

McNamara, K. E., & Des Combes, H. J. (2015). Planning for community relocations due to climate change in Fiji. *International Journal of Disaster Risk Science*, *6*, 315–319.

McNamara, K. E., & Gibson, C. (2009). 'We do not want to leave our land': Pacific ambassadors at the United Nations resist the category of 'climate refugees'. *Geoforum*, *40*, 475–483.

Methmann, C., & Oels, A. (2015). From 'fearing' to 'empowering' climate refugees: Governing climate-induced migration in the name of resilience. *Security Dialogue*, *46*(1), 51–68.

Moana Declaration. (2009). Moana Declaration: Pacific church leaders meeting statement on reset-tlement as a direct consequence of climate change. Retrieved from http://www.cws.org.nz/files/Moana%20Declaration.pdf

Nabobo-Baba, U. (2008). Decolonising framings in Pacific research: Indigenous Fijian Vanua research framework as an organic response. *Alternative*, *4*(2), 140–154.

Neef, A., Benge, L., Boruff, N., Pauli, N., Weber, E., & Varea, R. (2018). Climate change adaptation strategies in Fiji: The role of social norms and cultural values. *World Development*, *107*, 125–137.

Nichols, A. (2019). Climate change, natural hazards, and relocation: Insights from Nabukadra and Navuniivi villages in Fiji. *Climatic Change*, *156*, 255–271.

O'Keefe, P., Westgate, K., & Wisner, B. (1976). Taking the naturalness out of natural disasters. *Nature*, *260*, 566–567.

Oels, A. (2005). Rendering climate change governable: From biopower to advanced liberal government? *Journal of Environmental Policy and Planning*, *7*(3), 185–207.

Pelling, M. (2011). *Adaptation to climate change: From resilience to transformation.* London: Routledge.

Petz, D. (2015). Planned relocations in the context of natural disasters and climate change: A review of the literature. Retrieved from https://www.brookings.edu/wp-content/uploads/2016/06/Brookings-Planned-Relocations-Annotated-Bibliography-June-2015.pdf

Piggott-McKellar, A. E., McNamara, K. E., Nunn, P. D., & Sekinini, S. T. (2019). Moving people in a changing climate: Lessons from two case studies in Fiji. *Social Sciences*, *8*(5), 1–17.

Ransan-Cooper, H., Farbotko, C., McNamara, K. E., Thornton, F., & Chevalier, E. (2015). Being(s) framed: The means and ends of framing environmental migrants. *Global Environmental Change*, *53*, 106–115.

Swami, N. (2016, June). 63 Villages set for relocation. *The Fiji Times*. Retrieved from http://www.fijitimes.com/story.aspx?id=356455

Tanner, A. (2007). On understanding too quickly: Colonial and postcolonial misrepresentation of indigenous Fijian land tenure. *Human Organisation*, *66*(1), 69–77.

Tanner, T., & Allouche, J. (2011). Towards and new political economy of climate change and development. *IDS Bulletin, 42*(3), 1–14.

Tegart, W. J. M., Sheldon, G. W., & Griffiths, D. C. (1990). *Climate change: The IPCC impacts assessment*. Report prepared for IPCC by working group II. Intergovernmental Panel on Climate Change, Canberra.

Tuwere, I. S. (2002). *Vanua: Towards a Fijian theology of place*. Suva: Institute of Pacific Studies, University of the South Pacific.

United Nations Framework Convention on Climate Change. (2010). Report of the conference of the parties on its sixteenth session. Held in Cancún from 29 November to 10 December 2010, Cancún.

United Nations Framework Convention on Climate Change. (n.d.). Warsaw international mechanism for loss and damage associated with climate change impacts. Retrieved from https://unfccc.int/topics/adaptation-and-resilience/workstreams/loss-and-damage-ld/warsaw-international-mechanism-for-loss-and-damage-associated-with-climate-change-impacts-wim

United Nations High Commissioner for Refugees, Brookings & Georgetown University. (2015). *Guidance on protecting people from disasters and environmental change through planned relocation*. Washington: UNHCR, Brookings, Georgetown University. Retrieved from http://www.unhcr.org/protection/environment/562f798d9/planned-relocation-guidance-october-2015.html

Warner, K. (2012). Human migration and displacement in the context of adaptation to climate change: The Cancún adaptation framework and potential for future action. *Environment and Planning C: Government and Policy, 30*, 1061–1077.

INDEX

Note: Page numbers followed by "*n*" indicate end notes.

Printed in the United States
By Bookmasters